Destinations

DESTIN

ATIONS

*Essays from
Rolling Stone
by*

JAN MORRIS

• • •

NEW YORK

Oxford University Press / Rolling Stone

COPYRIGHT © 1980 BY ROLLING STONE PRESS
AND JAN MORRIS

First published, 1980

First paperback edition, 1982

Library of Congress Cataloging in Publication Data

MORRIS, JAN, 1926-

Destinations.

1. World politics—1975-1985—Addresses, essays, lectures.

2. Voyages and travel—1951-   —Addresses, essays, lectures.

I. Rolling stone. II. Title.

D849.M72   320.9'047   79-28492

ISBN 0-19-502708-6

ISBN 0-19-503069-9 (pbk.)

Photographers

LARRY WHITE (Washington, D.C.); HENRI CARTIER-BRESSON/Magnum (Delhi);
JILL HARTLEY (Panama); ANTONIN KRATOCHVIL (Los Angeles);
ALON REININGER/Contact (South Africa); G. RODGER/Magnum (London);
DAVID BURNETT/Contact (Cairo); BETTMAN ARCHIVE (Istanbul);
ERIC SILBERG/Alpha (Trieste); LARRY WHITE (Manhattan)

Printing (last digit): 9 8 7 6 5 4 3 2 1

PRINTED IN THE UNITED STATES OF AMERICA

Also by the author

. . . . . .

SPAIN

THE WORLD OF VENICE

THE OXFORD BOOK OF OXFORD

OXFORD

PAX BRITANNICA

CONUNDRUM

CONTENTS

· · · · · · · · · ·

AUTHOR'S NOTE

. . . .

IN 1974 I was asked by the editors of *Rolling Stone* magazine, then of San Francisco, now of New York, if I would like to write for them.

I was flattered and entertained by this unexpected approach. I was a middle-aged Anglo-Welsh writer of romantic instinct and distinctly traditionalist prose, based on a small seaside village in North Wales. *Rolling Stone* was the most thrilling phenomenon of contemporary American journalism, which had established its fortunes upon the economics of rock music, and found its readers among the lively, restless, affluent and stereophonic *avant garde* of young America.

I accepted the proposal at once, for I am fond of paradox, and the essays in this book are the product of our union. They *are* essays, but since *Rolling Stone* is a topical and indeed urgent kind of magazine, they are not timeless—they describe places at specific moments, in particular moods or conditions. On the other hand they are not exactly reportage, certainly not of the fashionable investigative kind: by the time I had pottered home to Gwynedd to write them, stopping off on the way, perhaps, to look at an interesting building in British Honduras, or go swimming in Corfu— by the time I got home with my copy I was far too late for any blow-by-blow reconstruction of events.

So I suppose they are, in a modest way, *sui generis.* To get their flavor best you must perhaps imagine them in their original setting, among the rock-and-roll gossip, the savage political satire, the advertisements for tweeters or source selectors, the learned reviews and the frequently incomprehensible sonic jargon which surrounds them in the pages of their remarkable patron. *Rolling Stone* is, by and large, a sharp and flinty organism: it has been my agreeable function, in writing these pieces, to temper some of its cutting edge with a few thousand words of moss.

–Jan Morris

JANUARY 1980

Destinations

THE
MORNING AFTER

There was an unmistakable feeling
of hangover to Washington, D.C., in the fall of 1974. The
long revelation of Watergate, partly so horrible, partly so beguiling, had
left the capital shaken but oddly nostalgic for its months of
disclosure. President Ford, having pardoned Richard Nixon for his
goings-on, was trying to restore to the political scene some of
its supposed wholesomeness, not to say alleged sanity.
Washington society was still obsessed with the minutiae of the great scandal.
By the time I got there the macabre party was over:
this is a portrait of the morning after.

. . .

WASHINGTON

· · · · · · · · · · · · · ·

The Morning After

[*1974*]

FAILING TO SOLVE any of the problems in the airline magazine's puzzle page, and soon exhausting all the faces upon which I could superimpose buck-teeth or sideburns, as we approached Washington, D.C., I turned to that beloved standby of the experienced traveler, the application for Diners Club credit cards. With a practiced hand I registered my name as Ethelreda B. Goering, my Amount and Source of Other Income as $8 million, Gold Mine, Transvaal, and as we landed I was delightfully debating whether to use as my personal reference His Holiness the Pope, Windsor Castle, Lhasa, or J.P.Morgan at the University of Lapland. ¶ Imagine then my pleasure when, arriving at my hotel that evening and opening the Washington Directory, I discovered the mayor of Washington to be Mayor Washington, the treasurer of the White House Correspondents Association Mr. Edgar A. Poe, and the doorkeeper of the House of Representatives Mr. William (Fish Bait) Miller. A concomitant of power is the privilege of eccentricity, and though in recent years Americans may have pined for rulers of more orthodox method, still to visitors from smaller and less potent states an early intimation of quirk is more a comfort than a threat—the gods make their victims mad, but their favorites unconventional.

Besides, it has a healthily deflationary effect on the stranger. The great Moslem travelers of the Middle Ages, when they approached the capital of some unimaginable Caliph or omniscient Sultan, fell as a matter of form or policy into a ceremonial prose, matching their cadences to the Master of the World, or adjusting their punctuation to the Commander of the Faithful. I had wondered myself, as I set off for Washington this time, what avedictory style might be best suited for the present Sublimity of the White House. When I first came to the city, President Eisenhower sat in the Hall of a Thousand Ears, and his style was easily, as you might say, approximated to. President Kennedy no less obviously demanded a mixed pastiche of Hemingway, Tolkien and Zane Grey, while President Nixon, of course, could only in courtesy be addressed in his own meaningful communicational media.

But President Ford offered the wanderer no text. Something faintly sanctimonious, perhaps? Something brisk and sporting? Something bland, something soothing, some literary equivalent of orange juice or rubdown, to honor his role as the Great Jogger? I could not make up my mind: and so, abandoning the precedents of ibn-Khaldun and ibn-Batuta, and encouraged by the evidence of the Washington Directory, I decided to skip the honorifics altogether, and simply say hi to Fish Bait—who turned out to be, by the way, an inescapable figure of Washington life, and who earned his nickname, so his office told me, during a shrimp- or worm-sized boyhood on the Mississippi shore.

Unreality, of course, whether comic, paranoiac or simply bizarre, is an attribute of capital cities, because power itself is so illusory. We look on the face of Nixon as of Ozymandias, and even Haroun-al-Raschid survives only in the fancy of his storytellers. At least, though, the Caliph could disguise himself when he wished, and walk anonymously through the marketplace of Baghdad, where the poets declaimed, the merchants haggled and all the jostle of the real world was available outside his palace gates. When President Nixon wished to do the same, he could only go to the Lincoln Memorial, slightly drugged it seems, and talk to the students in its sepulchral glow.

The idea of an artificial capital is, I believe, specifically American, though the nature of Washington is of course another legacy of those damned French. It was a rotten idea, disastrously copied in such dumps as Canberra, Brasilia and Islamabad, and inevitably creating in the nation's capital just the same blinkered introspection as one finds in new universities started from scratch on virgin rural sites. But though everyone claims to miss the stimulus of variety in Washington, like academics, politicians are terrified of outside competition, so that in practice all conspire to maintain the shrinelike posture of the place. It is a posture, altogether spurious, of dedicated zeal and memorial—a necromantic attitude, in fact, sustained by the commanding presence of the Arlington National Cemetery, Fame's Camping Ground as it says on its triumphal arch, and suggesting to me sometimes, not least when the carillon of the Central Union Mission rings out its hymns twice daily across the Mall, a premature hush of general elegy (though I was sorry to discover, when I inquired at the Mission door, that there was in fact no glazed lady carillonneur playing "Abide with Me" on the roof, only a man with a tape recorder at the reception desk).

From the center of that allegoric cemetery one may look out across the Potomac to the grand sweep of the capital beyond. Nothing could appear much less American, for while America is above all a country of verticals, artistic, economic, symbolic, phallic, imposed splendidly upon the passive landscape, Washington, D.C., is all horizontal. Nowhere is much flatter than Washington. The ground is flat. The style is flat. The architecture is deliberately flat. From up there in the Arlington cemetery the whole city seems to lie in a single plane, without depth or perspective, its layered strips of blue, green and white broken only by the obelisk of the Washington Monument and the Capitol dome, as the massed ranks of Arlington are interrupted only by the graves of specially important corpses. It looks like a city of slabs, rev-

7

erently disposed, and only the jets from the National Airport, straining themselves with difficulty out of the ambiance, throw a bold diagonal across the scene.

"Are all these," said a child to me outside Arlington House, surveying Fame's Camping Ground around us, "are all these *dead* guys?" "Dead," said I, "as mutton"—but at that moment her grandmother arrived, direct I would guess from Kalamazoo, and throwing me a distinctly accusatory look, as though I were undermining the loyalty of the young, she gave the child's nose a necessary wipe and hurried her down the hill to catch the Tour-Mobile.

The sentries at the Tomb of the Unknown Soldier are mounted by an infantry regiment known as the Old Guard, and I found them more haunting than the shades. I suppose new arrivals at Arlington are, so to speak, cosmeticized before burial, but however assiduously they are touched up for their last roll call, they could hardly be more theatrical than those soldiers still alive. Apparently shaven headed beneath their peaked caps, ominously sunglassed when the day is bright, expressionless, ritually stooped, they move with an extraordinary gliding motion that seems to require no muscular activity at all, but is controlled electronically perhaps from some distant command post—a slow, lunar motion, to and fro before the gaping crowds—a halt, a click of the boots, a stylized shift of the rifle from one shoulder to the other, a long pause as though the electrodes are warming up, and then, with an almost perceptible hiss, that slow spectral lope back to the other side of the memorial, while the tourists suppress a shudder.

Behind their dark glasses, I suppose, the soldiers know nothing of the sinister chill that surrounds them, and indeed when I later came across some of the Old Guard off duty at their barracks, they seemed nice, cheerful fellows. In the same way the obsessive nature of Washington is not always apparent to those who form part of it. "When I was just a little kid," a friend of mine told me at lunch one day, "I guess I wasn't more than ten or eleven years old, I used to dream to myself I could see my name there on the bedroom door—Senator W—!" I could hardly conceive such a fancy in a child's mind, but she saw nothing remarkable about it, and it is probably commonplace in Washington. Politicians are politicians everywhere, but only here is the political addiction so ingrained and so frank. Here one can observe its pursuit in every fanatic detail, from the gleam in the collective eye of the visiting debating society to the attendant stiffening when the great man speaks, from the swiveling heads over the cocktail canapés to the sweep of the big black cars at the Senate side.

To avoid getting hooked myself, for it is catching as well as habit-forming, sometimes I took the day off from politics, and did the tourist rounds: but for all the grandeur and meaning of the city, for all the endearing pride of my fellow visitors, still these experiences only heightened my sense of intrusion upon some immense private performance. Inorganic by origin, Washington is unnatural in behavior; but far from heightening everything as New York does, it spreads everything out, memorializes it, puts it in a park and reflects it in an ornamental pool. In New York I feel more myself than usual, in Washington much less, for when I look for my own reflection in this city, statues and symbols look back at me.

It is an alienating city. It lacks the corporate gift of hospitality. It is like one vast smokeless zone. Was ever genius less at home than in the National Gallery of Art, where the enigmatic Giorgione, the mad Van Gogh, the lusty Picasso hang forever antiseptically among the Garden Courts? Did ever Marlowe or Molière find a less likely stage than the Center for the Performing Arts, which suggests to me a cross between a Nazi exhibition and a more than usually ambitious hairdresser? I thanked my good fortune that this time I had arrived in September; at least those interminable cherries weren't out.

Nowhere in the world is so inexorably *improving*. Elevating texts and aphorisms, quotations from statesmen and philosophers, Thoughts for All Eternity nag one from every other downtown wall, and make one feel, especially perhaps if one has come in a high-school excursion bus, awfully insignificant. What giants there were in those days! How grandly they expressed themselves! How thickly they stand about! Innocent III, Napoleon, Moses and St. Louis supervise the Senate subway; clumps of heroes wrestle with their standards, horseback generals plan their strategies again on plinth and plaza across the capital. "Where Law Ends," booms the Department of Justice, "Tyranny Begins." "Taxes Are What We Pay for a Civilized Society," retorts the

Department of Internal Revenue. "Here Are the Ties That Bind the Life of Our People," the National Archives cry, and across the avenue the Mission responds, with an unctuous chime of the carillon: "Come to Me!"

When we came down from the top of the Washington Monument, even the elevator operator dismissed us with an injunction. "Let's all work," he said, "to clean up our country for the 200th anniversary just coming up." "Yes sir," we dutifully replied, "you're darned right—you hear that, kids?" He had not, however, finished yet. "And I'm talking," he darkly added, "about the mental aspects as well as the physical."

We had no answer to that.

Let me insert, if you will forgive me, two anecdotes of Westminster Abbey. One I report firsthand. I was standing once in a cluttered alcove of the fane, romantically topsy-turvy with statues of forgotten admirals, judges and miscellaneous rulers of the world, when I heard behind me the comment of an American visitor. "All it needs," she observed *sotto voce* but decisively, "is a good museum curator from the Middle West." A second quotation was given me by one of the Abbey's guides. "Sir," another American remarked politely to him one morning, "it occurs to me that this building looks remarkably like a church."

I throw them in because I am aware of a prejudice in my reaction to the Washington aesthetic. I stand with Chesterton for the rolling road, and prefer even the symmetry of the Greeks or the Georgians to have its nooks and serendipities. This is, I know, a taste common in my own particular culture, but rarer elsewhere, and I must bear in mind that the singular beauties of Washington, more than the beauties of less significant cities, lie in the eyes of their beholders. I can see that, for example, the motto inscribed on the Seabees memorial—*Can Do*—which seems slick or cheap to me, translates with perfect dignity as *On Peut*, and to a visitor from Rome, Vienna or Castile the Beaux Arts monumentality of Washington is no doubt only to be expected. We all see ourselves in America, and we see our own countries, our own civilizations, confirmed, denied or parodied in Washington, D.C.

The fantasy of the place is nourished, indeed, by the foreigners who frequent it. The presidents and prime ministers succeeding each other day by day at Blair House are like pilgrims come to consult the great oracle across the way. The embassies strung out among their flags and gardens on Massachusetts Avenue are pavilions of make-believe. It is all a parade! The Shah is indistinguishable from the Chairman to the maid who makes their beds. The embassies are built on air, with their agency-supplied manservants or K.G.B. chauffeurs, their government-issue carpets or regulation icons, their signed portraits of king or dictator among the dahlias on the grand piano, their ineffable hostesses, their suitable oil paintings, their envoys brought to this heady eminence by a lifetime of slog or a magazine of bullets, and the universal convention, sacrosanct in Washington, that their inhabitants are in some measure recipients of a divine or at least presidential grace.

I gave myself a walking tour of the Washington embassies, and highly diverting it was, being less an architectural exhibition than a display of national images. The most endearing building, I thought, was the Icelandic, which looks like a very comfortable boardinghouse in the outskirts of Reykjavik. The most alluring seemed to me the Turkish, which was designed in fact by the American, George Totten, but speaks deliciously of hookah and seraglio, and ought to be overlooking the Golden Horn instead of the Rock Creek Parkway. The most anthropomorphic is the Yugoslav, which bears a distinct physical resemblance to Marshal Tito, the most geographic is the Canadian, which bears a distinct physical resemblance to Canada.

Old-school loyalist that I am, of course I like the British embassy best, and am not in the least resentful, though perhaps a *little* surprised, to hear that in these difficult times they have installed in the ambassador's house that enervating contemporary device, air conditioning. No wonder a Washington posting no longer qualifies for hazard pay! Still, up there in Lutyens's country house, red Sussex brick in Washington NW, the diplomatic masque is unashamed, and English gentlemen still stand fastidious and self-amused beneath their chandeliers. When I first came to Washington, twenty years ago, that easy Oxford manner was a local cynosure. Ambitious Americans affected it, American aristocrats wore it like a uniform, Washington hostesses talked incessantly about dukely cousins or ancestral homes in Wiltshire.

Fashion is doubly fickle, though, when it partners power, and today most of the local Wasps, if they have not buzzed away altogether, have discreetly folded their wings. I met a few. I had coffee with A—, more indelibly English of accent, more unswervingly patrician of style, than any Englishman I have met for years. I renewed my acquaintance with B—, who spoke kindly of Harold Macmillan and asked what Lord Caccia was doing these days. I ran into the chairman of the Episcopalian Cathedral Garden Committee, who complained about the *dreadful* mess people made with Coca-Cola cans, adjured her dog Flicker to obey the garden regulations, and begged me not to notice the weeds. I met a retired colonel who told me to look out for an interesting essay he had contributed to the journal of the D.A.R. But gone, or at least adeptly modified, are the Anglophile enthusiasms which, only a generation ago, so largely set the social tone of the city. For better or worse, America has found itself since then, and the pretensions are home-grown now.

An ambassador nevertheless, as Sir Henry Wotton wrote, is a man sent abroad to lie for his country, and in every one of those plushy embassies, turreted or curtain-walled, rich in monarchic symbols or austere with socialist dogma, the envoys are doing their best to sustain their own deceptions. I went to the British embassy one evening to see the pianist Vladimir Horowitz presented with the Gold Medal of the Royal Philharmonic Society, brought to him on a cushion by a marvelously suave young secretary, and handed over with a graceful ambassadorial speech about violent times and the meaning of art. Mr. Horowitz seemed pleased, but instead of replying in kind sat down at the piano and played in a highly vibrant and indeed imperial manner *God Save the Queen*, making full use of the sustaining pedal.

There was a pause at the end of it, and instantly, as the last notes faded, I clicked the scene in my memory: and so I have held it there like a flash from a dream, the ambassador benignly at attention, the young diplomats rigid all about, the American guests clutching their champagne glasses, the great room aglow with carpets and portraits, the pianist's hand raised in a last grandiloquence—an ornate little vignette of Washington, where life so often shimmers through a gauze curtain, insubstantially.

Often time itself seems suspended in Washington. Superficially the current mutations show, from floppy moustaches in the National Press Building to mock folk art on the Georgetown sidewalks. Physically few cities have changed more radically in a lifetime: there are cabdrivers still on the road who remember the building of the Lincoln Memorial, and a city which fifty years ago was no more than an appendage to the Capitol is now a metropolis in its own right. Yet in the political heart of it, though the Presidents come and go, though the administrative style allegedly changes and the stance of government shifts, still the essence seems to stay the same. I was taken to lunch one day to a restaurant political people favor, and looking around at the other tables, seemed to see there precisely the same sober-tied lobbyists, identically the same boyish congressmen, with just the same haircuts and almost the same suits, as I had seen there eating unquestionably the same rockfish twenty years before.

They were *not* the same men. If I could see them side by side with their predecessors of 1954, I would doubtless notice differences of manner, dress, even bone structure. But set against the monumental presence of government, like mutes in a mausoleum they assumed a common identity. Even Nelson Rockefeller, one of the richest men in the world from one of history's most debatable dynasties, assumed it as to the manner born when he appeared before the committee inquiring into his suitability for the vice-presidency. So absolutely was he disguised in the capital's livery that seeing him sitting there among the humdrum rest of us, the world-weary reporters, the sycophantic senators, the policemen and the ushers, really I could hardly differentiate the Rockefeller person from all the others. More disturbing still, when I went to the theater that night, and saw Robert Preston belting out the opening song of the musical *Mack and Mabel* against a frenetic back-projection of the Keystone Kops, falling through manholes, sliding off roofs, driving cars into rivers and leaping from burning hospitals, at first it seemed to me that it was not Preston at all singing away amidst the chaos, but Rockefeller yet again.

In Georgetown especially, which is I suppose the most obsessively political residential enclave in the world, an extraordinary sense of sameness sometimes overcomes me. Georgetown is an innocent exterior disguising an immensely worldly, not to say tigerish community. Most of its houses are poky, inconvenient and unbeautiful, but a sort of rich inner glue of common interest and influence has permeated them, sticking them together through cracks in the brickwork, and making many of them feel less like individual houses than wings of some awkwardly dismembered mansion. Outside, too, their often undistinguished fronts have been successfully disguised with foliage, shutters and colonial lamps, giving the whole district so powerful a sense of unity that its streets have become more or less interchangeable, and I came to feel that if I got the address confused, and went to the wrong house for dinner, nobody would notice anyway.

There are spontaneous parts of Georgetown, modest parts too, but the dominant characteristic of the quarter is a rich premeditation. Good taste is everywhere: original style, not often. Georgetown's culture is the culture of politics. It is all in the game. It flows watchfully with the tide, abstract to pop, kinetic to representational, *Time* one year to *Rolling Stone* the next. I doubt if there are, for instance, just at the moment anyway, many Victorian narrative pictures in the Georgetown drawing rooms; I wonder how often Mendelssohn, for example, is played on the Georgetown hi-fis; I doubt if, let us say, Somerset Maugham is prominently displayed in many Georgetown bookcases. Washington taste is much like Washington ambition: calculated.

Within the cramped opulence of the Georgetown setting, which is a kind of lush mirror image of the Capitol scene, the faces of the Washington activists are shaded still further into anonymity, lost among their peers and followers, so that even the affection of marriage, parenthood or friendship seems to lose its truth. It is like a shadow world. At one Georgetown dinner I was introduced to a man I seemed to think I knew. Had I met him in Europe somewhere? Was he a colleague from the distant past? Or was he, as so often happens these days, not a personal acquaintance at all, but an actor from some television serial whose face is familiar to us all? He seemed a nice man and I did not like to hurt his feelings, but I did venture to ask what was the name again. "George McGovern," I was told. Ah yes.

The ultimate self-deception is the deception of permanence, and

Heaven knows this is not unique to Washington. Every empire has assumed its own eternity: within a decade of each other both Churchill and Hitler spoke of their respective empires lasting a thousand years apiece. I am sure there are many people in Washington who have envisaged their capital destroyed by a nuclear missile, a fate for which it seems almost expressly designed, but I suspect there are a few politicians who see their ambitions, their successes and their professional sorrows merely as transient contributions to decay. It seems so important, no doubt, when your name goes on that door at last; it seems so desperate, when you lose that election; it seems so magic a moment, when the House Majority Leader recognizes you in the elevator, or the *Washington Post* profiles you, or you get that job on the senatorial staff or the committee payroll. It is all a parade! Nowhere in the world, I think, do people take themselves more seriously than they do in Washington, or seem so indifferent to other perceptions than their own. Whether they are granite reactionaries or raging revolutionaries, they find it hard to see beyond.

As a corrective to this most fundamental error, I used sometimes to go and sit on the grass beside the Mall, where the tourist coaches stop beside the great round pool below Grant's statue, and the white mass of the Capitol looms portentously above it all. I am a cultist of the *genii loci*, those misty and marvelous spirits which are, I believe, literally conjured into being by the force of human experience: and though the Capitol is not very old by mystic standards, still there can be few buildings on earth more compelling to such sprites, so that on the right day I could almost see their vaporous trails circling the great dome, or intercepting each other with comic gestures above the crowning figure of freedom (for they know better than any of us how little liberty has to do with politics). I was awed by the thought of them there, and the high intentions which had for nearly two centuries attended that site, and when I found the ground a little dusty, and cast around for something to sit on, for a moment I really wondered if it would be improper to place my bottom on a map of The Nation's Capital.

The point about the *genii loci*, though, is that they outlive their creators. I could not easily imagine Washington actually deserted, but as I sat there in the hot sun I did not find it hard to imagine the city past its heyday. There is an Indian feeling to Washington on a hot fall day, when the grass is browned by the long summer, the trees have lost their flowers, and the taxis are bouncing desolately through the dust of the new subway excavations—a slight sense of Calcutta, say, where the monuments of another greatness look out forlornly across the parched Maidan. Then I saw Washington too frayed in decline: the gleaming white of the Capitol gray and fretted, the pool blotched with scum, the cherry trees dead in their twos and threes, litter blowing across the grass and slogans scrawled on the statues' plinths. Then I saw the remaining spaces of the Washington plan filled in not with ostentatious halls and galleries, but with the jerry-buildings of an impoverished bureaucracy, and I saw potholes in those ceremonial boulevards, and beggars sleeping disregarded in the shade of the Washington Monument, and two or three mangy dogs nosing about the rubbish outside the Federal Court House.

But as I sat engrossed in this melancholy fancy, I heard a camera click. "Thanks, ma'am," said the cheerful young man with his girl, and instantly I remembered that illusion is a prism: for to them, who was I but your perennial Washington tourist, from Iowa or Arkansas, sitting on her map to keep her skirt clean, a history teacher perhaps, or a realtor's wife of artistic yearnings, sketching the Capitol in her notebook, recording patriotic emotions, or resolving once more to keep America beautiful in a mental as well as physical sense?

The Elder Statesman, being rather deaf, had to lean over the sofa to conduct the conversation, but was not deterred. "Who's that? What? Sure, I remember when Jack cut off aid there. Sam didn't agree. Ted did. De Gaulle didn't want it. I thought we should. What? Who's that? Sure. I remember that very well—the Bay of Pigs—the U-2— Eisenhower didn't have any idea—Khrushchev didn't know—Sam said yes—Dulles said no—I told the committee it couldn't be done. When? Who d'you say? Sure, some people say it was the Truman Doctrine, but it wasn't, only Jack/Sam/Lyndon/Harry said look, if we don't get there as sure as hell there'll be trouble with Nasser/Chiang/Nehru/Thieu. Which? When d'you say? Sure, I met him that evening. Macmillan was there, Gromyko was there, Winston was there, Stalin was there, Napoleon said look, Gladstone said wait a minute, Robert E. Lee was there, Lincoln said to me, I said to the Kaiser, Metternich said not on your sweet life, Bismarck walked out—he was a very difficult guy to deal with. . . . What's that? Which? Sure, yes, I'd love some, no sugar thanks. . . ."

For of course there is to the gigantic fantasy of Washington a hardly less enormous element of truth. If I have romanticized that monologue toward the end, I have not distorted its message—which is that like it or not, Washington is the summit of the Western world. The great seldom seem so great when one meets them face to face, and in Washington especially they seem to shrink in the flesh—the only man I saw in the city who struck me at once with the magic aura of leadership was the cantor or precentor of a group of Hare Krishna devotees. Nevertheless the names that Washington so loves to drop really are the names that will survive in the history books, and that statesman across the sofa was truly reminiscing about the stuff of legend. His wife was there too, and her conversation was hardly less Pepysian or Nicolsonian. "I do think," she said "—and I've just this minute run into him at the Italian Embassy reception—I really do think Henry's getting a *little* too fat."

My own sense of hierarchy is skeptical, even condescending, so that this kind of small talk raises in me more a giggle than a gasp: but I pulled myself together whenever I could and reminded myself that in Washington more than anywhere, perhaps, the great game of politics is played for human lives and happiness. So infectious is the rhythm of the capital, so compelling, I can well see, is the fascination of its charades, that it takes a conscious effort of the will to translate its illusions into reality (not least, as I later discovered, in the presence of Henry, who is not too fat at all, I don't think, and who is so genuinely entertaining a man, with so smoky a wit, that one can hardly grasp the titanesque nature of his employment). There is a car that drives around the town towing a coffin inscribed with the text "The Death of Philippine Democracy." In a city accustomed to the comings and goings of Immortals, such a little cortège goes unremarked. I obliged myself, though, when it passed me one day, to wonder just what it meant, and what tenuous chain of appeal it represented. At one end of the demonstration stood the White House, the fount of all mercy, whose incumbent was commonly supposed to have achieved office by a deal with his predecessor, a common crook, but who would one day be honored in this city, no doubt, whatever his shortcomings, with a Memorial Grove, Archive or Sculpture Garden. At the other end of the message lay—what? Men in prison? Wives distraught? The knock at the midnight door? I did not, to be honest, know much about the state of Philippine democracy, but just to speculate about the connection between the state of human happiness in the Manila backstreets and the condition of human power in the Oval Office was a useful exercise in perspectives.

Here is another. I shared a taxi into town one day with a lady in a blue silk turban who was visiting Washington and was about to meet her daughter for lunch at a Hot Shoppe. Down the great thoroughfares we drove, and all the memorials of the American splendor passed us one by one, granite and concrete, obelisk and colonnade. My companion drew my attention now and then to a White House or a Treasury, but it was as we approached the Capitol itself, and were deploring the state of things in general, that she spoke the words I best remember: "I sometimes wonder, oh, what kind of a world are we bringing our children into, when you have to pay 20¢ for a donut?"

Twenty cents for a donut! Even Americans bleed.

Even Washingtonians. Even Georgetownees. Even White House-holders. Nothing brought me more sensibly down to earth during my stay than poor Mrs. Ford's mastectomy, a suffering which most of us, I suppose, would willingly forgo presidential status to do without . . . wouldn't we? As one whose immediate instinct is to pardon anyone for anything—to understand is to forgive—and who believes that while the good of human conduct goes into the grand repository, the bad just goes to waste, I was always touched by the true if misguided loyalty of Julie Nixon, and see in it still a more important element of that sad and squalid saga than all the collusions of graft or the temptations of tyranny. In Washington there are many reminders, even now, of the old American instinct toward simplicity. I was reassured to find that an ordinary-looking boat moored down at the Navy Yard, which I took to be a lighthouse tender, perhaps, was in fact the presidential yacht

Sequoia, a far cry indeed from the gilded private liners of the European monarchies. Even the White House itself is a happy antidote, for though Jefferson thought it big enough for a couple of emperors, a Pope and a Grand Lama of Tibet, by the standards of princely mansions it is a fairly modest house, a house where, it seems to me, a family could decently and happily live, browsing through the library (or rather the Learning Resources Center), pottering through the garden, or sitting on the lawn with long cool drinks watching the Philippine caskets go by.

For there is, of course, an ordinary, human side to Washington life, deeply buried though it often seems. The shambled districts that I remember southwest of the Capitol have all been swept away, indeed, and replaced by plazas, malls and Award-Winning Developments, but there are still wide districts of Washington, even inner Washington, that feel like parts of a real city, aloof to the central contagion. On 7th Street SE, within sight of the Capitol, genial butchers still offer cracklings and homemade sausages beneath the shabby high-ribbed roof of the Eastern Market (even if, beside the fruiterers, the Washington Consort *does* advertise its forthcoming performance of Early 17th Century Flemish Madrigals). On K Street NW, beneath the Whitehurst Freeway, the freight trains rumble among the waterside cobbles for all the world as though Georgetown were still the little river port of its origins (even if Rive Gauche, just a block away, *does* charge $10 without tax for a straight filet mignon). At Fort McNair, within the dire shadow of the War College, a most agreeable row of early Victorian villas stands beside the Washington Channel, white and wholesome, like village houses around a green. Even in the central shopping streets I sometimes feel myself to be, not in the capital of the Western world, but in some characteristic small city of the South, blistered with heat, where politics aim no further than the next mayor and sheriff, and there is nowhere to go on Sunday but church, the drugstore or the evangelist's tent outside of town.

The rich and the poor, transcending politics, do exist in Washington, and often seem equally immune to its deceptions. To the very, very rich the ambitions of Capitol Hill can doubtless seem trivial or peripheral. "What do you want most in the world?" Mr. Joe Hirshhorn was asked on the night the vast Hirshhorn gallery was opened in the very heart of monumental Washington, adding his name forever to the roster of the great. "Money," he replied. Hardly a stone's throw away, closer still to the Capitol, I remarked to a hot-dog vendor one day what a fantastic place it was to have a stand. "Sure is," he agreed, "fantastic up till Labor Day anyways, 60 or 70 dollars in a single morning. . . ." "Garbage is garbage like anyplace else," said the refuse collector when I asked him if he ever found secret documents in the litter bins.

Such earthy truisms mean more in Washington. For myself I long ago concluded that generally speaking the only important part of life is the private part, and that public ambition is seldom worth the cherishing. This of course disqualifies me from participation in Washington's affairs, but at least it makes me a detached observer. So I tried hard, during my stay in the city, to flake away the surface of the civic conduct and reach the substance beneath: and if I sometimes found that surface and substance were indistinguishable, I often managed to penetrate the display, to reveal a loyal daughter, a 20¢ donut or alas a cancerous node beneath. Even in Washington, D.C., all is relative. "Nothing alters life so absolutely," I overheard a woman saying at Billy Martin's Carriage House, "as having your ears pierced."

"I'll take you," said a kind friend, "to the *real* Washington." He has a piquant humor, and I rather hoped that in this all too familiar threat he was referring to the Wax Museum. But no, instead he took me up Fourteenth Street to show me the gaps and parking lots created in the race riots of 1968, and back via T Street, where one or two black prostitutes, blinking in the cruel light of the afternoon, hung unhopefully around the lampposts.

An inescapable reality of Washington is its blackness. When I first came to the city it somehow did not show. Today it is all-intrusive, and one can hardly miss its underlying conflicts either. Old-fashioned phrases like "Get out of the way, you dumb nigger," or "Don't blow your horn at me, you shit," mingle hourly with the historic texts: in no American city, at least in the past five years, have I felt the old antipathies so viciously. This is partly perhaps because the District of Columbia is still, in a political sense, hardly more than a fief of Congress —a black plantation around the Hill. And it is partly because it is neither exactly a Southern city, nor a Northern, so that two inherited sets of mores clash here, leaving everyone uncertain. I read somewhere that Washington, a city of some 750,000 people, is now the largest black city outside Africa, and for my taste much of its real elegance, most of its true originality, springs from its black awareness. If I want to know the way in Washington, I try to ask a black: for I like the directness of the response I am likely to get, the flash, the style of it.

I looked in one evening at a posh black function at the Washington Hilton, and was greeted with a brilliance that made the poor Georgetown socialites seem dowdy. What terrific strapping women! What gorgeous ruffled shirts! How quick the smiles and explosive the laughter! What energy! What self-esteem! In downtown Washington the fury of blackness communicates itself often in violence, and there is probably no city in the world more thickly policed than Washington, where every street seems to have its prowling patrol car, and the air is meshed with howls, blurps and radio signals. In the upper echelons of black society, though, that dynamism is expressed in very different, more formidable terms, and brings back to Washington a reality that possesses, I like to think, some of the original American excitement. (Though of course it is only *half*-black, the American Negro having interbred so frequently with whites and Indians, and one of the lesser ironies of the place is the attitude of the African students at Howard University, who view the junketings of Washington black society with a distinctly mordant eye.)

I went to the House of Representatives to the 200th anniversary celebration of the First Continental Congress, a ranging shot for the coming bicentennial barrage. The ceremony did not at first impress me, for there is nothing so flaccid as American pageantry. The congressmen looked pasty, as though most of them needed a good night's sleep, or some fresh vegetables for a change. The fife and drum band, in wigs and redcoats, looked downright ridiculous. The representatives who read a fraternal message from the Senate were inaudible. The potted palms they had stacked around the Speaker's desk made the Chamber look like the setting for a palm court trio.

Presently, though, when the band had played its opening piece, the chairman had spoken his introduction, and I was beginning to doodle, a very unexpected voice broke the spell. It was a rich, clever voice, reading with great skill and intensity a passage from Jefferson—"Mr. Jefferson," as he is still apparently known in these parts, as Mr. Rhodes is remembered in Africa. I looked up from my notebook then, and turned my attention to the speaker. She was a youngish, stoutish, vigorous-looking black woman, whose very posture on the rostrum seemed to express a combination of defiance and resolution, and made everybody else look flabby. I left after her speech, for I thought the academics billed to follow her might be bathetic by contrast, and I am glad I did: I had never heard before of Barbara Jordan (D-Texas), but of all the politicians I saw in Washington, she is the one I am least likely to forget.

She was not the only woman, either, who seemed to me to bring an emphatic new distinction to Washington life. Women have changed in most places, of course, in the past twenty years, but nowhere more radically or more significantly than they have in Washington, D.C. When I first came to the city the feminist movement was, so to speak, in abeyance, its theoretical political objectives achieved, its practical social targets not yet formulated. There were women in Congress, of course, but Washington was still in the hand-that-rocks-the-cradle era, or more pertinently, the hand-that-makes-the-table-arrangement phase. The Monstrous Regiment marched still. I remember vividly my first Washington hostesses when, young and terribly British myself, I arrived with unimpeachable letters of introduction and found myself swirled into the Georgetown vortex. Thickly made up and diligently fashionable they greeted me then, and their skirts were precisely the Paris length, and they celebrated their importance in diamonds and pearls, and stood graciously at the senatorial side, inexorably pursuing their husbands' interests.

They survive, and have grown yet more gracious and even more diamondal with the passage of the years, but far more impressive nowadays is the new Washington breed of free women, to be found in every rank or station. I hope I am not biased in admiring them so. I hope I am not naïve, either, for I do see that in the course of their progress toward what I myself take to be the evolutionary goal of androgyne, they may retrogress sometimes, or pick up bad habits from the old hands. But for the moment anyway they seem to me the most trustworthy people in Washington, the people who see life in its truest perspective, the people whose opinions I most valued, whose advice I most welcomed, and whose explanations of the American electoral system I found most nearly comprehensible.

Having newly realized their own potential in this most male-dominated of Western cities, they have the frankness of confidence: they are comrades still, the best of them, one with another, and they are genuinely inspired more by principles than by profits. Also the Washington game is more immediate for them: they are the players now, only yesterday they were the pawns. It is a grand and moving phenomenon, I think, here in the old shrine of individualism, to see one half of humanity coming into its own at last, on a plane of intention and sensibility far beyond the theatricals of women's lib.

But of course I *am* biased. I believe the traditional feminine principles of gentleness, loyalty and realism to be the best ones for politics: here in Washington, combined as they now can be with power and opportunity, I believe them to be the hope of the world.

It occurred to me one day that Washington seemed to go to bed rather early. When I asked why, I was told it was partly because the streets were unsafe at night, but partly because so many Washingtonians were émigrés from the country, used to getting up at six to milk the cows, spread the muck, cut the cane or open up the corner store. I liked this romantic explanation, without much believing in it, and certainly the pretensions of Washington are often redeemed by a small-town, even a country feeling.

Most Americans, it seems, were comforted during the Watergate hearings by the homey philosophy of Senator Sam Ervin. For myself I dislike the genre almost as much as I detest the idiom of Mr. Nixon's kind, and distrust it rather more. But there is a kind of family charm to the presence in the capital of all those provincial politicians. I love to see them ushering constituents around the Capitol, benign and avuncular, and to observe the endearing combination of the condescending (for they are after all Elected Representatives of the People) and the wheedling (for they do after all need votes) with which they shake hands with their respectful visitors at the end of the tour—"We sure are obliged to you, Congressman"—"We certainly are, Sir"—"I shall never forget this day, Congressman"—"*Fine, just fine, great to have you along. . . .*" Meeting a likely looking gent in a Capitol corridor, I tried a gambit myself, as a speculation. "Morning, Senator," I said. "Hullo there young lady," he instantly replied. "Having fun?"—and off he strode to his office, chomping, alas for my purposes, not an actual, but at least a metaphysical cigar.

There are two big Washington airports. From the lovely Dulles Airport the international flights leave, and some people find it exciting to watch them taking off for Rio or Frankfurt, London or Dakar. I much prefer the lesser allegory of the National Airport, beyond the Arlington Cemetery. When L'Enfant laid out Washington, he conceived it as a series of hubs from which symbolic highways would radiate not merely across the capital, I suppose, but far across the nation too—just as Washington's original highway, the Potomac, took the traders past the Georgetown wharfs into the Appalachian hinterland. A much more telling hub now, though, is that airport: nothing is more suggestive in Washington than to watch the jets come in from the American interior, from the states with the magical names, from the prairie clusters and the desert sprawl, from all the huge body of America to this, the marble heart of it. Washington sophisticates tend to scoff, when I express this lyric pleasure to them. But there, I like that sort of thing.

Another thing I like is the disrespect which survives the pomp of Washington. I do not mean the specific disrespect of broadsheet, poster or black comedy: I mean the older, deeper disrespect for circumstance in general, which used to be, for half the world, the very meaning of this republic. One tends to forget the flow of this ancient current, I must say, when the presidential caravan sweeps out of the White House with its cohorts of policemen and bulging bodyguards, but in a way it is what Watergate was all about, and it is not dry yet. "Yeah," said a woman loudly and complacently, stepping back from a china cabinet during our tour of the White House. "Just what I thought—*chipped!*" The apotheosis of the presidency proceeds apace, despite the Nixon heresies, but still in Washington, one sometimes feels, the old instincts are only lying dormant.

The most appealing evidence of this, for the stranger, is the railway-station feeling of Congress itself. I love to wander around its corridors and contrast its cheerful informality with the stately self-esteem of lesser assemblies. What fun to ride the subway train from one side to the other, ruffled in the sub-Capitolian breeze, while the train driver reads his paperback thriller backwards and forwards through the legislature! What a laugh to add your contribution to the restroom graffiti—Cindy loves Ron, or Happyness Is Elvis! How agreeably improbable, to be eating your bean soup in the basement of Congress! Of all the national parliaments I have ever visited, only one rivals the jollity of Capitol Hill, and that is the National Assembly at Reykjavik, where the page boys in jeans and sweaters will run out and get you a bag of chips, if you ask them nicely.

Here is a scene I enjoyed. We are back at the Rockefeller inquiry, in the Old Senate Office Building. The issues are tremendous. The talk is of vast corporations, incalculable funds, life, death and the integrity of the presidency. In the middle of it all, crouching between the chairman's table and Mr. Rockefeller's desk, beneath the high classical vaulting of the inquiry room, with its draped satin curtains, its ornate moldings, its massed ranks of television lights, its majestic Stars and Stripes—in the middle of it all one of the photographers finishes his film, and removing it from his camera, sticks it in an envelope where he crouches.

Turning momentarily from the scene before him, but keeping one eye on the action, he throws this small package halfway across the room to a leather-jerkined young man standing in the aisle holding a crash helmet—who, deftly catching it, and chewing the while upon his gum, puts it in his pocket and in a leisurely and preoccupied manner, chewing all the way, saunters out of the assembly, past the policeman at the door with the Revolver Sharpshooter Badge, through the vast pillared hall, down to his motorbike parked outside. The inquiry proceeds, and by the time that insouciant messenger has kicked his bike into action, we have moved on from the deaths of the Attica prisoners, and the political meaning of great wealth, to discuss the pardoning for crimes unspecified of the 37th President of the United States.

So the realities assert themselves, and we are brought to the core of

Washington. The most fascinating aspect of this capital, the fire of it, is the fusion between what is true and what is false, what is all too real and what is hallucinatory. Balance is the point of Washington—between rulers and ruled, between the three branches of government, between war in the Middle East and the death of Local Resident, 90, between what is magnificent in the American idea, and what is despicable in the American practice. It is the perpetual juggling of antitheses that gives the city an excitement far beyond its architecture, and makes every day in Washington, if scarcely a festival, at least an event.

Today the city is in the aftermath of nightmare, and is still only half wakened from it. Often when one emerges from a particularly ghastly and convincing dream, it is at once a relief and a perverse delight to re-enact its details in the mind—even to embellish them, if you are of an inventive turn. Washington is doing this now. Its people do not realize that though the whole world, like a solicitous friend attending an acid trip, observed its ordeal from the outside, only in Washington was the hideous dream an immediate personal experience. So they are, to be frank, a bit boring about Watergate. They mull it over and over, reliving all its Gothic thrills. Perhaps the real world feels anticlimactic to them, and they half wish they were back in the frightful limbo of the night before.

I was startled by this phenomenon. I had supposed that, with Nixon gone and his accomplices discredited, Washington would be settling with relief into a more composed routine. I expected a contemplative, if shaken community: I found instead a nest of zealots. There was a venom still in the air, something more poisonous I thought than mere political reaction. I had experienced moments of political trauma before —the McCarthy hearings in this same city, the Suez debacle in Britain, France's abdication among the *colons* of Algeria—but I had never felt quite so insidious a sense of bitterness and repulsion as I felt in Washington now. I ventured sometimes, foolishly, to express some of my soppier inbred prejudices, like forgiving and forgetting, or making a fresh start, but I soon discovered that just at the moment the liberal ethic is hardly at a premium in Washington. Gentle and civilized old friends of mine declared not merely that they despised or resented Nixon, but that they *hated* him. One could only compare him, said one distinguished commentator, to a hyena. "I don't know about these Nixons," a hotel porter said to me. "If you cut them, would blood come out?" "I'd no sooner pardon that guy," somebody else told me, "than I'd pardon a rattlesnake."

This is immature language. I thought it at once childish and frightening, and in some way suspect. What were these passions so furiously unleashed? They could hardly be moral disapproval, since everyday politics in America, everyday society in Washington indeed, is riddled as everyone knows with corruptions no less contemptible. The commentator who can only liken Nixon to a hyena is a self-proclaimed thief. Mr. Hirshhorn of the eponymous Museum, upon whom all Washington society embarrassingly fawns, is a convicted stock manipulator. Mr. Abe Fortas, who was obliged to resign from the Supreme Court for a dubious indiscretion in 1969, is doing very nicely with his Georgetown law firm. And if Mr. Nixon's coarseness of language offends the sensitive, it was after all the earnest Mr. McGovern, for whom the very reporters wept in idealistic sympathy, who told a heckler during the 1972 election to go kiss his ass (or, as I prefer to spell it myself, being a traditionalist in these matters, his *arse*). To be shocked by President Nixon's conduct is, in the context of 20th-century America, pure hypocrisy. To be surprised, sheer gullibility.

What then? Many thoughtful people, no doubt, believe themselves to have narrowly escaped a true political catastrophe: the establishment of a personal tyranny, equipped with all the paraphernalia of a police state. Many more feel themselves to have been above all hoodwinked. Hell hath no fury like a voter fooled, and the vast majority of Americans, after all, though you would hardly guess it from the Washington conversations, judged Mr. Nixon their best available leader—that Washington, D.C., as it happens, plumped in 1972 for George McGovern only goes to prove, I fear, the superior skepticism of the blacks. Others again are simply enjoying the peculiar American appetite for blood and honey, which gnaws another's ignominy as it licks another's success.

Slowly I grew to differentiate these various responses, and to commiserate with some of them, for I recognize this particular nightmare to have been true. What I found more disturbing was the popular feeling of a general betrayal, expressed so often in Washington through the myth of conspiracy. The conspiratorial strain, like the violent strain, has figured largely in the American past, not least because it has so often been founded upon hard fact. The Elders of Zion may be imaginary, but the Mafia distinctly is not, and the present taste for things eerie and unexplained has given extra force to the sense that evil secret energies are webbed beneath the surface of political life. Sometimes my informants specialized in single conspiracies. Sometimes they apparently lumped together all the tragedies of the sixties and seventies, all the scandals and assassinations, the cover-ups and the revelations, the wars and even the illnesses in one hazed but embittered conception. Johnson had Kennedy murdered, Nixon had Wallace shot. Connally was behind it all, Mitchell was only a front, Ford was in it, Liddy was at Dallas, Calley knew Haldeman, Ruby was a classmate of Dean—"Did you ever stop to think about this: Why did McGovern choose Eagleton in the first place? You think he didn't know about that guy's head-shrink? *Sure he knew. . . ."*

On a higher level this instinct turns into a conviction that *everyone* has something to hide, an unfortunate conviction in political terms, for it is undeniably true. Faith in analysis is strong in America, and the notion that some truths are best left fallow is not popular in the capital. I was at a dinner table one night when one of the investigative reporters who are the contemporary lions of Washington was discussing new targets—Kissinger, Ford of course, Rockefeller, nobody had ever *really* done Rocky. . . . I found it a depressing conversation. Who was there, I bleakly asked, what single leader, to whom they could give their loyalty and trust, without sensing the need for an exposé? But answer came there none, for they had changed the subject by then, and over a particularly delicious and innovative sole with orange sauce, were back to Watergate once more.

There is no denying the stimulation of this extraordinary mise-en-scène, where truth and innuendo, fact and legend are all intermingled. It is like a political Hollywood: faces familiar to the world are the commonplaces of its sidewalks, and the tour buses take their sightseers to Watergate precisely as they circumambulate the Homes of the Stars—as my Washington guidebook says, there is no better place than the Army and Navy Club "to catch a glimpse of high-ranking officers off duty." The Washington actors are perpetually onstage, and their audience too is half drawn into the performance, so that the sense of theater binds every aspect of the city together, and makes it difficult even for visiting hedonists to remain altogether detached. Even I expressed a political opinion once or twice in Washington, and nearly always found it, whether it expressed the reactionary or the radical in me, Welsh intuition or English decadence, instantly and conclusively squelched. Coals are hard to sell in Newcastle.

I went to the opening of the Watergate cover-up trial, when Messrs. Mitchell, Haldeman et al. appeared before Judge Sirica in the Federal Court House. During the lunch recess I found myself descending the courtroom stairs behind John Ehrlichman, who courteously opened the door for me before passing with his wife into the sunshine of Constitution Avenue. Against all my better instincts, for in me the urges of an investigative reporter are not simply atrophied, they are actually reversed, I decided to follow the couple down the avenue and see where they went. At first a small pack of photographers pursued them like seagulls following a trawler, dismissing them at a street corner with genial insincerities—"Thanks a lot," "Take care," "Have a good lunch." Then they were all alone, and in the bright sunshine they walked hand in hand toward the Federal Triangle.

Nobody looked twice at them. Nobody noticed them, so far as I could tell. Not a secretary nudged her companion as they passed, not a hardhat stared from the subway works. Ehrlichman's name and face were familiar wherever newspapers are read. He was standing trial for one of the most shattering political crimes of the century. Only months before he had been one of the most powerful men in America. He had been called the Göring to Nixon's Hitler, the jackal perhaps to the hyena. Yet nobody noticed. I was oddly touched, sentimentalist that I am, by the sight of that fated couple waiting for the traffic lights to change, and felt a momentary urge to reach out to them with a smile or a touch of the sleeve: but I remembered who I was working for, and restrained myself with a shudder as, hand in hand still, they crossed the Mall and disappeared for their half-hour of privacy into the National Gallery of Art. ("You think they didn't know you was watching? *Sure they knew. . . .*")

He was a bad, bad man, my friends told me reprovingly, when I confessed to this little episode. Hand in hand, they said, was the oldest cliché in the game. Heart's no use without head, they said. Mercy demands justice, they told me. Well, I know it, and it is a chill fact about the Washington stage that the villains up there are not acting. Here the melodrama is true. That really is the Pentagon, scowling beyond the river. Ring 351-1100 and the nasal, bored voice of the operator really will announce "Central Intelligence." This is the city of the wiretap, the bodyguard and the foreign spy, where assassination is a daily possibility, where the Pentagon disposes of its missiles and the Navy Department its submarines. Here in Washington indeed, just down the road from my hotel, is the black box which, at a word from the White House, can wreck the world. There's *Grand Guignol* for you!

Capital of a violent nation, Washington is accustomed to violent values. Its general air is easygoing, but its bad men are truly bad, and brute force lies always near the heart of it. The climax of the public tour of the FBI headquarters, in the Federal Triangle, is a demonstration shoot by a marksman, who shuts himself in a glass-walled range, muffles his ears with a headset, and shoots at a paper target in the shape of a human torso, first with a revolver, then with a submachine gun. He was using demonstration bullets actually, our guide explained when I attended this display, to make a cleaner hole: the ones they used in real life ripped the target about a little too much. Our marksman that day, an amiable man who looked like a dentist, perhaps, or a bank teller approaching retirement, shot very accurately indeed, placing all his bullets within what we were told was the most desirable area, around the heart and lungs; and presently, opening his glass door and pressing a button, he brought his torso target winging spookily and horribly deathlike back toward us on a runner—"Like I say," our guide repeated, "in real life it'd be more torn about." In the kindliest way he removed it from its fastening and folded it into a tidy package: and looking around his smiling and grateful audience, and choosing the smallest infant in the front row, with a quip about playing hooky from school that day he presented the child with the mangled evidence of his skill. "Real neat," the little boy's mother thought. The tour is, so they told me at the gate, one of the most popular experiences the Nation's Capital has to offer.

30

If there is something infantile to all these dramatics, the bombs, the wiretaps, the FBI machismo, well, there is something juvenile of course to the whole paraphernalia of power, wherever it is pursued. (The only wholly adult statesman I have ever heard of was Lord Salisbury, who once said that his notion of British foreign policy was to drift gently downstream, now and then putting an oar out to prevent a collision.) In Washington the silliness of it is only intensified by the volatility of America itself, which seems to me at once the genius and the absurdity of the republic. America is the land of the instant flattery, the absolute rejection. Here more than anywhere fashions shift, and opinion follows its leaders of the day. Where are the protesters of yesteryear? Where are the McCarthyites of the decade before? A cause vanishes, and so does its fervor; an issue arises, and there are convictions to match. A single New York critic can destroy a play; a single Washington columnist can destroy a reputation; a nation which votes a man into office by an overwhelming majority in 1972 can discover him to be a common criminal by 1974. The American pendulum, whose pivot is in Washington, swings not simply side to side, but erratically backwards and forwards too.

It seldom, though, goes round in circles. It is hard to be bored in Washington. Every morning breaks the excitement anew. Nothing is ordinary. The moment I left the trail of the Ehrlichmans that day, I encountered another familiar of the Washington scene, equally ignored by the lunchtime crowds. He was a very serious-looking man of Jewish cast, dressed entirely as President Lincoln and walking purposefully in the direction of the White House—where else? He carried a briefcase under his arm, inscribed, so far as I could without rudeness make out, with the name Abraham B. Lincoln: and this was satisfyingly puzzling, in a city of cryptic mysteries, for as anyone knows, Abe Lincoln has no middle name.

A transcendental quality is part of modern American life. It goes with space travel, with electronics, with drugs, with contemporary art and humor, with the knowledge always at the backs of our minds, especially in Washington, D.C., that we have the power to blow the world up. The nature of reality has shifted too, so that illusion has acquired new substance, and neither space nor time nor matter can lightly be defined (let alone truth).

So the delusions of Washington, if they are delusions, are the delusions of America, just as America's own faults and merits are, in a less intense or underdeveloped degree, common to us all. One reads constantly that the American public is pining for a thorough reform of political life, an end to corruption in high places. But the corruption of Watergate is different only in application, not in kind, from the general mayhem. The big lie is the small lie magnified, and I suspect it to be the only true political aphorism that a nation gets the leaders it deserves. What is FBI surveillance but investigative reporting from the other side? Who in Washington has not bugged, if not another's private telephone, at least another's private business? White House doublespeak is only the old Georgetown flattery, employed in another genre. It is only a step, if a big one, from pretending to like a picture you loathe to charging the state for improvements at San Clemente.

For myself I have come reluctantly to believe that these values are inherent to democracy, when it reaches a particular stage in its development—or decay. But because America does not yet share this morose persuasion, or at least prefers not to recognize it, on my last afternoon in Washington I went along to Capitol Hill to watch President Ford address a joint session of Congress about his economic policies. I suppose one might say this was the ultimate in Washington occasions—the First Citizen addressing the Legislature of his fellow countrymen, and presenting for their approval his plans for the community. At least that is how I viewed it. The 38th presidency was another attempt, a late attempt, to prove that the system worked, that the Washington balances still made for the good of the nation, that the whole grand idea of America, so imperishably represented in Washington's images and epitaphs, was not just a sorry and discredited sham. President Ford was trying to prove that dishonesty was an American aberration, not an American norm. "We will be good," he seemed to be saying, like Queen Victoria before him, and the nation echoed him in the jargon of the day —*you gotta believe!*

I was not convinced about the system that afternoon, but I was convinced by President Ford. He is no orator, no economist either I suspect. His speech was full of speech-writer's ham: wunnerful young people— zeroing into problems—time to intercept—pitching in with Uncle Sam.

In his lapel he wore a footling ad-man's badge saying "Win," an emblem he appeared fondly to suppose would soon sweep the fifty states. When he shook hands with his old colleagues of the House, or accepted their ovation with a disarming smile, I knew as well as everyone else that the bonhomie was charged with political nuance and deceit. He is not a handsome man, nor a man of inspiration, and he has not a quarter of the magnetism of that Hare Krishna chant leader, nor half the awful fascination of his predecessor.

Yet he stirred me. There! There among the ghosts and shadows, there in that great hall smoked with the fires of glory as of fraud, there in the very center of the American meaning, he seemed to me to be doing his best. Hard though I tried, I simply could not imagine him standing there, as Nixon might have stood, discredited and abused. I think it all too likely that the whole ornamental façade of Americanism, all its Declarations and Dedications and Bicentennial Festivities, has become hardly more than a gigantic publicity device, like Mother's Day, like monumental Washington itself. But if Gerald Ford is a bad man, if those investigative tigers ever discover anything really discreditable about him, if the motives of the 38th presidency prove to be anything but honorable, if he fiddles his tax returns or even tells a heckler to go kiss his ass, then I will, upon demand, sadly eat this essay.

The object that moved me most in Washington, more than the Declaration of Independence, dim lit above its altar at the Archives, more than Grant brooding on his tall horse above the Mall, more than Giorgione's *Adoration of the Magi* (which, as a matter of fact, I do not believe to be the work of that master)—the object that most moved me was the minuscule capsule in which the first American space traveler was projected out of the earth's gravity, hunched on his pad among his dials. I looked at it for a long time on its stand at the Smithsonian, wondering at the courage that once inhabited it, and contemplating the vast pyramid of money and brains of which it was the apex. As I did so I subjected myself to another of those self-summoned visions to which I am prone, and I imagined myself leaving Washington strapped in its padded chair. Up I went with a swoosh, up through the splintered museum roof, and presently the domes and obelisks were flattened below me, and the great gardens and boulevards were retreating fast, and the

Potomac was only a silver thread, and all the big radial roads were spinning, spinning through my window, until the very shape of Washington was lost in the mass of the world, and the haze of cloud, and the dim blue blur of space.

Nothing was left in my mind then but the echoes of the capital, distantly pursuing me—*Sure, I remember it well—Rocky, nobody's really done Rocky—you look terrific—that louse?—oh, what a world to bring children into!—that hyena?—I mean that in a mental as well as a physical aspect—if you cut them would blood come out?—they rip the target about a little—E Pluribus Unum—come to me!—ask Fish Bait—20¢ for a donut!—sure he knew* . . . ever more faintly, ever less strident, until at last all those harsh discords were stilled into harmony, and were only another hum in the music of the spheres.

Move along lady, please. Give the kids a chance. Christ, the dumb bitch.

. . . .

MRS. GUPTA
NEVER RANG

*Indira Gandhi was in power in Delhi in 1975,
but though she had clamped the country under a State of
Emergency, harshly limiting the press and imprisoning much of the
opposition, to the stranger the Indian capital felt much the same
as ever. There is not much in this essay to reveal which particular
regime governed India at the time of its writing: Delhi is one of those
cities whose age, manner and disposition easily absorb the
transient styles of its successive rulers.*

· · ·

DELHI

· · · · · · · · · · · · · · · · ·

Mrs. Gupta Never Rang
[*1975*]

"YOU SEE," SAID THE GOVernment spokesman, "you may liken Delhi to the River Ganges, it twists and turns, many other streams join it, it divides into many parts, and it flows into the sea in so many channels that nobody may know which is the true river. You follow my train of thought? It is a metaphysical matter, perhaps. You will do best to burrow under the surface of things and discover what is not revealed to us ordinary mortals! In the meantime, you will take a cup of tea, I hope?" ❧ I took a cup of tea, milkless, very sweet, brought by a shuffling messenger in a high-buttoned jacket with a scarf around his neck, and between pleasantries I pondered the spokesman's advice. Indians, of course, love to reduce the prosaic to the mystic. It is part of their Timeless Wisdom. For several centuries the tendency has variously baffled, infuriated, amused and entranced travelers from the West, and India is full of pilgrims still, come from afar to worship at the shrines of insight. But *Delhi*? Delhi is not just a national capital, it is one of the political ultimates, one of the prime movers. It was born to power, war and glory. It rose to greatness not because holy men saw visions there but because it commanded the strategic routes from the Northwest, where the conquerors came from, into the rich flatlands of the Ganges delta. Delhi is a soldiers' town, a politicians' town, a journalists', diplomats' town. It is Asia's Washington, though not so picturesque, and lives by ambition, rivalry and opportunism.

"Ah yes," he said, "what you are thinking is quite true, but that is the *surface* of Delhi. You are an artist, I know, you should look *beyond*! And if there is anything we can do to help your inquiries," he added with an engaging waggle of his head, "you have only to let us know. You may telephone us at any time and we will ring you back with the requisite information in a moment or two. We are here to help! That is why we are here! No, no, that is our duty!"

Certainly Delhi is unimaginably antique, and age is a metaphysic, I suppose. Illustrations of mortality are inescapable there, and do give the place a sort of nagging symbolism. Tombs of emperors stand beside traffic junctions, forgotten fortresses command suburbs, the titles of lost dynasties are woven into the vernacular, if only as street names.

One of the oldest and deadest places I know, for a start, is the crumbled fortress-capital of Tughluqabad in the city's southern outskirts. For a single decade it was a place of terrific consequence, for nearly seven centuries since it has been a gray wasteland of piled stones and ruined alleyways, a *memento mori* by any standard, inhabited only by the disagreeable monkeys which are the familiars of Delhi, and by a melancholy watchman who, recently transferred by the Archaeological Survey from some more frequented historical monument, now sees nobody but the apes from one day to the next.

Or consider, in another kind of allegory, the Lodi Gardens. These are popular promenades, but they are also the cemetery of the Lodi kings who thrived in the early 16th century. Here death and life consort on familiar terms, and especially in the early morning, when Delhi people go out for some fresh air before the sun comes up, they offer some piquant juxtapositions. All among the memorials the citizens besport themselves, pursuing their Yogic meditations in the tomb of Sikander Lodi, jog trotting among the funerary domes, exercising their pampered dachshunds beside the Bara Gumbad Mosque or pissing, in the inescapable Delhi manner, behind the mausoleum of Mohammed Shah.

They used to say, to express the marvelous continuity of Delhi, that seven successive capitals existed here, each superimposed upon the last. Nowadays they are always finding new ones, and the latest tally seems to be fourteen. Few foreigners and still fewer Indians have ever heard of most of the dynasties represented, but here and there across the capital some of them have left not merely tombs or ruins but living remnants of themselves. Embedded, for instance, in one of Delhi's smarter quarters, almost within sight of the Oberoi Intercontinental, is the Moslem village shrine of Nizamuddin, built in the time of the 14th-century Sultan Ghiyasuddin Tughluq and still as holy as ever.

Through tortuous mucky lanes one approaches it from the busy highway, past the statutory Indian lines of beggars, crones and saddhus, through the spittle-stained portals where the old men stare, and into the intricate jumble of courts, tombs and arcades that surrounds the mosque of Nizamuddin and its sacred pool. Here mendicants lope around on knobbly staves, saintly scholars are at their books, sweet old ladies sit outside tombs (they are not allowed in, being female), and in the mosque there hustles and brushes the muezzin, an indefatigable goblin figure with white eyebrows and dainty tread. Nothing here is unpremeditated. All moves, though you might not guess it, to an immemorial schedule: the prayer call comes precisely to time, the rituals are meticulously ordered, even the whining beggars have their appointed place in the hierarchy, and when I left the precincts the imam gave me his visiting card—his name is Al Haj Hazrat Peer Qazi Syed Safdar Ali Nizami and his cable address is HEADPRIEST DELHI.

Even more a living relic, so to speak, is the Begum Timur Jehan Shahzadi of Darya Ganj, in the old walled city of Delhi. This lady is a Moghul princess of the dynasty which made Delhi its capital in the 17th century and built the very city, Shahjehanabad, in whose labyrinthine recesses she lives now. Just go to the Old City, her son-in-law

had assured me, and ask for the Begum Jehan's house: and though in
the event this proved insufficient advice and I spent half an afternoon
stumbling through the high-walled maze of Shahjehanabad, vainly presenting the inquiry, still I relished the form of it and thought it was
rather like knocking on the door of the Great Pyramid, asking for
Cheops.

I found her in the end anyway, ensconced in her front sitting room
between portraits of her imperial forebears: a short, decisive old lady
with a brief mischievous smile and an air of totally liberated self-
possession. There is no pretending that this princess lives much like a
princess. Her old house, into which her family moved when they were
ejected by later conquerors from their imperial palace, is a beguiling
shambles in the old Islamic style: a couple of rooms in the Western
manner for the convenience of visitors, the rest more or less medieval—
a wide decrepit courtyard, a dusty trellised vine, thickly populated
chambers all around. There are granddaughters and sons-in-law and undefined connections; there are skivvies and laundrymen and assorted
sweepers; there are children and dogs and unexplained loiterers in doorways. Forty or fifty souls constitute the tumbled court of the Begum
Timur Jehan, and through it she moves commandingly in green trousers,
issuing instructions, reminiscing about emperors, traitors or ladies of the
harem, and frequently consulting her highly organized notebook, all
asterisks and cross-references, for addresses or reminders.

Like HEADPRIEST DELHI she lives very near the earth, close to the
muck and the spittle, close to the mangy dogs and the deformed indigents in the street outside. Delhi is scarcely an innocent city, for on
every layer it is riddled with graft and intrigue, but it is distinctly
organic, to an atavistic degree. An apposite introduction to the city, I
think, is provided by Map Eight of the *Delhi City Atlas*, which marks a
substantial slab of the municipal area as being Dense Jungle: though this
is now a city of a million inhabitants, it feels near the bush still. From
many parts of it the open plain is in sight, and the country trees of India,
the feathery tamarisks and ubiquitous acacias, invade every part of it—
the animals too, for squirrels are everywhere and monkeys, buffalos,
cows, goats and a million pi-dogs roam the city streets peremptorily.

There is simplicity everywhere, too, for rural people from all India flock into Delhi for jobs, for help, to see the sights. There are Sikhs and sleek Bengalis, Rajputs ablaze with jewelry, smart Gujaratis from the western coast, beautiful Tamils from the south, cloaked Tibetans smelling of untanned leather, clerks from Bombay smelling of aftershave, students, wandering sages, clumping soldiers in ammunition boots, black-veiled Moslem women, peasants in for the day from the scorched and desiccated Punjab plains. Endearingly they trail through their national monuments, awe-struck, and the attendants intone their monologues hoping for tips, and the tourist buses line up outside the Presidential Palace, and the magicians prepare their levitations and inexplicable disappearances in the dusty ditch below the ramparts of the Red Fort.

This is the Gandhian truth of India, expressed in Delhi chiefly by such reminders of an earthier world beyond the city limits. Though I fear I might not give up my electric typewriter without a struggle, still I am a Gandhian myself in principle, and respond easily to this suggestion of a vast Indian naïveté, stretching away from Delhi like a limitless reservoir, muddied perhaps but deeply wholesome. The Gandhian ethic is rather outmoded in India, in fact, and the Mahatma himself seems to be losing his charismatic appeal, but still I liked the inscriptions in the visitors' book at Birla House, where he died in 1948 (his body was displayed to the public on the roof, illuminated by searchlight), and where many a country pilgrim reverently pauses. "My heart heaving with emotion," wrote P. H. Kalaskar. "Moving indeed," thought A. K. Barat. Several people wrote "Felt happy." One said "Most worth seeing place in Delhi," and when, quoting from the master himself, I contributed "Truth is God," the inevitable onlookers murmured, "very good, very good," nodded approvingly to each other and touched my hand in sympathy.

Delhi is a city of basic, spontaneous emotions: greed, hate, revenge, love, pity, kindness, the murderous shot, the touch of the hand. Its very subtleties are crude: even its poverty is black and white. On the one side are the organized beggar children who, taught to murmur a few evocative words of despair like "hungry," "baby" or "mummy," succeed all too often in snaring the susceptible stranger. On the other are the courtly thousands of the jagghis, the shantytowns of matting, tentage and old packing cases which cling like black growths to the presence of Delhi.

There are beggars in Delhi who are comfortably off, and people too proud to beg who possess nothing at all, not a pot or a pan, not a pair of shoes. I saw one such man, almost naked, shivering with the morning cold and obviously very ill, huddled against a lamppost in Janpath early one morning. He asked for nothing, but I felt so sorry for him, and for a moment so loved him for his suffering, that I gave him a ten-rupee note, an inconceivable amount by the standards of Indian indigence. He looked at it first in disbelief, then in ecstasy and then in a wild gratitude, and I left him throwing his hands to heaven, singing, praying and crying, still clinging to his lamppost, and sending me away, slightly weeping myself, to coffee, toast and orange juice ("You'll be sure it's chilled, won't you?") at my hotel.

The voice of the people, Gandhi used to say, is the voice of God. I doubt it, but I do recognize a divine element to the Indian poverty, ennobled as it is by age and sacrifice. Indians rationalize it by the concept of reincarnation, and I see it too as a halfway condition, a station of the cross. "In the next world," I suggested to my driver after a long and exhausting journey into the country, "I'll be driving and you'll be lying on the back seat," but he answered me with a more elemental philosophy. "In the next world," he replied, "we'll *both* be lying on the back seat!" For even the inegality of Delhi, even the pathos, often has something robust to it, a patient fatalism that infuriates many modernists but is a solace to people like me. It is disguised often in Eastern mumbojumbo, preached about in ashrams to gullible Californians and exploited by swamis from the divine to the absurd: but it is really no more than a kindly acceptance of things as they are, supported by the sensible thesis that things are not always what they appear to be.

But pathos, yes. Delhi is the capital of the losing streak. It is the metropolis of the crossed wire, the missed appointment, the puncture, the wrong number. Every day's paper in Delhi brings news of some new failure, in diplomacy, in economics, in sport: when India's women entered the world table-tennis tournament during my stay in Delhi, not only were they all beaten but one actually failed to turn up for the match. I was pursued in the city by a persistent and not unattractive

Rajput businessman. I thought him rather suave as I fended him off, in his well-cut check suit and his trendy ties, confident of manner, worldly of discourse: but one day I caught sight of him hors de combat, so to speak, muffled in a threadbare overcoat and riding a battered motor scooter back to his suburban home—and suddenly saw him, far more endearingly if he did but know it, as he really was, smallish, poorish, struggling and true.

He dropped me in the end anyway, perhaps because I developed an unsightly boil in my nose—men seldom send roses to girls with red noses. The side of my face swelled up like a huge bunion, and I was half red and half white, and sniffly and sad and sorry for myself. In this condition, self-consciously, I continued my investigations, and at first I was touched by the tact with which Indians in the streets pretended not to notice. After a day or two, though, I realized that the truth was more affecting still. They *really* did not notice. They thought my face quite normal. For what is a passing grotesquerie, in a land of deformities?

"Certainly," said the government spokesman, perusing my list of questions, "by all means, these are all very simple matters. We can attend to them for you at once. As I told you, it is our duty! It is what we are paid for! I myself have to attend an important meeting this afternoon—you will excuse me I hope?—but I will leave all these little matters with our good Mrs. Gupta and all will be taken care of. I will telephone you with the answers myself without fail—or if not I myself, then Mrs. Gupta will be sure to telephone you either today or tomorrow morning. Did you sign our register? A duplicate signature here if you would not mind, and the lady at the door will issue you with the requisite application form for a pass—it will make everything easier for you, you see. Have no fear, Mrs. Gupta will take care of everything. But mark my words, you will find the spiritual aspects of our city the most rewarding. Remember the River Ganges! As a student of history, you will find that I am right! Ha ha! Another cup of tea? You have time?"

Even he would agree, though, that the spiritual aspect is hardly predominant in New Delhi, the headquarters of the Indian government and the seat of Indian sovereignty—the newest and largest of Delhi's successive capitals. This was built by the British, and despite one or two sententious symbolisms and nauseating texts—*"Liberty Will Not Descend to a People, A People Must Raise Themselves to Liberty"*—it is a frank and indeed noble memorial to their own imperial Raj. It is not anomalous even now. For one thing it was built in a hybrid style of East and West, to take care of all historical contingencies, and for another, Britishness is far from dead in Delhi. Delhi gentlemen, especially of the sporting classes, are stupendously British still. Delhi social events can be infinitely more English than Ascot or Lords. The following scrambled-names puzzle appeared recently in a Delhi magazine: LIWL FFFEY (a comedian); UALNIJ YHLXEU (a zoologist); ARMY SHES (a pianist); HIIPPLL LLEGAADU (a historian). Only two classes of people on earth could solve this riddle without reference books: Britons of a certain age, Indians of a certain class.

Besides, the grand ensemble of New Delhi, the Presidential Palace flanked by the two wings of the Secretariat, has adapted easily to the republican style. It was the greatest single artifact of the British Empire, perhaps its principal work of art, and there are men still alive in Delhi who spent all their working lives building it. I met one, a rich and venerable Sikh contractor, and he recalled the great work with immense pride, and spoke affectionately of its English architects, and said it never once occurred to him to suppose, during all the years he worked upon it, that an Indian would ever be sitting in the halls of the Viceroy's Lodge.

Seen early on a misty morning from far down the ceremonial mall, Rajpath, New Delhi is undeniably majestic—neither Roman, its architects said, nor British, nor Indian, but *imperial*. Then its self-consciousness (for its mixture of styles is very contrived) is blurred by haze and distance and by the stir of awakening Delhi—the civil servants with their bulging briefcases, the multitudinous peons, the pompous early-morning policemen, the women sweepers elegant in primary colors, the minister perhaps (if it is not *too* early) in his chauffeur-driven, Indian-built limousine, the stocky Gurkha sentries at the palace gates, the first eager tourists from the Oberoi Intercontinental, the entertainer with his dancing monkeys, the snake charmer with his acolyte children, the public barber on the pavement outside Parliament, the women preparing their washing beside the ornamental pools, the man in khaki who, approaching you fiercely across the formal gardens, asks if you would care for a cold drink.

Then the power of India, looming above these dusty complexities, is unmistakable: not only created but instinctive, sensed by its foreign rulers as by its indigenous, and aloof to history's permutations. Of all the world's countries, India is the most truly prodigious, and this quality of astonishment displays itself afresh every day as the sun comes up in Delhi. Five-hundred-and-eighty-million people, three-hundred languages, provinces from the Himalayan to the equatorial, cities as vast as Bombay and Calcutta, villages so lost in time that no map marks them, nuclear scientists and aboriginal hillmen, industrialists of incalculable wealth and dying beggars sprawled on railway platforms, three or four great cultures, myriad religions, pilgrims from across the world, politicians sunk in graft, the Grand Trunk Road marching to Peshawar, the temples of Madras gleaming in the sun, an inexhaustible history, an incomprehensible social system, an unfathomable repository of human resource, misery, ambiguity, vitality and confusion—all this, the colossal corpus of India, invests, sprawls around, infuses, elevates, inspires and very nearly overwhelms New Delhi.

Searching for a corrective to such cosmic visions, I thought I would investigate the roots or guts of New Delhi, instead of contemplating its tremendous aura, so I inveigled my way not into the State Hallroom or the Durbar Hall but into the kitchens of the Presidential Palace, by way of an obliging aide-de-camp and a compliant housekeeper (for as dubious flunkies repeatedly murmured as I made my way downstairs, "It is not allowed to visitors"). At first I thought I had succeeded in finding humanity among that majesty, for the way to the kitchens passed through a labyrinth of homely offices, workshops and storerooms and cupboards, supervised by smiling and apparently contented domestics. Here were the Pot Cleaners, scouring their big copper pans. Here were the Linen Keepers, standing guard on their pillowslips. Here were the Washing Up Men, ankle deep in suds themselves, and here the Bakers invited me to taste the morning's loaf. I felt I was passing through some living exhibition of Indian Crafts, diligent, chaste and obliging.

But even before I entered the kitchens proper, a clanking and grand aroma brought me back to the realities of New Delhi, for in the palace of Rashtrapati Bhavan, Downstairs is scarcely less consequential than Up. These kitchens are imperial institutions themselves, half Western, half Eastern, colossal in scale, lordly in pretension. Armies of cooks seemed to be laboring there. Foods of a dozen cuisines seemed to be in preparation. Batteries of aged electric ovens hummed and whirred. There were squadrons of deep freezers and battalions of chopping boards and armories of steel choppers. The cooks and their underlings bowed to me as I passed, but not obsequiously. It was with condescension that they greeted me, one by one along the preparation tables, and when at last I reached the sizzling center of that underworld, I felt myself to be more truly at a crossroad of the empires than anywhere else in Delhi—for there, just around the corner from the English ovens of the viceroys, they were smoking over charcoal braziers, scented with wheat grain, the aromatic yellow pomfrets that were a grand delicacy of the Moghuls.

So even in the kitchens power presides, in a traditional, ample sense. Delhi is full of it, for this republic, which came to office in a loincloth, rules in a gaudier uniform. Nehru said that modern Western civilization was ersatz, living by ersatz values, eating ersatz food: but the ruling classes of Delhi, the politicians, the businessmen, the military, have mostly adopted those values without shame. Gandhi said that his India would have "the smallest possible army," but Delhi is one of the most military of all capitals: when I looked up some friends in the Delhi telephone book, I found that under the name Khanna there were four generals, an air commodore, twelve colonels, a group captain, twelve majors, three wing commanders, four captains, one commander, three lieutenant commanders and a lieutenant.

Nor is Delhi's display just a façade or a bluff. India often seems to outsiders a crippled country, emaciated by poverty and emasculated by philosophy, but it is only a half-truth. We are told that half India's population is undernourished and three-quarters illiterate: that leaves nearly 180 million people who are well fed and literate. The Indian gross national product is the tenth largest on earth. The armies of India are very strong and are largely equipped from Indian factories. I went one day to the Delhi Industrial Fair, housed in a series of modernist ziggurats directly across the street from the gateway of the ruined city Purana Qila, and there I discovered that India makes not only warships, railways engines and aircraft, but Carbicle Grinders too, Lapping Machines and Micro-Fog Lubricators ("I'll take that one," said I flippantly, pointing to an electric transformer as big as a cottage, "please send it to my hotel"—and diligently the salesman took out his order form).

Power corrupts, of course, and in India it corrupts on a grand scale. At the top, the whisper of nepotism or opportunism repeatedly approaches Central Government itself. At the bottom, graft harasses the street hawkers of the city, who can scarcely afford the protection money demanded by the police. Even the stranger to Delhi feels the rot: in the arrogant petty official declining to look up from his newspaper, in the stifling addiction to red tape and precedent, in the affectations and snobberies which, as they thrive in Washington's Georgetown, flourish here too in the districts south of Rajpath.

As it happens, I am rather an addict of power. I do not much enjoy submitting to it or even exerting it, but I do like observing it. I like the aesthetics of it, colored as they so often are by pageantry and history. I am everybody's patriot, and love to see the flags flying over palace or parliament, Westminster or Quai d'Orsay. I am very ready to be moved by the emanations of power in Delhi—the sun setting behind the Red Fort, the grand mass of New Delhi seen across the dun plateau or the ceremony of Beating Retreat on Vijay Chowk, when a dozen military bands pluck at the heart with the Last Post and "Abide with Me."

Nobody cries more easily than I do, when the bugle sounds or the flag comes down, but somehow I do not respond to the old magic in India. The British, rationalizing their own love of imperial pomp, used to claim that it was necessary to retain the respect of Asiatics. It availed them nothing, though, against the "half-naked fakir," as Churchill called Gandhi, and now too the magnificence of Delhi seems paradoxically *detached* from India. How remote the great ensigns which, enormously billowing above their embassies in the diplomatic enclave, testify to the presence of the plenipotentiaries! How irrelevant the posturings of the grandees, hosts and guests alike, the Polish defense minister greeted by epauletted generals, the Prince of Wales inevitably winning his polo match, the resident Congress party spokesman puffed up at one press conference, the visiting minister of national reorientation condescending at the next.

And most detached of all seems the unimaginable bureaucracy of Delhi, battening upon the capital—a power sucker, feeding upon its own consequence or sustained intravenously by interdepartmental memoranda, triplicate applications, copies and comments and addenda and references to precedent—a monstrous behemoth of authority, slumped immovable among its files and tea trays. Much of it is concerned not with practical reality at all but with hypotheses or dogma. Forty government editors are engaged in producing the collected works of Gandhi, down to the last *pensée*—they have got to volume fifty-four. Hundreds more are concerned with plans, for there was never a capital like Delhi for planners—the Multilevel Planning Section, the Plan Coordination Division, the Plan Information Unit, the Social Planning Unit, the Project Appraisal Unit, the Socio-Economic Research Unit, the Program Evaluation Organization, the National Sample Survey Organization, the National Survey Organization, the Central Statistical Organization. Big Brother is everywhere, with a slide rule, a clipboard and a warning in small print. "This map," says one Delhi tourist publication severely, "is published for tourists as a master guide and *not as legal tender*"—and there, in its mixture of the interfering, the pedantic, the unnecessary and the absurd, speaks the true voice of Indian officialdom.

But this is an essential part of the Indian mystery, always has been, probably always will be. Delhi is too old to care anyway, and takes the system as it comes. Which viceroy or president had he most enjoyed serving, I asked one antediluvian retainer at Rashtrapati Bhavan. He shrugged his shoulders with an almost perceptible creak. "I serve the government," he said. "It is all the same to me." With this indifference in mind I went that afternoon to a murder trial which, to much publicity, was proceeding then in the New District Court, a kind of permanent bad dream in concrete in the northern part of the city—filthy, cramped, dark and suffocatingly overcrowded. Here authority was at its most immediate and most awful. The case concerned the alleged murder of a well-known south-of-Rajpath lady by her husband, a fashionable eye surgeon, assisted by his mistress and an assortment of

vagabond accomplices. It was a true *crime passionel* with thuggish over-
tones, and at least five people faced, there and then, the ultimate
penalty. The judge was a grave and clever Sikh, turbaned and spectacled.
The court was jammed with a festering, jostling audience, hungry for
the salacious, the macabre and the terrible. The white-tabbed attorneys
droned and argued, the watchmen barred the door with staves, the accused sat in chains along the side of the court, shackled to their guards.

Yet fearful though their predicament was, they did not seem awe-
struck nor even alarmed. They were like sightseers themselves, of their
own tragedy. They yawned occasionally. They exchanged comments.
They laughed at the legal jokes. And sometimes, feeling the strain of
the long day, they raised their manacled wrists to their warders' shoulders and, placing their cheeks upon their hands like sleepy children,
dozed through destiny for a while.

"I will find that out for you, of course," said the government spokesman. "It will be no problem at all. You see, it is something I am not
exactly sure of myself, but we have many sources of information. Do
we have your telephone number? Ah yes. I have temporarily mislaid it.
Would you give it to me again? Rest assured, dear lady, I shall find out
this information, together with the answers to your earlier questions,
and shall telephone you for certain, if not this afternoon, then tomorrow
morning first thing.

"I don't know if you are familiar, you see, with the *Bhagavad-Gita*?
As a student of the Gandhian philosophy you would find it very beautiful: and you would find it exceedingly relevant to your article about
Delhi. It is self-awareness, you see, that is the key. Oh madam, you are
laughing at me! You are very wicked! But never mind, you will see, you
will see! And in the meantime you may be quite sure," he concluded
with his usual charming smile and reassuring shake of the head, "that
I will be telephoning you with this information, or if not I myself, then
our good Mrs. Gupta is sure to. It is not very spiritual but we must do
our duty!"

There is a species of telephone operators' English, often heard in
Delhi, which is not exactly an articulated language at all, but a sort of

elongated blur. Indian English proper, of course, is one of India's cruelest handicaps, for it is so often imperfect of nuance and makes for an unreal relationship between host and visitor, besides often making highly intelligent people look foolish (CHINESE GENERALS FLY BACK TO FRONT, said a celebrated Indian headline long ago). But the elliptical, slithery kind is something else again, and has another effect on its hearers. It makes one feel oddly opaque or amorphous oneself, and seems to clothe the day's arrangements in a veil of uncertainty.

This is proper. One should not go fighting into Delhi, chin up and clear eyed. Here hopes are meant to wither and conceptions adjust. A single brush with a noseless beggar is enough to change your social values. Just one application for an import license will alter your standards of efficiency. After a while graver mutations may occur, and you will find yourself questioning the Meaning of It All, the Reality of Time and other old Indian specialties. "You will see, you will see!" Most disconcerting of all, you may well come to feel that the pomp and circumstance of Delhi, which struck you at first as illusory display, is in fact the only reality of the place! All the rest is mirage! Everything else in the Indian presence, north, east, south, west, across the Rajasthani deserts, down to the Coromandel beaches, far away to the frontiers of Tibet, everything else is suggestion, never to be substance.

I pick a Delhi newspaper at random. Crowd Loots Colliery. Police Kill Dacoits. Dacoits Loot Pilgrims. Students Raid Cinema. Farmers Arrested during Agitation. Teachers Boycott Examination. Police Fire on Crowd. Mizo Rebels Spotted. Peace Feelers for Naga Rebels. A State of Emergency exists in India, but one is hardly aware of it for this is a country always in emergency, crossed perpetually by dim figures of faith and violence, prophets of revolution, priests of reaction, saints and spies and fanatics, moving here and there through a haze of hatred, idealism and despair. Experts Visit Bomb Blast Site. Police Charge Crowd. 600 Arrested. Government Minister Has Asthma.

Sometimes these shadows reach into Delhi itself, and chaos feels uncomfortably close. While I was there the hereditary Imam of the Jama Masjid, the greatest mosque in India, was engaged in a quarrel with the government and was even heard inciting his congregation to political dissent over the loudspeakers of his minaret during a visit to the neighborhood by Mrs. Gandhi herself. His family have been incumbents of the Imamate since the mosque was founded by Shah Jehan in 1650, and are great figures in the Moslem community: nevertheless he was arrested, and in the ensuing riots at least six people were killed (always add a zero, an Indian acquaintance nonchalantly told me, if you want the true figure) and at least 600 locked away for safety's sake.

It happened that I was wandering around the purlieus of the mosque on the day of the arrest, and bleak was the sensation of déjà vu with which I watched the riot police, brandishing their guns and batons, heavily clambering out of their trucks. But more ominous still, I thought, was the spectacle of the mosque itself a few days later. They slapped a curfew on the area, and when I next passed its outskirts, along the crammed and filthy pavements of Netaji Subhash Marg, where the beggar families crouch day and night beneath their sacking shelters and the teeming junk bazaars crowd around the Chandni Chowk—when I looked across to the Jama Masjid, I saw its great shape there silent and eerily deserted—gone the milling figures of the faithful on its steps, gone the stir of commerce and devotion that habitually surrounds it, empty all the stalls and shops, the kebab restaurants, the fortunetellers, the silversmiths, the tanners and the cobblers. All were empty, and the mosque looked like some immense captive champion, brooding there in solitary confinement.

Yet even this all-too-real reality seemed a deception upon the composure of Delhi. I never feel insecure there, even when the riot police are storming by. The only citizens who frighten me are those damned monkeys, so beguiling of motion, so threatening of grimace. Delhi people treat these beasts with distinct circumspection, crossing roads to avoid them or bribing them with peanuts to go away, and in this, it seemed to me, poor Indians behave toward monkeys much as Europeans behave toward poor Indians—especially as, the monkey god Hanuman being an important figure of the Hindu pantheon, some element of conscience is presumably involved. This disconcerting parallel gave me an unexpected sense of membership, and every time a monkey bared its teeth at me I felt like saying, "Wait, friend, wait—I'm the European, it's the poor Indian you want!"

For the Indian sense of hierarchy, which so contributes to the bafflement of India, provides for each rank of society a kind of comradeship; and in Delhi especially, which is like a shadow play of India, one senses the hidden force of it. The Untouchables of the capital—Harijans, Children of God, as Gandhi called them—live in well-defined colonies on the edge of the city. Though I knew better intellectually, emotionally I somehow expected, when I drove out there one afternoon, to find them a people made morose and hangdog by their status. In fact they turned out to be a very jolly lot, welcoming and wreathed in smiles, and looking at least as cheerful as the average member of the Socio-Economic Research Unit, say. Why not? They might be Harijans to the world outside but they were doubtless Brahmins to each other.

In the same way Delhi, preoccupied with its own diurnal round of consequence and command, is paradoxically protected against that dust storm of controversy, threat and misfortune which hangs always, dark and ill-defined, over the Indian horizons. That blur or slither of Delhi, which begins as a mystery and develops into an irritation, becomes in the end a kind of reassurance. After trying three times, you give up gratefully. After expostulating once or twice, it is a pleasure to accede. You think you can change the system? Try it, try it, and when the elaborations of Delhi have caught up with you, when you realize the tortuous significances of the old method, when it has been explained to you that only Mrs. Gupta is qualified to take the money, that Mr. Mukerjee is prevented by custom from working beside Mr. Mukhtar Singh and that Mr. Mohammed will not of course be at work on Fridays, when it dawns upon you gradually that it has been done more or less this way, come conqueror, come liberation, since the early Middle Ages, with a relieved and affectionate smile you will probably agree that perhaps it had better be left as it is.

As it is! India is always as it is! I never despair in Delhi, for I feel always all around me the fortification of a profound apathy. The capital is essentially apathetic to the nation: the nation is aloof to the capital. By the end of the century there will be, at the present rate of increase, nearly 1000 million people in India, and I think it very likely that there will have been a revolution of one complexion or another. But the traveler who returns to Delhi then will find the city much the same, I swear, will respond to much the same emotions, indulge in just the same conjectures, bog down in just the same philosophical quagmires, and reach, if he is anything like me, about the same affectionate and inconclusive conclusions.

"You see? You see? Did I not say so? You are thinking metaphysically, as I foretold!" Well, perhaps. But the government spokesman proved his point better himself, for neither he nor Mrs. Gupta ever did ring.

AN IMPERIAL
SPECIMEN

*Panama in 1975 was approaching one of the
great turning points of its history, the conclusion of an
agreement with the United States which would give it control, after
almost seventy years, of the Panama Canal, hitherto an
American enclave. The proposed new treaty was already an
inflammatory subject of debate in the U.S. itself, but
recognizing in it elements all too familiar to me from the history of
my own country, I decided to treat the Panama Situation
not as a political issue, but as a specimen
of a particular historical "genre."*

· · ·

PANAMA

· · · · · · · · · · · · · · · · ·

An Imperial Specimen

[1975]

THEY HAVE A TV PROGRAM in England in which a panel of eminent antiquarians inspects curios and objets d'art presented for its assessment by eager collectors. *"Nice enough little piece,"* they say. *"You inherited it from your grandmother did you Mrs. Thompson? Well, it's not quite a first-class example, I don't think—something a little greenish about the glaze, wouldn't you say, Francis?—but still a nice little thing, very pleasing, well worth hanging on to Mrs. Thompson."* ¶ In such a consultative capacity, as an aficionado of historical curiosities, did I fly into Central America one day to inspect that well-known collectors' item, that controversial but beguiling example of diplomatic craftsmanship, the Panama Situation. I will not pretend to you that it was always a specialty of mine. When I awoke in my hotel room in Panama City the morning after my arrival, I did not know whether it was the Atlantic or the Pacific Ocean I could see extending, bounded by hump-backed islands and speckled with shrimp boats, grayish and steamy outside my window. It was the Pacific actually, but as the waiter said when he brought my breakfast, I need not feel ashamed of myself—hardly anybody knows for sure.

Geographically Panama, which occupies the narrowest sliver of land in Central America, is a confusingly contorted country. Dividing as it does, almost symmetrically, North from South America, and calling itself, almost incessantly, the Bridge between the Oceans, it ought to run north and south, but instead goes perversely, and unreliably, east to west. The Pacific is south of Panama, the Atlantic north; the sun rises over the Caribbean; to go to the States from Panama City one sets off, ignorantly protesting, in a southwesterly direction. Moreover, the country is surrounded by states whose location most people are vague about, like Costa Rica and Colombia, besides having a history that few foreigners can grasp, a population rather less than Detroit's, and a name that nobody knows the meaning of, some translating Panama as "Lots of Fish," some as "Many Butterflies," and some rather feebly as "Big Trees."

Nevertheless, the moment I stepped out into the drizzle of Via España (for it was the rainy season and those shrimp boats lay there hangdog and apparently waterlogged in the bay), I recognized the genre. The Panama Situation is a late classic of the imperial form. It possesses all the true imperial elements: a distant and tremendous dominant power, an anxious settler community, a subject people united only in resentment, dubious historical origins, a sleazy tropical setting, above all a specific raison d'être.

In the annals of Empires there is no artifact more charged with passion and purpose than a canal, for great works of irrigation and navigation were always hallmarks of imperial grandeur, and sometimes its excuses too. Wherever Emperors ruled in foreign parts, they commemorated themselves with mighty waterworks, as though to demonstrate their mastery not merely over the lesser breeds, but over nature herself. In Mesopotamia the rulers of Babylon brought the desert to life; in Egypt the Pharoahs linked the Mediterranean with the Indian Ocean;

grand aqueducts marked the progress of Rome across Europe; in India the Victorians summoned new provinces into existence by their monumental dams and conduits. The Suez Canal, though the British did not actually build it, became so inescapable an emblem of their imperialism that the phrase "East of Suez" was a synonym for Empire itself, and the Empire's desperate attempt to keep control of the waterway became in the end its bitter curtain call. Nearly always the constructions were destined to outlive their sponsoring sovereignties, and when all the substance of command had faded, the drums were silenced with the rhetoric, then the great work lingered on, crumbling more slowly down the centuries, like the last ironic smile of the Cheshire cat.

The greatest single work of the American Empire is the Panama Canal, the fifty-mile waterway which, bisecting the Republic of Panama, links the Pacific and the Atlantic oceans, and has for more than sixty years given the United States an overwhelming presence at the junction of the Americas. The Canal is the truest meaning of the Panamanian Republic, though Panamanians hate one to say so, but no less is it a terrific expression of American imperialism in its original and simplest sense, older by far than the complexities of Vietnam, the CIA or the conglomerates. It was bred by Big Stick out of Manifest Destiny, two thoroughbreds of American assertion with which, around the turn of the 20th century, the Americans hoped to keep up with the galloping European Empires. *"Take up the White Man's Burden,"* Rudyard Kipling had abjured the Americans, and nobody responded more boisterously to the call than Theodore Roosevelt, "Theodore Rex," who had already more or less arranged the acquisition of the Philippines, and was to see in the construction of the Panama Canal, with its emphasis on skill, strength and usefulness, a truly Kiplingesque consummation of American splendor.

Like most great imperialist enterprises, it had murky beginnings. It was an old dream, of course—for generations people had thought of piercing the isthmus, and Panama indeed had come into existence as a place of transit between the Atlantic and the Pacific. Here the conquistadors girded themselves for their assaults upon the Inca kingdoms, and here, by mule track from one coast to the other, the booty was assembled for shipment to Spain or plunder by English pirates. Here the gold-rush men staggered through swamp and jungle on their way to California, and here, as far back as the 1850s, the Panama Railroad Company of New York laid a line across the isthmus and carried $750 million of gold bullion back to the East from California. The Panama Situation, by which this ancient function became subject to American expansionist instincts, was born in the early 1900s. Until then Panama had formed part of a province of the Colombian Republic, subject to the neglectful authority of Bogotá: it was the prospect of the Canal, giving the isthmus an incalculable international importance, which enabled the local nationalists to break away and establish their own hopeful if infinitesimal state.

Here was the American chance. Ferdinand de Lesseps, the French genius of the Suez Canal, had already begun work on a cutting through Panama, but had made a terrible mess of it all, sinking deeper every year in shame and corruption—the Panama Scandal, it is called in the French history books, and it is said that de Lesseps's bribery of the French press was so thorough that even *L'Écho des Sociétés Chorales* got its payoff. The Company went bankrupt, and so in 1903 Washington stepped in. By guaranteeing the independence of the new Panama Republic, by a frank flourish of the Big Stick in fact, President Roosevelt arranged that the Panama Canal would be a great work of American enterprise, a marvel to posterity and an earnest of American greatness forever. As Suez was to the British, Panama would be to the United States; not just a commercial enterprise, not only a strategic convenience, but a grand talismanic truth, the ships of all the nations passing symbolically beneath the Stars and Stripes from one half of the world to the other. "I took Panama!" Teddy Roosevelt cried, and he was echoing, consciously perhaps, Disraeli's celebrated report to his monarch, when with a loan from the Rothschilds he bought Britain's way into the Suez Canal: "Madam, the Canal is yours."

A proper degree of skulduggery was involved. The Panamanians, being inexperienced in power politics, had employed a French commission agent, the astute Philippe Bunau-Varilla, to present their case to Washington, offering in effect a canal concession in return for cash and protection. Bunau-Varilla had good personal reasons for wanting an agreement, since he stood to gain financially himself, and he had very soon drawn up the terms of a treaty. By the time the Panamanian leaders got to Washington themselves, he and John Hay, the U.S. secretary of state, had already signed it. The entire future of the Panamanian state had been decided by a Frenchman and an American; and Hay himself frankly told the Senate, when the treaty came up for ratification, that it was "very satisfactory, vastly advantageous to the United States, and we must confess, not so advantageous to Panama." The Senate, naturally, ratified it at once, for what it promised the Americans, give or take an interpretation or two, was not just the right to build and operate a canal across the isthmus of Panama, but the right to establish a colony of their own around it, with all the rights of sovereignty, inalienable, complete and in perpetuity.

The Panamanians were paid a modest fee—$10 million down, $250,000 yearly annuity—and could certainly be assured that no revengeful Colombian gunboat would be permitted to bombard Panama City. But the Americans were given sovereign powers over a swath of land ten miles wide running clean across the new Republic, dividing it absolutely in half. The Panamanians would have no share in the profits of the Canal: the Americans would have the right to do almost anything they pleased in the Canal Zone, to have a monopoly of all transisthmian communications forever, and even to keep order within the Panamanian cities of Colón and Panama City, which were not in the Zone at all.

Roosevelt was delighted. The uncompleted French works, with the railroad, were handed over to the United States government, represented by a Panama Canal Commission, and before long 45,000 men had poured into Panama, from the States, from the West Indies, from Spain, even from Greece and Italy, to build the all-American canal.

In 1906 Roosevelt went down in person to inspect progress. It was the first time an American President had ever left the country during his term of office, and it was like a Pageant of Destiny in some celebratory festival; all among the dredgers and the steam hammers, the toiling thousands of workers, the jungle clearings and the swamp causeways, the President strode bull-like and resolute, in knickerbockers and straw hat. Here was the American Empire, the White Man's Burden heroically shouldered! Sweeping irresistibly through marsh and shrub, defying disease, employing all the latest instruments of science and engineering, tremendously the Americans were cutting their ditch between the oceans. It was, said Roosevelt, one of the great works of the world. More than that, declared the editor of *Panama and the Canal in Picture and Prose*, it was "the most gigantic engineering undertaking since the dawn of time." The Canal was the equivalent of a ditch ten feet deep and fifty-five feet wide clean across the United States, Maine to Oregon, or a hole 16.2 feet square from the North to the South Pole. It was Colossal! It was Historical! It was AMERICAN!

Seventy years later it is still there, and in essence nothing much has changed in the relationship between Panama and the United States. But a situation that seemed the very latest thing in 1906, the most modern product of expansionist policy, is now a period piece. Though it can still give pleasure to enthusiasts like me, and still raise a frisson in true-blue all-American hearts, still good taste has outgrown it over the years— don't you agree, Francis? It has lost its atavistic punch, and is riddled anyway, I am sorry to have to say, with rot and woodworm.

The natives are restless, for the Republic of Panama has greatly changed its temper since those hapless delegates, morosely surveying the terms of their treaty, returned to their bewildered compatriots in 1903. They are frustrated, unfulfilled, and their national life has come to revolve around a grievance—as though in a subtle and insidious way they have been deprived of potency.

There is a shabby corner of Panama City which effectively conveys, I think, this flavor. It is down by the markets, in the old Spanish part of the city, and is pervaded by a powerful odor of dismembered bullock and gutted codfish, but it is not without beauty either, for here the wooden tenements open out to reveal a small shingly beach upon the bay, a fine sweep of sea, and the white high-rise buildings of the city's posher quarters to the east. This is a busy place, but not frenzied. There is something expectant to the scene, something calculated perhaps, as though everyone is waiting for an interesting event to occur—as though the whole city is waiting, indeed, for some grand and undefined denouement.

In the market entrance a leisurely row of men and women is selling lottery chances, sitting on the ground with legs stretched out, carpeted by green and yellow tickets. Facing the beach are a couple of open-fronted cafes, at whose counters one or two layabouts are meditatively or perhaps narcotically slumped. Whorelike ladies are here and there, giggling mildly with construction men or swapping symptoms with colleagues, and from the door of the marine police station a couple of lean gendarmes, heavily armed and darkly spectacled, look broodingly across the square, as though they are wondering whom to electrocute next. Above the beach there is a pile of rubbish; and there in ghoulish concentration half a dozen vultures pick away among the garbage, looking for bones and offal, or perhaps corpses, sometimes flapping their huge wings in appreciation, or taking off heavily among the rooftops, trailing strings of gristle.

Yet if it is a squalid scene, smelly too, it is very easily transformed. The Panamanians are people of great charm, and any one of those stagey characters, tart, cop, hardhat or beachcomber, will respond with grace to a greeting or an inquiry. Physically Panama may not be a very prepossessing Republic, but it has a quick and courteous style, even down there among the scavengers. Can it be you yourself, you momentarily wonder, that they have been expecting, like one of those theatrical tableaux that need only a director's click to bring them to life? But no, when they have given you your directions, and you look back upon the scene as you walk away toward the cathedral, that spell of anticipatory suspension has fallen upon it once more, and everyone is waiting for Godot again.

Panama lacks *settledness*. Perhaps it always has. Perhaps it is something to do with its functions of transit. It has always attracted the rootless, raffish kind, from the lusty Welsh pirate Henry Morgan, who with his compatriot John Morris sacked Old Panama in 1671, to the Spanish developers, American bankers, Russian cultural delegates and French arms salesmen who still fish hopefully in its somewhat polluted waters. Panama is a community of gamblers, jockeys, boxers and cockfighters, a place where characters habitually disappear to, or re-emerge from, in old-fashioned thrillers. Its greatest institution is the National Lottery, which holds the entire population in its grip, and it has traditionally been a great entrepôt of the drug trade, in whose profit, if we are to believe a line of gossip peddled almost everywhere in the modern world, many of its most prominent citizens have shared (you do know, don't you, about the Archbishop of Canterbury and the Corsican Connection?).

It lives for, by, around and because of the Canal, just as its churches, convents and caravanserai arose around the mule tracks of the Spaniards. Tourist guides speak glossily of mountain resorts, delectable island beaches, unspoilt Indian tribes and colorful country markets, but really Panama *is* the Canal. "If you're going to Gibraltar, dear," says one lady to another in a favorite Victorian cartoon, "you must on no account miss seeing the Rock"; and similarly one might say that if you are visiting Panama, you should keep your eyes open for the Canal. Probably a third of the population lives in one or other of the two Canalside cities, Colón at the Atlantic end, Panama City at the Pacific, and the whole texture of their lives, their manners and mores, their outlooks, their incomes, is influenced by the presence of the waterway.

This makes for an embattled feeling, too, as though they are struggling always to keep their dignity, or even their identity. The city of Colón is bisected by a rather grand boulevard, tree lined and ornamented with heroic statuary, Nationhood, Motherhood, Christopher Columbus, that kind of thing; but all around the Paseo del Centenario oozes the contagion of the Canal, in duty-free zones and sailors' bars, in yachts impounded for drug smuggling and seamen arrested for midnight brawls, in Hindu emporia and cut-price camera shops, in the shrill and gaudy bustle of Front Street, where generations of travelers have come ashore to be deftly clipped or comforted. Educated Panamanians try hard to maintain their Castilian poise, but it is hard to seem very composed on the edge of all this racket, and diligently though the National Cultural Institute presents its folk festivals and piano recitals, wittily and caustically though the Panama bourgeoisie observes the passing charade, still it must be said that the Republic of Panama, as Lord Rosebery once observed of the entire African continent, is not much of a place for a gentleman.

Wistfully they keep trying. I was taken to the theater one night to see the Cuban National Ballet, with its celebrated *première danseuse*, Alicia Alonso. It is a dear little theater, exuberantly embellished with gilt and flourishes, and the balletgoers were dressed in their slinky best and greeted each other with cousinly enthusiasm, since they all seemed to be related; but no less than that seamier ensemble beside the market, I thought, did the occasion seem to express some sense of yearning, some *jamais vu*. When the music struck up it was played only on a wavering record player, and the ballet itself turned out to be largely propaganda, emancipated peasants greeting a golden dawn, or marching shoulder to shoulder toward the revolution. The Panamanians greeted these exhortations halfheartedly, and there was some booing, not from the gallery but from the dress circle, where Aunt Elisa sat decorously with her nephew the professor.

Panama is a kind of police state, but not the most awful kind, for unlike some of its neighbors it has an easygoing tradition of politics. The family oligarchy which, until 1968, ran the place in quadrillelike succession was venal perhaps, but not often cruel: the revolutionary government which has succeeded it does not, I am assured, habitually murder its opponents, or incarcerate too many critics on its penal island. Exile rather than execution is the rule, and sometimes a dissident even returns from banishment and lives happily enough ever after.

Still, all the paraphernalia of despotism is there. The press is entirely controlled, all political parties are banned and the statutory portraits of the chief, General Omar Torrijos Herrera, gaze lugubriously from cobblers' shops and gas stations. There is a genial president of the Republic, who keeps live white herons in the hall of his presidency beside the sea, their cages lined daily with clean white copies of the morning newspapers. There is a ministry of civilians, mostly from the middle classes. There is even an impotent National Legislature, in a showy new Legislative Palace. The true core of the state, though, the state itself perhaps, is the National Guard, part army, part police, which brought General Torrijos into power seven years ago and keeps him there now.

This all-powerful gendarmerie is no joke. In other countries there is often something tragicomic about military despotisms, with their preposterously epauletted generalissimos and their strutting, puffed-up majors, but there is nothing laughable about the National Guard of Panama. Expensively equipped, well trained and disciplined, it is like a formidable praetorian guard implanted immovably in the heart of the Republic, with fingers in almost every Panamanian activity. Its elite battalions, the Tigers and the Pumas, are enough to scare any dissident into conformity, and its intelligence is said to be omniscient, so that people think twice before telling anecdotes about it.

The fortress headquarters of the force is in El Chorrillo, another of the less inviting quarters of Panama City, and a baleful place it is, being surrounded by slums, gas storage tanks and the city prison. As it happens I spent a couple of hours inside it, for I had arranged to meet the guard's chief of security, Colonel Manuel Noriega, and since he never in the event turned up, a common enough Panamanian practice, I was left to kick up my heels and pursue my fancies deep in his bunkerlike suite of rooms—now and then looked in upon by obliging orderlies, soothed by music from a local uplift program called the *Bright Sounds of Inspiration*, but otherwise all on my own.

How strange, to sit alone in the lair of an unknown security chief! I had heard conflicting reports of Colonel Noriega. He was sinister, he was not bad really, he had hypnotic eyes, watch out for his hands, he liked art, he knew all about interrogation. Certainly he looked after himself in his bunker. Steel doors enclosed it, with armed sentries and closed-circuit TV in his outer office, within the shuttered gates of the building itself, within the guarded wires of the headquarters compound. It was bugged, no doubt, and it had no windows, only skylights. The longer I sat there, and the more boldly I opened doors and peered around the place, the more vividly I seemed to see the absent colonel, and perhaps the autocracy he enforced. Here, through the left-hand door, was the sybaritic side of him, the sensual side, all done up in chrome and white leather, with thick sexy carpeting, and bright pictures of girls and landscapes, and a well-stocked cocktail cabinet, and a very strong suggestion of self-indulgence. Here, through the right-hand door, was his machismo: his big black TV console, with its six steady pictures of exits and entrances, his library of books on counterinsurgency and military intelligence, a huge photograph of himself parachuting out of an aircraft, and above the door an automatic rifle of the Egyptian Army, brought home from Sinai by the Panamanian contingent to the UN peace-keeping force.

Here and there I diffidently pottered, while the *Bright Sounds of Inspiration* wallowed on, and gradually there overcame me a feeling of despair, familiar to any student of the ends of Empires. Those adolescent symbols of manhood and virility! Those second-rate pictures! Those manuals of violence and repression! We are ruled by children, I thought, and all the agonies of state and ideology are only games for little soldiers.

At 3:30 next morning, before the dawn broke, there was a rap at my door, and looking out of my hotel window I saw two National Guardsmen pacing around the deserted patio far below. I feared the worst—perhaps they had put me on film down at the colonel's bunker?—and, jumping swiftly back into bed again, took my usual emergency action and pulled the sheets over my head.

Nothing more happened, but still for a moment I had experienced the chill uncertainty that is the worst part of autocracy. The Panama Situation, like many another experience of late imperialism, is especially disturbing because nobody knows what lies beyond it. What kind of a place will Panama be, if ever it is resolved? Will the traveling prove more gratifying than the arrival? The revolutionary government is a government of pragmatic response, rather than original initiative. Beyond a generally reformist or populist bias it has no true ideology of its own. If it has a communist emphasis, and certainly several of its civilian members have Marxist sympathies and backgrounds, that is partly because in imperialist situations communism habitually thrives. General Torrijos himself has invested in that least Marxian of properties, an estate in Spain (bought indeed, I am told, from the widow of Cuba's fascist reactionary colonialist puppet, Batista). Stylistically his models have varied from Moshe Dayan to Fidel Castro, and in recent pictures he looks for all the world like any other Pentagon general posing for a publicity handout. Ideologically he probably belongs, if he belongs to any company, only to the eclectic society of the dictators, living more by charisma than conviction. He does not often appear in Panama City these days, preferring his seaside estate some sixty miles out of town; but his bodyguard is always thick around his villa in the capital, and in his trellised garage there one may see his gleaming white Jaguar, ready perhaps for hasty getaways.

All these uncertainties, though, these unexpressed yearnings and expectancies, these unsatisfied aspirations, the very tone and temperament of modern Panama, find their focus in the presence of the Canal. It is the alien-controlled Canal which has, paradoxically, deprived the Panamanians of their vocation and their self-esteem; it is the Canal which binds them together; it is the Canal which enables the dictator to command their loyalty and pride.

Colonia Americana . . . No! runs the chorus of one of the regime's official Revolutionary Marches:

> Es nuestro el Canal
> No somos, ni seremos
> Di ninguna otra Nación.

—"We are not, nor shall we be, of any other nation." For in a world turned upside down since Teddy Roosevelt's day, the Panamanians look with an ever-growing resentment toward the imperial presence deposited, like some vast pyramid from earlier ages or a survivor from some vanished species, gigantically in the middle of their little state.

The Republic of Panama grants to the United States all the rights, powers and authority within the zone mentioned and described in Article II of this agreement . . . which the United States would possess and exercise if it were the sovereign of the territory within which said lands and waters are located to the entire exclusion of the exercise by the Republic of Panama of any such sovereign rights, power or authority.

The American presence in Panama is based upon two abstractions: power and pride. Both are inescapable. For most of its length the Canal Zone, 553 square miles of it, is remote from large Panamanian settlements, but at its two extremities its border forms the limit of a Panamanian city. Suddenly, across a city street, or at the end of an avenue, the Latin jumble of life evaporates, the rickety dark tenements disappear, the rubbish-strewn gutters give way to almost obsessively tended lawns and everything is plumper, richer, duller—*as if these streets,* the Panama poet Manuel Orestes Nieto has written, *and their stop lights/ and highway signs/were controlled by computers/from Washington itself.* In the days of that other Empire, the British Raj in India, Englishmen of imagination often liked to escape from the ordered incorruptibility of their own territories into the jumbled domains of the independent and often atrocious maharajahs; and I must say that whenever I crossed the unmarked frontier out of the Republic of Panama into the Canal Zone, I felt I was taking a retrograde step, out of reality into pretense.

An impressive pretense, mind. The Panama Canal is exceedingly well run, to a textbook precision. The United States Defense Department not only operates the Canal itself, it also governs the Canal Zone. In its representatives are all virtue and authority delegated. The governor of the Zone, usually a lieutenant-general of engineers, is also president of the Panama Canal Company. The company may sound like a corporation, and indeed a representative of the *New York Times* was down there recently soliciting its advertising, but it is really wholly owned by the Defense Department: its toll rates are decreed by Washington and are supposed only to cover the cost of working the Canal. There is no private property in the Canal Zone and no private commerce. Even the supermarkets are government owned, and when you expect a Zone TV program to break for soap powder or shampoos, instead you get advice about calling the Fire Brigade, or elevating messages about the history of the 193rd Infantry.

It is a terribly institutional place, run so authoritarianly that there is not even a school board, let alone an elected legislature. Its judges, its radio announcers, its storekeepers, its railwaymen, its funeral parlor managers are one and all government servants. It is thick with notices, mostly prohibitive—CONSUMPTION OF ALCOHOLIC LIQUOR IN ANY VEHICLE IS PROHIBITED, SWIMMING IS NOT PERMITTED BETWEEN DAWN AND DUSK—and even its friendly neighborhood signs are apt to have an organizational flavor, like WELCOME TO THE DREDGING DIVISION. The Canal Zone is intensely *bland*. Panamanians often find it stifling in its pallor. Its architecture is mostly a kind of Hispanic Beaux Arts, and most of its buildings seem to look more or less the same, whether they are Lock Control Stations or Mrs. Dugdale's residence, but the governor's house is very desirable in white clapboard, with flower-painted fans and awned patios, while the headquarters of the company and government, standing magnificently on a crest above the company town of Balboa, looks half like the Forbidden City of Peking, and half like a post office (there is a large statue of Theodore Roosevelt in its central rotunda, and when I offered to wipe its nose, the cleaning lady being unable to reach that high, she said, "Yeah, he does get kinda snotty").

This is a truly imperial enclave, jammed with expertise and experience. It has been doing the same job for sixty years now and it all goes with a very professional glide. The great lock gates swing smoothly open. The sluices spill their overflow. The tugs adeptly maneuver. The pilots, leaning from their bridges as they pass through the locks, murmur a pleasantry over their walkie-talkies or wave a languid hand to Joe in the control tower. Down at marine headquarters the great register of vessels builds up year by year, so that the computer knows not simply the size, speed and shape of a ship, but the way she handles too, her mechanical idiosyncrasies, even the kind of meal the pilot is likely to get. Well oiled, well practiced, well documented—the Canal Zone Regulations fill 314 pages of the Federal Code—the mechanism has come to seem organic, as though the passing of the vessels is a natural phenomenon, and the locks are no more than steps in the landscape, or a convenient kind of cascade.

Teddy was right, though—it really was one of the world's great works when they built it long ago. It was cut through some of the nastiest country in the world, so unhealthy that 25,000 men are said to have died during the construction of the Panama Railroad, infested with noxious insects and jealous reptiles, lethal with malaria and yellow fever, tangled with jungle and soggy with swamp. It entailed building the biggest dam in the world to create the largest man-made lake, digging the largest excavation in history through the Continental Divide, and raising and lowering ships, by the largest locks ever conceived, 85 feet up at one end of the Canal, 85 feet down at the other. The very idea of the Canal was inspiring: Goethe himself had responded to the poetry of it, long before, and James Bryce the historian called it "the greatest liberty man has ever taken with nature."

Everything, Balboa on the Pacific to Cristobal on the Atlantic, was made to a pattern, giving the work an aesthetic unity too—Frederick Law Olmsted, the creator of New York's Central Park, approved the landscaping—and method, consistency, care, were embedded into the

Canal's very structure, making it a kind of philosophical enclave, too, in that tropical environment. Everything was self-sufficient, self-reliant; only one percent of the labor force was Panamanian, and the Canal was built almost without reference to the Panamanian government. The Canal's own surgeons eradicated yellow fever from the Zone, having discovered that it was carried by mosquitoes. The Canal's own engineers invented the electric "mules" which, like land-borne tugs or the horses of earlier waterways, manipulated ships through the locks. And through all the great work, which took ten years to complete, there ran that conscious thread of American destiny, as the skills, guts and dollars of the United States drove the great ditch through the Divide to link sea with shining sea. It was a deliberately imperial enterprise. They called one of the construction towns Empire.

Almost from the start, too, the Americans saw it not just as a waterway, but as a power base. This was inevitable. Just as the possession of Suez enabled the British to keep a grip on the whole Middle East, so Panama was America's key to the command of the Americas. It obviated the need for a two-ocean Navy and it gave the Washington strategists an invaluable foothold in Latin America. They have never looked back. American forces have been based in the Canal Zone since 1911, and since 1963 Quarry Heights, just over the Zone border outside Panama City, has been the headquarters of United States Southern Command, responsible for all American military activities in Central and South America.

There is no pretending that this base is there for the defense of the Canal itself, as the original treaty allowed. Its purpose is strategic, a command post for the whole of Latin America, a staging point, a training camp, a military laboratory. Every kind of military establishment has used the Canal Zone, from medical research teams to intelligence agencies, and today it teems with activities overt and concealed, and bristles with military acronyms—USARSA and IAAFA and COMUSNAVSO, MILGPs and MAAGs and MTTS and TATs. Here the Army has its Jungle Training School. From here the Green Berets dispatch their counterinsurgency training teams throughout Latin America—among their most successful pupils were the Bolivian rangers who hunted down Ché Guevara. Here, too, is the School of the Americas, specializing in counterrevolution (or as the military put it, "internal security and civic action requirements"); its alumni include many a Latin American security chief, war minister and intelligence director, and it is particularly busy at the moment training Chileans to keep their country in order. There are schools of Air Force technique too, and tropical laboratories of several kinds, and from the Canal Zone are coordinated all the contingency plans for American intervention in Latin American affairs, with or without the help of the CIA.

For within the Zone, in the very heart of Latin America, the American establishment may do what it pleases. It is like having a room of one's own, with one's very own lock and key, and a private telephone line, inside one's neighbor's house. The hills around Quarry Heights bristle with masts, aerials and suggestive bumps, and are tunneled through, like Gibraltar, with secret caverns; and whenever I looked up to those grassy knolls, beyond the parklike lawns of Balboa, the royal palms and the monument to Colonel George Washington Goethals Erected by His Fellow Americans—whenever I looked up there, I seemed to hear the hum of the ciphered messages, on their way to Washington, and see the wary flicker of their electronics.

These are reasons, right or wrong, for the American presence in the Canal Zone. Below them lie emotions. "It is not the critic that counts," Theodore Roosevelt cried when he visited the Canal in 1906. "The credit belongs to the man who is actually in the arena; whose face is scarred by dust and sweat and blood; who knows the great enthusiasms, the great devotions, so that his place shall never be with those cold and timid souls who know neither victory nor defeat. . . ." This kind of rhetoric, imperfectly enunciated, still infuses the Americanism of the Canal Zone. Deeper by far than the goings-on of Green Berets or MILGPs lies an old American pride in achievement. This gives the Zone community a very old-fashioned, almost touching air, a nostalgic assertion of myth that is a kind of mirror image of Panamanian aspirations across the border—the one people hungering for a chimerical fulfillment, the other pining for a half-legendary past. The average age of American civilians in the Zone strikes me as fairly high and their affinities are often with the South, with New Orleans, which is almost the Canal's home port, so to speak, with Louisiana upon whose laws the Zone's legal system is patterned. They are likely to be patriots, Veterans of Foreign Wars, bicentennialists, people of the Flag and the Oath, family men, lodge members. They read the Panama edition of the *Miami Herald* over cheeseburgers in government canteens, and award second prizes to artifacts called Things and Strings in exhibitions of work by the National League of American Penwomen. Their husbands attend the Nathaniel J. Owen Branch of the American Legion. Their daughters go to proms. They are not Ugly Americans, not at all, but you might judge them, well, *plain*, perhaps.

I have much sympathy for them, for in all these attitudes they are only being true to themselves. They have been brought up to believe that they are serving a great American institution, the Panama Canal. It is as American in their eyes as Kleenex or George Wallace, and for them it reflects the American genius, the American dream, as truly today as it did when the first ship sailed through it. There is a plaque in the headquarters rotunda put up there in 1955 by the American Society of Engineers. "A Modern Civil Engineering Wonder of the U.S.," it says of the Panama Canal, and never for a moment does it suggest that the Canal is not in the U.S. at all. Americans built it, Americans run it, Americans own it; many of its American employees seldom enter the Republic of Panama from one year to the next—there used to be a policeman who boasted he had never set foot in the place for thirty years. Of the 15,000 people who work the Canal today, 12,000 are Panamanians, but none of them are senior executives and only two of the two hundred Canal pilots are local men. The Panama Canal remains what it always was: a self-sufficient self-reliant, self-perpetuating, American organism.

And this conviction is accentuated by the unchanging nature of the Canal itself. In fact it is fast getting out of date, being too small for many modern ships, so that the big container vessels have to squeeze their way through the locks like Victorian dames in bustles edging their way through drawing-room doors. There have long been plans to build a newer bigger one, probably without locks at all, but in the meantime the Canal still works exactly as it always did, often with its original equipment. The original dials and gauges, familiar to generations of American operators, still record the rise of the lock water in the high control towers. The electric mules still trundle archaically up and down, Japanese built in their latest models but still doing precisely the same job they always did. It is a very dated wonder and this adds a true pathos to the pride its servants have in it. They live in a world where Big is still Beautiful, where engineering marvels can still move the spirit, where a statistic is still believed, and you can still raise a gasp with the revelation that the stone handled in the construction of the Panama Canal would be enough for 28 Giza pyramids, or 190,438 average American homes. Manifest Destiny is alive, well and rather endearing in the duplexes of Balboa and Cristobal.

There they stand then, at the end of 1975, the classic opponents in an archetypal performance of Empire. They have been opponents from the start, ever since it dawned upon the Panamanians that the 1903 Treaty had robbed them of a birthright, but the animosity has built up steadily through the years, through the brave American heyday, through the chicaneries of banana republic and conglomerate, through the ignominies of Vietnam and Watergate—through a whole era of history in which imperialism as an idea has been discredited, and America as an imperial power has lost faith and persuasion.

The Panamanians now demand an altogether new relationship. They do not, at the moment anyway, demand the immediate withdrawal of American power from the Zone; but they want the arrangements to end altogether by the year 2000, and in the meantime they want to see the Canal gradually handed over to Panamanian control, they want substantial parts of the Zone given back to them and they want Panamanian sovereignty fully recognized. There is absolutely no way in which they can enforce these demands physically, the disparity between the two peoples being as great as ever—140 to 1. Today for the first time, though, they may well enforce them diplomatically, for Panama now has behind her the support of many countries and the threatened encouragement of many more.

When the British were fighting to keep control of Suez, the antagonism was complete, Britons and Egyptians having very little in common, seldom mixing, and pursuing diametrically opposite aims. In Panama it is different. For one thing, though the Canal Zone forms so distant an enclave within the Republic, still it is not physically insulated. Anyone can cross from one side to the other. There are no barriers, check points or wire fences, not even a *cordon sanitaire* (though in Panama City the wide highway called Avenida de los Mártires does form an unfortunate sort of No Man's Land, avidly photographed for TV documentaries, between the lawns of Quarry Heights and the fetid tenements of El Chorrillo). Many Panamanians commute from the Republic to the Zone—some Americans, too. There have been thousands of intermarriages over the years, so that for myself, as I wandered around the Zone, I often found it hard to know whether a cop, a functionary or even a soldier was American or Panamanian. The cultures overlap, as the British and the Egyptian never did: half America has grown up with the awareness of a Spanish past and all Panama has grown up with the consciousness of a gringo present. These antagonists are anything but strangers. They know each other very well indeed, and have more in common than they care to admit.

Then again, though Panamanians prefer not to recognize the fact publicly, they share many self-interests. General Torrijos would not be the chief he is without his American military training. Colonel Noriega perfected his machismo at the School of the Americas. The National Guard is armed with American weapons and advised by an American military mission (MAAG, I think. or it may be MILGP): when its battalion went to the Middle East, every item of its equipment was supplied by the United States, even down to the *socks*. The revolutionary government itself might well have been overthrown by now were it not for tacit American support (interspersed, they tell me, by CIA threats to have the chief of state contracted for, but then we all know how effective *they* are).

Economically, it pays Panama handsomely to be within the American orbit, and especially perhaps beneath the guns of the Canal Zone. The U.S. dollar is official currency, the Panamanians never having printed their own banknotes, and it is unlikely that USSOUTHCOM would ever let the Republic disintegrate into chaos; but the Panamanians impose few prissy restrictions on exchange, interest rates or accessibility, so that the canny investor in Panama City can enjoy the best of many worlds. Wherever you look in the capital there is a foreign bank or a company headquarters, and the Panamanian flag is so particularly convenient that more than 1000 merchant ships, nearly all American owned, gratefully fly it. Panama enjoys the highest living standards in Central America, and there is no denying that this is partly because the Americans are there.

So it is an amorphous emergency, blurred at the edges, slow in coming. There have been the customary riots now and then, the standard breaking of Embassy windows, the normal breaking of diplomatic relations, the usual student protests. The Avenida de los Mártires was renamed for Panamanian students killed in a 1964 affray—it used to be called Fourth of July Avenue. There have been several attempts to replace the Treaty, and it has been repeatedly modified, each time to give the Panamanians a little more self-respect or a little more cash; but only now is the confrontation really coming to a head, each side knowing that if a limit is not soon set upon the American presence in Panama, real trouble is on the way. On the American side intentions remain half-veiled. On the Panamanian side they are very clear: the Americans must be out of Panama altogether in twenty-five years, leaving the Republic of Panama in complete control, technically, economically and militarily, of the Most Gigantic Engineering Undertaking since the Dawn of Time.

If you drive from Panama City to Colón, along the highway magnificently called the Carretera Transistmica, you are traveling more or less parallel with the Canal, without entering the Canal Zone (for a Treaty modification of 1955 kindly allowed the Panamanians to have a road of their own across the isthmus). Everything is highly Panamanian. The villages you pass through are cheerfully wayward, littered with 7-Up signs, buses with pictures, banana-sellers' booths and ravaged, abandoned automobiles. The country is jungly, hummocky and unlovely. There is a kind of aimless shabbiness to it all, shambled, benevolent but not picturesque. At one or two places, though, a side road will take you to a vantage point above the Canal itself, and there, spread out before you between the hills, you may see an almost allegorical antithesis. There the tiled houses of the Americans nestle in their gardens. There the big ships sail across Gatun Lake, their high funnels and superstructures gliding grandly among the islands. There are the trim installations of USGOG or AMPLIG or COMSWAM. There everything seems cool, ordered, prosperous and private. It is like looking through the lodge gates at some unapproachable estate.

The Panama Situation, like so many of its kind, is embodied in *contrast*. Of course not all the Americans of the Canal Zone are stinking rich—none of them indeed are as rich as rich Panamanians. They are, however, undeniably exclusive and they have made the Zone a world of their own. Once you cross that Zone border, though you may be only a hundred yards from your own home, nothing is Panamanian. The signs, the systems, the language, the ambiance—all are American. If you are caught speeding, you will be taken before an American judge in an American court. If you need a cup of coffee, you will be unable to buy one without a Zone card. The Stars and Stripes fly everywhere—only since 1964 has the Panama flag flown within the Zone, and even now it does not often show.

It is the apparency of it all that is so provocative. It so happens that in Panama City a spit of the Zone protrudes directly in front of the Legislative Palace, so that while the Legislature is within the Republic, the lawns before it are in the Zone. On that very spot the Zone authorities, every morning of the year, hoist the American flag—in tandem, indeed, with the Panamanian, but giving the distinct impression, to foreigners as to touchier Panamanians, that they claim a tacit suzerainty not just over the Zone but over Panama itself.

In fact the Americans are not sovereign even within the Zone. Even M. Bunau-Varilla did not allow for that. They are the owners of the Canal Zone soil, just as a householder owns the title to his garden, and they possess all the rights of government, the Panamanians having specifically given up all claim to power or authority. But the United States was given those rights, even in 1963, only *"as if it were the sovereign of the territory."* America did not acquire the Canal Zone in the sense that she acquired Alaska, say, or Hawaii. She enjoys no sovereign right of cession or conquest, which is why the Zone never became a territory of the United States. The American presence in Panama is analogous only to the Treaty Ports of pre-revolutionary China, where the several powers, while dimly recognizing the sovereignty of the Celestial Kingdom, ruled themselves and the local citizenry by their own laws and with their own authority. And just as the foreign garrisons, clubs, parks and department stores of Shanghai now seem like images of another age, so the American presence in the Canal Zone is already one of history's anachronisms.

Legally the Americans might maintain the status quo indefinitely. "We own this place," as one Canal Zone resident explained it to me, "it's as simple as that. It's ours for all time. It's a bit of America." Perhaps even a court of law, though, would not hold Panama to such an agreement, concluded in such doubtful circumstances, in such different times. The 1903 Treaty is a true text of the Imperial Age, presupposing that Western civilization would dominate mankind for centuries: but only a Frenchman and an American, perhaps, deciding between them the entire future of a third country, could make its provisions, like Rome herself, actually *eternal*! Even Hitler envisaged only a 1000-year Reich! Even Churchill, contemplating the British Empire's finest hour, gave it only a millennium!

> Take up the White Man's Burden,
> And reap his old reward
> The blame of those ye better
> The hate of those ye guard!

You must not suppose that I do not understand. I know the glory of the distant flag! I have heard the bugles call! From the island of Períco, at the Pacific end of the Canal, there is a magnificent view of Panama Bay and the Canal entrance. From there the scene looks immensely powerful. The city straggles eastward along the shore, ramparted and steepled at one end, skyscrapered at the other; the lawns and villas of the Canal Zone, topped with aerials and ringed around by harbor installations, run away to the west. The high steel arch of the Bridge of the Americas takes the Pan-American highway magnificently across the waterway, and through the humpbacked islands offshore, sometimes green and blue in the sunshine, sometimes black with sudden rainstorms, ships are always moving, steadily and silently out of the Pacific.

High on the flank of Períco, shut off by wire fences and severe in-

junctions (TRASH AND LITTER GENERATED IN THIS AREA WILL BE
DEPOSITED IN YELLOW TRASH CANS) there stands an observation post,
the first American station on the Pacific side; it has probably been there
since the Canal was built. Its platforms are open-fronted and it perches
on the hillside with a campaigning air, a hammocky, mosquito-net,
semaphore and heliograph, sepia, Sam Browne air. I could not see if
anyone was actually on watch beneath its eaves, when I went out there
on my last afternoon in Panama, but I was powerfully moved anyway
by the spectacle of that ever loyal lookout, ever watchful, ever faithful
down the years. What generations of Americans looked proudly out
from there, in the days when American power really was the hope and
glory of the world! It seemed to me to stand in the truest line of the
imperial monuments, the best of the genre, the line of the Khyber and
Hadrian's Wall, the Saharan forts and the Venetian castles—the kind
that make you wonder what kind of men once served their Empire
there, how bravely they stood their ground, and how gracefully, when
the time came, they pulled the flag down and departed.

· · · · · · · ·

THE
KNOW-HOW CITY

Los Angeles was a surprise to me when I
went there for ROLLING STONE *in 1976. Though I had often*
visited the city, and written about it once or twice, I had never stayed so
long before, and I found my responses greatly
changed. Like most people, I had thought of it before as vulgar,
un-beautiful and above all formless. Now I discovered
it to be . . . well, read on if you please!

· · ·

LOS ANGELES

· · · · · · · · · · · · · · · · ·

The Know-How City

[1976]

LOS ANGELES IS THE CITY of Know-How. Remember "know-how"? It was one of the vogue words of the forties and fifties, now rather out of fashion. It reflected a whole climate and tone of American thought in the years of supreme American optimism. It stood for skill and experience indeed, but it also expressed the certainty that America's particular genius, the genius for applied logic, for systems, for devices, was inexorably the herald of progress. ❧ As the English had thought in the 1840s, so the Americans thought a century later. They held the future in their hands and brains, and this time it *would* work. Their methods and inventions would usher not only America herself but all mankind into another golden age. Know-how would be

America's great gift to history: know-how to rescue the poor from their poverty, to snatch the colored peoples from their ignominy, to convince the nations that the American way of free enterprise was the best and happiest way of all. Nothing was beyond know-how. Know-how was, if not actually the substance of God, at least a direct derivative.

One city in America, above all others, came to represent this enviable conviction. There has never been another town, and now there never will be, quite like El Pueblo de Nuestra Señora la Reina de Los Angeles de Porciúncula, Southern California, where the lost American faith in machines and materialism built its own astonishing monument.

Los Angeles, in the generic sense, was a long time coming. It is not a young city. Spaniards were here before the United States was founded, and I never get the feeling, as I wander around L.A.'s vast, amorphous mass, that it lies thinly on the ground. It is not like Johannesburg, for instance, where almost within living memory there was nothing whatsoever. Nor does it feel transient or flimsy, like some of those towns of the Middle West, which seem to have no foundations at all, but await the next tornado to sweep them away in a tumble of matchwood. In Los Angeles there are reminders of a long tradition. There is the very name of the city, and of its euphonious streets and suburbs—Alvarado, El Segundo, Pasadena, Cahuenga Boulevard. There is the pattern of its real estate, still recognizably descended from the Spanish and Mexican ranches of long ago. There is its exotic taste in architecture, its patios and its deep eaves, its arcades, its courtyards. There are even a few actual buildings, heavily reconstructed but still authentic, which survive from the first Spanish pueblo—swarmed over by tourists now, but fitfully frequented too, I like to think, by the swaggering ghosts of their original caballeros.

A sense of age informs the very setting of L.A. From the air the city looks like some enormously exaggerated pueblo itself: flat, sprawling, rectilinearly intersected, dun colored, built of mud brick by some inconceivable race of primitives, and behind it the tawny mountains run away in a particularly primeval way, a lizardy, spiny way, their dry expanses relieved only by the flicker of white on a snow peak here and there, or the distant glimmer of a lake. In a huge amphitheater the city lies, accessible only by passes through the surrounding ridges, rather like a gigantic mining camp: and through the veil of its own artificial mist, suggestively whirled about and blended with the California sunshine, it looks across its golden beaches toward that most enigmatic of the oceans, the Pacific (never called the sea in Los Angeles, always "the ocean").

There is nothing Johnny-come-quick to this scene. Los Angeles is a complex merger of separate settlements, containing within its scrambled presence eighty different municipalities, and sprawling district by district, decade by decade, over its central plain and into its foothills. The witty Mr. David Clark, when he named his book *L.A. on Foot: A Free Afternoon*, was ironically emphasizing the amoebic immensity of the place, territorially among the largest urban settlements in the world, and psychologically one of the most involved. Though I would guess that nine-tenths of its buildings were erected in the 20th century, still Los Angeles is, like some incurable disease, a balefully organic phenomenon. Its streets are forever nibbling and probing further into its perimeter hills, twisting like rising water ever higher, ever deeper into their canyons, and sometimes bursting through to the deserts beyond. If the city could be pried out of its setting, one feels, it would be like a dried mat of some bacterial mold, every bump, every corner exactly shaped to its landscape.

This is partly because the landscape itself is so individual, so that unlike Chicago, say, or Paris, Los Angeles is inconceivable anywhere else. But it is also, I think, because this city genuinely springs out of its own soil, possesses a true genius loci and forms a kind of irreplaceable flash point: the point on the map where the intellectual, the physical and the historical forces of American history met to produce—well, combustion, what else? Whatever happens to L.A., it will always be the city of the automobile and the radio, showbiz and the Brown Derby restaurant, the city where the American ideal of happiness by technique found its folk art in the ebullience of Hollywood. It is essentially of the forties and the fifties, and especially perhaps of the World War II years, when the American conviction acquired the force of a crusade, and sent its jeeps, its technicians and its Betty Grables almost as sacred pledges across the world. Los Angeles then was everyone's vision of the New World: and so it must always remain, however it develops, a memorial to those particular times, as Florence means for everyone the spirit of Renaissance, and Vienna speaks always of fin de siècle.

Across the car park from the remains of the original Spanish pueblo, where the Mexican souvenir shops now huddle profitably along Olvera Street, there stands Union Station. This was the last great railway depot to be built in the United States, completed in 1939, and one of the most handsome. Cool, tall, elegant, and nowadays restfully unfrequented by trains, it has patios green with flowers and trees, shaded colonial-style arcades, and is rather the sort of railway station a multibillionaire might devise, if he wanted one at the bottom of the garden. In this it is very proper, for while paying graceful respect to L.A.'s origins and pretensions, it honors too the first and fundamental quality of this city: organized, stylized movement.

It was not liberty that Los Angeles cherished in its prime, or at least not absolute liberty. A spiritual culture can be anarchical, a material culture must be disciplined. Implicit to the promise of technological fulfillment was the necessity of *system*, and L.A. soon became a firmly ordered place. The original Los Angeles public transport system, the electric trains and streetcars of the early 20th century, drew together the scattered settlements of the time, bringing them all into cityness.

When the car arrived the mesh was tightened, and L.A. built its incomparable freeways. These remain the city's grandest and most exciting artifacts. Snaky, sinuous, undulating, high on stilts or sunk in cuttings, they are like so many concrete tentacles, winding themselves around each block, each district, burrowing, evading, clambering, clasping every corner of the metropolis as if they are squeezing it all together to make the parts stick. They are inescapable, not just visually, but emotionally. They are always there, generally a few blocks away; they enter everyone's lives, and seem to dominate all arrangements.

To most strangers they suggest chaos, or at least purgatory, and there can certainly be more soothing notices than the one on the Santa Ana Freeway which announces MERGING BUSES AHEAD. There comes a moment, though, when something clicks in one's own mechanism, and suddenly one grasps the rhythm of the freeway system, masters its tribal or ritual forms, and discovers it to be not a disruptive element at all, but a kind of computer key to the use of Los Angeles. One is processed by the freeways. Elevated as they generally are above the flat and centerless expanse of the city, they provide a navigational aid, into which one locks oneself for guidance. Everything is clearer then. There are the mountains, to the north and east. There is the glimmering ocean. The civic landmarks of L.A., such as they are, display themselves conveniently for you, the pattern of the place unfolds until, properly briefed by the experience, the time comes for you to unlock from the system, undo your safety belt, and take the right-hand lane into the everyday life below.

The moment this first happened to me, Los Angeles happened too, and I glimpsed the real meaning of the city, and realized how firmly it had been disciplined by the rules of its own conviction.

Confusing, nevertheless, the Santa Ana with the San Diego Freeway, missing the exit at Bristol, mistaking Newport Avenue for Newport Boulevard, getting in the wrong lane at Victoria, miscounting the traffic lights on 22nd Street, an hour late exactly I arrived for lunch with the world's greatest authority on European naval history in the early 20th century.

Through apparent chaos to unmistakable authority. This was a not uncharacteristic Los Angeles experience. Expertise is the stock in trade of this metropolis, and behind the flash and the braggadocio, solid skills and scholarship prosper. There are craftsmen everywhere in L.A., craftsmen in electronics, in film-making, in literature, in social science, in advertising, in fashion. They say that in San Francisco there is less than meets the eye: in Los Angeles there is far more, for the reputation of the place makes no allowance for this corporate diligence and dexterity. Here Lockheed makes its aircraft. Here NASA makes its space shuttle orbiter. Here is UCLA, one of the most fertile universities in the Western world. Here the McCulloch Corporation has patented a device to pop the golf ball *out* of the hole, to save its owner stooping. This is no place for dilettantes. Even sport is assiduously, sometimes grimly, pursued: the tennis players of Beverly Hills joylessly strain toward perfection, the Malibu surfers seldom lark about, but take their pleasures with a showy dedication.

I went one morning to Burbank Studios to see them filming Neil Simon's macabre comedy, *Murder by Death*. This is one of those movies in which everyone is a star, and the set was cluttered with familiar figures. There was Truman Capote, described in the studio publicity as "acclaimed author and international celebrity," huddled with a young friend in a corner and wearing a wide-brimmed hat. There was Peter Falk, charmingly chatting with Elsa Lanchester. Alec Guinness looked truly gentlemanly, David Niven looked almost too elegant. Ray Stark the producer looked preternaturally successful, Robert Moore the director looked alarmingly gifted.

I am antipathetic to the famous, though, and I found that my eyes kept straying from these luminaries to the two sound technicians who, just off the set, sat nonchalantly over their equipment wearing headsets and reading the trade papers. One was called Jerry Jost, the other Bill Manooth, and they had both been in the business twenty years and more. How calm they looked, I thought, how sure of themselves, how easily aware of the fact that nobody in the whole world could do their job better than they could! They had seen the stars come and go, they had helped to make flops and winners, they had suffered every temperament, they had seen the film industry itself in boom and decline. Sometimes they looked up to exchange a pleasantry with a passer-by, sometimes they turned a page of the *Hollywood Reporter*: but they were always alert when the moment came, always watching their quivering instruments, always ready to mouth the magic word "Speed!"—which, with its assurance that they had got things right, gave the signal to that whole assembly, director, cameraman, actors, Capote and all, to proceed with their flamboyances.

For somewhere near the heart of the L.A. ethos there lies, unexpectedly, a layer of solid, old-fashioned, plain hard work. This is a city of hard workers. Out on the hills at Santa Monica, overlooking the Pacific Ocean, the writer Christopher Isherwood and the painter Don Bachardy share a house, sunlit and easygoing, with a view over the rooftops and shrubberies of the canyon. In such a place, with such occupants, in such warm and soothing sun, with the beach down the road and Hollywood up the freeway, it might seem a house for cultivated indolence, interminable wit around a swimming pool, long cool drinks with worldly neighbors before lunch. Not at all. "We are *working* people," Isherwood says, and so they literally are: each at his own end of the house, each with his art, the one surrounded by his books, the other by his brushes and pictures, carefully and skillfully they work through the day, friends and fellow laborers.

I very much like all this. It suggests to me, unexpectedly, the guild spirit of some medieval town, where the workers in iron or lace, the clockmakers and the armorers, competed to give their city the glory of their trades. All the mechanisms of Los Angeles are like apprentices to these matters: the robot lights and the TV cameras, the scudding helicopters, the laboring oil pumps bowed like slaves across the city, or the great telescopes of Mount Wilson, brooding among their conifers high above the city, which in the years before the Second World War more than doubled man's total knowledge of the physical universe.

It is true that this expertise is sometimes rather dated, but then L.A. is essentially a survivor of earlier times, and one is constantly plucked back to that simpler world of the forties, when values were surer than they are now, and the attainment of wealth or fame seemed the true gauge of contentment.

One citizen who honors those values still, in life as in principle, is Ed Davis, the celebrated police chief of Los Angeles. He is an inescapable figure there. I doubt if there is another police chief in the world better known among his citizenry. Powerful, controversial, dogmatic, his name entered almost every conversation I had about the city, and aroused powerful reactions everywhere. He was a pseudofascist reactionary. He was a great police chief. He was bigoted, unbalanced, hysterical. He was a staunch upholder of right and decency. He was a brute. He was a father figure. He ought to be shot. He ought to be President.

So I arranged to meet him, and arriving one sunny morning at police headquarters, familiar to everybody in Western civilization from a thousand prime times on TV—arriving in those hallowed halls, trodden before me by Sergeant Friday—arriving there reverent and docile

("Say," they told me, "there was a cop here from England only the other day—he was *dazzled* by the level of crime we have here")—dazzled then, by the historic ambiance, I proceeded to the *piano nòbile*, where Davis was attended by his faithful middle-aged secretary Helen and by sundry lesser acolytes.

He was on the whole the most impressive man I met in L.A., but impressive in a faintly forlorn way. It is not that he really believes, as he once claimed, that hijackers should be publicly hanged at L.A. airport, or that he really harbors malice when he speaks of "raving faggots" or inveighs against illegitimate massage parlors: what dates him, and gives him a paradoxical poignancy, is his apparent belief that Order can somehow *cure* society's ills. He talked to me of crime in intellectual terms—"situation ethics," "symbionic relationships," "the new morality," and he argued that even victimless crimes are like cancers on the body public: but he is really animated, I think, by an old-school, traditional faith in the redemptive power of discipline. He is a man of unchallenged technique, but like the technique of the automobile which has made L.A. what it is, it is the technique of an older America. It is not yet discredited—Ed Davis really has kept organized crime to a minimum in his city—but it is distinctly outmoded.

I thought him, for all his force and brilliance, rather a nostalgic figure, pining for the days of faith and family: and nostalgia too blurs the realities of Hollywood, the Versailles of Los Angeles, and peoples it forever with the royalty of another era, the Astaires, the Tracys, the Garbos, and nobles of even earlier vintage. Now as always the tourist buses circumnavigate the Homes of the Stars, and the touts peddle their street plans on Sunset Strip. Now as always Hollywood feeds upon narcissism, cosseted in sycophancy and sustained by snobbery. Scattered over the Hollywood Hills, and over the Santa Monica Mountains into the San Fernando Valley, the houses of the movie people stand sealed and suspicious in the morning, the only sounds the swishing of their sprinklers, the snarling of their guard dogs, or perhaps the labored breathing of their gardeners: and in their garages the cars are profligately stacked, Jag beside Merc, Rolls upstaging BMW. Hollywood prefers its own world to ours, loving and living, generation after generation, its own fairly tawdry legend.

I stayed in the middle of it all, and soon came to feel how period a piece it was. My hotel was the Chateau Marmont, a monument in itself, built in the French manner half a century ago, and directly overlooking Sunset Boulevard. Everyone in Hollywood knows the place. That's where Bogart proposed to Bacall, they say, that's where Garbo used to stay, Howard Hughes had a suite there, Boris Karloff loved it, Valentino preferred the penthouse. It is impregnated with showbiz, from the gigantic antiques in the downstairs lounge to the strains of the electronic organ from the pop group practicing in the garden bungalow: but what seems to the aficionado amusingly evocative seemed to me only a little threadbare, the ghostly thread of the stars did not make up for the lack of a dial telephone, and I often found myself pining for an honest downtown motel, where never a Gable raised his eyebrow, or a Garland threw a tantrum.

Every morning, too, I walked across the boulevard to have my break- fast at Schwab's, "The World's Most Famous Drugstore." Everyone knows Schwab's, too. Schwab's is where Lana Turner was discovered, sitting on a barstool. Hardly a Hollywood memoir is complete without a reference to Schwab's, and it is heavy with the old mystique. Elderly widows of émigré directors reminisce about Prague over their cornflakes. Young men in jerkins and expensive shoes ostentatiously read *Variety*, or greet each other with stagey endearments and expletives. Ever and again one hears across the hubbub, in the whining intonations peculiar to not very successful actors offstage, an exchange of critiques—"I love her, she's a fine, fine actress, but it just wasn't *her*"—"Well, but what can you expect with Philip directing, she needs *definite* direction"—"True, but shit, it just made me *puke*, the way she did that last scene. . . ." Nearly everyone seems to know nearly everyone else at Schwab's: I used to drink my coffee at the counter, until I found this instinct for in- timacy too cloying for comfort, and took to sitting at a table with the divorced wife of a Mexican set designer who shared my enthusiasm for Abyssinian cats.

If fetish and nostalgia often make for vulgarity in L.A., they often make also for homeliness, in the English sense of the word—a commu- nity feeling, a domesticity. Even Hollywood is far less repulsive in its private aspects than in its public goings-on. This is largely because Los

Angeles is a haven, to whose doors people have come from all over the world. It is a fraternity of refugees. Isherwood, showing me the view from his window one day, remembered the days when Stravinsky, Schönberg, Brecht and Aldous Huxley had all lived in the city out there. Hardly a day goes by without the death of some celebrated European resident, driven here long ago by war, ambition or persecution, and the British consul general told me that within his area there live more than 50,000 British subjects, some of whom fly Union Jacks from their roofs. San Francisco, up the coast, has an intimacy of a totally different kind, a hereditary or environmental closeness, bound up with the beauty of the place and the allure of its traditions. There is no such grace to the brotherhood of L.A. This is a charmless city really, humorless, often reactionary, a city without a gentry. Its comradeship lies only in a common sense of release or opportunity, tinged with a spice of holiday.

I used to buy my bread at Farmer's Market, a rambling enclave of stalls and tables off Wilshire Boulevard, and sitting over an orange juice afterward, nibbling bits off the end of my loaf, loved to watch the Angelenos go by. Often, of course, they were not Angelenos at all, but Japanese businessmen being shown around by bored local agents, or package tourists in wild sunglasses and kerchiefs, or bookish Europeans from UCLA deep in *Sociological Ratios in Southern California*. But there were always plenty of indigenes too, and they were instantly recognizable, not so much by their looks as by their posture, for they displayed all the somewhat impatient complacency of people who have discovered a Promised Land, and don't want to miss a minute of it. Though there are obviously lots of unhappy people in L.A., lots of dispossessed blacks, unemployed layabouts, junkies and nuts and winos and miscellaneous *bêtes noires* of Mr. Davis's department, still by and large this strikes me as a happy population—determinedly happy, perhaps. Nobody I met wanted to go back to New York or Detroit. With its Middle West squareness, its Manhattan bitterness, its imported touch of the European and its glorious Pacific sun, L.A. seems to please most people in the end —or for the moment.

In particular it provides a cheerful refuge for the jollier kind of American widow or divorcée, and many of these belatedly liberated souls frequent Farmer's Market. I often talked to them. There was a certain sameness to their appearance: in their bright blouses, leather jerkins, rather too tight slacks and rather too rakish sailor caps, bowed often by arthritis but resolutely vigorous of step, most of them looked more or less like Mr. Capote except, of course, for the layered makeup ineffectually disguising their cod-skin complexions. To their attitudes though there was a sprightly element of freedom. Briskly, gaily, talkatively they walked around the stalls, a pumpernickel loaf here, a bag of cashews there, and often they exchanged rather throaty comments with acquaintances about last night's movie or tomorrow's meeting of the Democratic party.

For such citizens L.A. offers an unexpected security, for its hard efficiency provides a bedrock, so to speak, upon which they can safely reconstruct their lives. It is nourished by the certainties they were weaned upon, like the pre-eminence of gadgetry or the goodness of capitalism. For all its cosmopolitan excitement, to a far greater degree than Chicago or San Francisco, let alone New York, it is still a provincial American town. "Did you know," one Farmer's Market lady asked me, supposing me, I imagine, to be a bit lost for social satisfactions, "did you know that the telephone company offers a free tour every day? My, that's a rewarding way of spending an afternoon!"

More exotic refugees share an intenser camaraderie. Members of the alternative society, for instance, seem to live rather in phalanx, perhaps because Mr. Davis sees no moral necessity for them. Southern California indeed has a long tradition of religious tolerance, sprouting cults, sects and rites like vivid fungi, and L.A. itself welcomes eccentrics if they are rich and famous enough. Your honest dropout, though, your simple hash man, often finds the atmosphere inhospitable, and among the more poignant corners of the metropolis is Venice, a struggling enclave of unorthodoxy on the ocean south of Santa Monica. It is a forlorn kind of suburb anyway, for it is the remains of a fin-de-siècle attempt to re-create the original Venice, "Venice Italy," upon the Pacific coast. A few Renaissance arcades remain, a Ruskinian window here and there, and there is a hangdog system of canals which, with their low-built bridges, their loitering ducks, their dog-messed paths, their smells of silt and dust and their air of stagnant hush, really do contrive to preserve a truly

Venetian suggestion of decay. Here we seem to see a philosophy with its back to the wall. It is like a caricature of itself, squeezed into this ocean beachhead by the colossal pressures of Los Angeles, and the society that frequents the place, too, suggests to me a culture on the verge of dissolution.

On the other hand, aliens in the older sense, foreigners that is, stand amazed still at the munificence of L.A. In some immigrant cities—in Toronto, for example, perhaps the archetypical melting pot of our time —your newcomer from Turkey or Sweden generally views his new home cynically, simply as a place to make money. I do not get this feeling with L.A.'s immigrants. They seem to see it still as a place of hope and blessing. I went one night to one of those Hollywood parades one used to see on newsreels long ago. Nothing much had changed. The long motorcade crawled down Hollywood Boulevard in a welter of self-esteem, with drum majorettes and elephants and Scottish pipers and U.S. Marines and belly dancers and coveys of movie personalities in antique cars who stopped now and then to be interviewed by TV men— "Hey Bob, great to see you! How's everything? Isn't this a great parade?" "Sure is, Jim, fantastic, just great, and I wantya to meet my family, Jim, my wife Margie, this is my son Jason, my daughter Laureen!" "Great, fantastic, great to meet all you folks, nice talking with you, Bill." "Sure thing, Jim, sure is a great parade, fantastic. . . ." The echoes of the bands trumpeted across town, the belly dancers spangled their way past Grauman's Chinese Theater, and overhead the helicopters clanked and circled, playing their searchlights upon the junketings below.

I was touched by the crowd that watched this display, for I felt in it a truly innocent wonder. Its people came from everywhere. There were a few of my Market friends ("I forgot to mention this morning, dear, that the Municipal Cleansing Department offers a very interesting lecture tour Tuesday mornings"); but there were Mexicans, too, in bright ponchos with babies on their backs, and lots of Italians, and Hindus talking impeccable English, and Greeks talking Greek, and there was a Scotsman in a kilt looking maudlin when the pipers went by, and a man who looked like a Zulu chief, and a voluble family who seemed to be talking Finnish, or perhaps Basque, and there were thousands of that particular neo-American blend, of no particular color, no specific race, no exact dialect, the *Homo californii*; and though the cops strode up and down fiercely slapping their nightsticks against their thighs, still everybody seemed genuinely, guilelessly delighted to be participants in such an unmistakable Angeleno spectacle.

I stayed till the very end, and the last I saw of the parade were the winking red lights of the police cars which brought up the rear, blinking away slowly down the boulevard as the crowds flooded off the sidewalks to follow them.

Much of L.A.'s expertise is devoted to such display. The Goodyear dirigible loiters effortlessly over town (I could not get a ride in it, alas, the Goodyear PR person never having heard of *Rolling Stone*). The freeways often seem to me to be as much showmanship as engineering. Sunset Strip, "the Billboard Center of the Western World," is one and a half miles of unremitting posters, 78 when I was there in the sixteen blocks between Crescent Heights and Doheny Drive: every day most of them seem to be changed, as one might replenish the drawing-room flowers, and marvelous is the professionalism by which the billboard men, with their slender cranes and their hefty trucks, bisect the torsos of rock singers, demolish romantic countrysides, split rodomontades or separate superlatives to hoist those tremendous announcements down in their several sections and trundle them away to oblivion or Las Vegas.

Yet Hollywood itself, its fact and its reputation, its studios and its publicity machine, is a family of sorts, not always very loving indeed, and frequently incestuous, but still bound by a common loyalty to its own legend. Its members often speak of it with true affection, especially if they are old. As the glamour of success fades, as the meaning of money blurs, so Hollywood memories acquire a mellower force, and elderly directors, dowager stars, speak of old Hollywood as others might remember happy school days, or Edwardian society. Age is paradoxically venerated in Hollywood, and one is told without pejoration that So-and-So is living in a home for aged actors, or assured with respect that Miss Estelle Winwood really *is* in her 93rd year. The new breed of entertainer often seems awkwardly anomalous, almost alienated, in this hierarchical community: which is why the Hyatt hotel on Sunset Boulevard, where the rock bravos tend to congregate, was long ago nicknamed the Continental Riot House.

Sometimes the camaraderie is oddly attractive. I went one day to a taping of the *Carol Burnett Show*, itself approaching institutional status after so many years on the screen, and found it an endearingly domestic occasion. Miss Burnett the star was married to Mr. Hamilton the executive producer, Miss Lawrence the ingenue brought her baby along. Everyone had known everyone else for years, and easily broke into a sort of family badinage: so that when somebody playfully pretended to sock somebody else on the jaw, even the sound effects man, somewhere out of sight, instantly contributed an impromptu *thunk*. Though it is currently the longest running show on television, and one of the most consistently successful, it suggested to me a rehearsal for some unusually polished but still folksy high school show, so that when Miss Burnett happened to tell me that she was dining that evening with Sir Alec Guinness and Lord Olivier, I felt like saying "Lawsy me, Carol, lucky old you. . . ."

At other times the bond can be sickly, or comic, or a bit morbid, or even creepy. I went to a Democratic party meeting in Beverly Hills which reminded me almost eerily, in its sense of inbred continuity, of the McCarthy era in Hollywood twenty years ago. There were the very same writers and directors, I swear, whom we used to see pale before the inquisitor's gaze; and there were their dauntless, loyal wives, no longer in dirndls and home-weave blouses indeed, but suitably beaded and denimed instead; and there was the same curl of pipe smoke in the air, with the same progressive smiles, and the same ladies went around getting signatures on petitions or propagating similar liberal causes—"Can we persuade you to support the Council for Universal Rights?"—"May I ask you to sign this petition on behalf of the Coalition for Handgun Control?"—"You do *know* about CDC, don't you, *so* important we feel"—until the chairman called for silence, and there stepped handsomely to the rostrum, just as he might have braved Senator McCarthy's furies long ago, that young crusader of today's Los Angeles joustings, that very antithesis of reaction, Jane Fonda's husband, whose name I momentarily forget.

The Los Angeles ethos is intensely infectious, and transmutes everything it touches. It can be great fun. The J. Paul Getty Museum of Art, for instance, which is housed in a dazzling re-creation of a Roman villa above the sea at Malibu, often excites the scorn of critics and connoisseurs, but delights people of more urbane taste. The Rolls-Royce motorcar, elsewhere in the world a symbol of dignity and reserve, becomes in Los Angeles, where it probably proliferates more than anywhere else, a young person's runabout, to swish up the drive to the Beverly Hills Hotel, or weave around the staid Cadillacs on the Palisades. Even the Californian cultists are easily Los Angelized, when they venture from their communes and mountain churches into the purlieus of the great city. The flaming sign on the Santa Ana Freeway announcing the Amazing Prophecy Center does not look in the least out of place, and I was not at all surprised to learn that America's largest incense factory, Spiritual Sky Scented Products Inc., was the property of the Hare Krishna community (acronymically ISKCON—International Society for Krishna Consciousness).

I visited the factory, as a matter of fact, to see just how easily the mantra and the head knot would adapt to L.A.'s style of capitalism, and found that fusion had easily been achieved. The lady at the reception desk was dressed in full Indianified costume, and the company memo pads ended their list of practical alternatives (Take Action / See Me / Call Me / File) with the hardly less clear-cut spiritual injunction, clean across the bottom of the page in vaguely Oriental lettering, HARE KRISHNA, HARE KRISHNA, KRISHNA, KRISHNA, HARE, HARE / HARE RAMA, HARE RAMA, RAMA, RAMA, HARE, HARE. The plant manager was dressed more or less for Rotary, and told me that the Spiritual Sky line emphasized the incense America wants and loves—strawberry flavor especially: but when I pressed him on more spiritual matters, in no time at all he had pushed the *Wall Street Journal* aside and was enthusiastically explaining to me the principles of his Divine Master—rather wistfully, I thought, as though the management of Spiritual Sky was in the nature of a penance.

Just as often, though, the L.A. treatment only coarsens and degrades. It was no coincidence that so many of the Watergate acolytes were alumni of Los Angeles advertising agencies: the aerosol charm of John Dean, for instance, who entertained me most kindly to Dr.

Peppers in his Laurel Canyon hideaway, blends very easily into the ambiance, and I suspect that Mr. Nixon himself, if ever he turned up in Farmer's Market, would be ecstatically welcomed. "Smartness," in the opportunist sense, the importance of image, the search for celebrity whatever its cause—all these are true L.A. characteristics, and are contagious. Many vegetarian restaurants, I am told, opening to a regular sacrament of organic ideals, soon degenerate into convenience foods, and even death of course becomes a packaged product up at Forest Lawn, where the Wee Kirk o' the Heather offers consolation in Tim of Sorrow, and Companion Lawn Crypts provide the ultimate security of Reinforced Concrete. The TV game shows of Hollywood have evolved an entire language and ritual of falseness, from the stylized jumpings, handclappings and mock-bashfulness of the competitors to the palatial languor of the ravaged showgirls who act as ladies of the prize chamber.

For myself, I am left with an uneasy feeling even about Disneyland, where the most advanced technical resources, the most brilliant administrative systems, are used simply to animate a gigantic charade. The sham treads uncomfortably upon the heels of truth, and one begins to wonder whether a dummy castle from Snow White, a make-believe New Orleans restaurant, even a nonalcoholic mint julep, might not be as good, and as true, as the real thing. I found this inescapable illusion rather suffocating, and was revived, as I staggered from the King Arthur Carousel to the Casey Jr. Circus Train, through Tomorrowland to the Bear Country, only by the presence of the peripatetic bands, blues, brass or Mexican, who really were undeniably alive and irreplaceable by electronics even in L.A.

Saddest of all, for a visitor from over the water, is the spectacle of the liner *Queen Mary*, perhaps the most celebrated of all ocean steamships, which lies in the harbor of Long Beach in a condition of induced elation, as though she has been pumped full of stimulants. She has had the L.A. treatment with a vengeance. Her innards ripped out, her funnels replaced, part of her turned into a hotel, part into a museum, jazzed up, repainted, publicized, projected, she cost almost twice as much to turn into a tourist center as she cost to build as a ship, and has been losing money ever since. Would it not have been easier, the municipality is sometimes asked, to build a new one? It would, they gravely reply, but then it would have lacked *curiosity quotient*.

Curiosity quotient! It is arguably better than scrapping her, I suppose, but still I thought the experience of the *Queen Mary* infinitely depressing. How silly, the mock-nautical uniforms! How pitiful the spectacle of that lifeless bridge! How drear, the prospect of nuptials in the Wedding Chapel (*Promenade Deck: Wedding Coordinators and Ordained Minister*)! This was the pride of the Clyde when I was a child, this was the ship which, speeding through the wolf packs in the gray Atlantic, safely took half a million Americans to the liberation of Europe! Now she lies there tarted up and phony, the victim of a culture which, in the intoxicating mastery of its know-how, so often uses it ignobly.

And, unexpectedly, when I examine my feelings about this tremendous and always astonishing city, I find them inextricably shot through with regret. This is not, I think, a usual reaction to Los Angeles, and I am moved to it partly because I come from a temporarily discomfited civilization myself—"worrying the carcass of an old song," as the poet R. S. Thomas described us Welsh, "gnawing the bones of a dead culture."

Nobody driving down Wilshire Boulevard, say, or watching the surfers spring into the Pacific, could call the culture of L.A. dead. It is full of vitality still, full of fun and wealth. The refugees are still flocking to this haven beyond the deserts, the men of brilliance are still at work in labs and laboratories and studios from Malibu to Irvine. Almost every development of Western thought, from space research to comparative linguistics to Transcendental Lung Control, finds its niche, its expression and its encouragement somewhere in this metropolis. Surveyed in the morning from one of its mountain belvederes, Los Angeles really does look one of the classic cities, one of the archetypes. Its streets and houses and bridges and buildings seem to lie there *differently*, massed differently, differently integrated, sprouting here and there peculiarly with the clumps of their urban centers, and hung over already, as the sun rises over the deserts, with the particular chemical haze whose very name, smog, was a Los Angeles invention.

Then it looks unmistakably a world city: and it will represent forever, I think, the apogee of urban, mechanical, scientific man, rational man perhaps, before the gods returned.

For it is past its prime already. It has lost the exuberant certainty that made it seem, even when I first knew it, unarguably the City of the Future, the City That Knew How. None of us Know now. The machine has lost its promise of emancipation, and if L.A. then seemed a talisman of fulfillment, now it is tinged with disillusion. Those terrific roads, those thousands of cars, the sheen of the jets screaming out of the airport, the magnificent efficiency of it all, the image building, the self-projection, the glamour, the fame—they were all false promises after all, and few of us see them now as the symptoms of redemption.

There is one monument in L.A. which hauntingly commemorates this failing faith. It is the queer cluster of pinnacles called the Watts Towers, and it stands in one of the shabbier parts of town, way out on 107th Street, beside the railway tracks. Simon Rodia, an Italian immigrant, built these arcane artifacts single-handedly, taking more than thirty years to do it. He made them of cement, stuck all over with bits of glass and pottery, strengthened by frames of scrap metal and wound about with curious studded spirals, rather like precipitous roller coasters. When he had built them he surrounded them with an irregular cement wall, like a row of tombstones, so that the whole ensemble has the air of a temple or shrine, rather Oriental in nature.

It is very dusty there, and all around are the unpretentious homes of black people, so that you might easily suppose yourself to be in some African railway town, in the Egyptian delta perhaps. Few cars go by. You can hear children playing, and dogs barking, and neighbors chatting across the way. It is like a simple country place, before technology arrived: and just as the Watts riots of the sixties were a protest against the failure of technique to give contentment to poor people, so the Watts Towers, years before their time, were a symbolic *cri du coeur* against the computer tyrannies to come.

Mr. Rodia was a prophet: and when he had built his towers he slipped away from Los Angeles once and for all, and went to live somewhere quite different.

Southern Africa

· · · · · · · ·

THE SIEGE
STATES

*In the spring of 1977 I went to southern Africa,
and wrote these two essays about states under siege. There
was nothing essentially new to the situation. South Africa had been
isolated in the world for years, thanks to its inveterate racial
policies, while it was more than a decade since Ian Smith
of Rhodesia, by declaring the independence of his country from Great
Britain, had given notice that the whites there would hang on
to complete power for as long as possible. In 1977, though,
the pressures were intensifying, and in both countries I was haunted—
stimulated too, to be honest—by the feeling that things
were coming to a head, that abscesses were presently to burst, and that
one of the most fateful political stories of our time
was on its way to a denouement.*

· · ·

SOUTHERN AFRICA

I. Black, White and Fantasy in South Africa

[1977]

The Siege States

HIGH ABOVE PRETORIA, the administrative capital of the Republic of South Africa, there stands a squat bulbous monument on a hill, commanding the wide windswept highlands of the Transvaal—5000 feet up on the high veld, 400 miles from the sea, in one of the most splendidly African parts of the African continent. This is the supreme shrine of the White Man in South Africa. Built into its massive stonework, as coins and newspapers are buried beneath the foundations of bridges, is the deepest rationale of apartheid, the intricate political device —part mysticism, part economics, part confidence trick— by which the white race maintains its supremacy over the blacks in the southernmost part of the continent. Everywhere else the white race, once master of half the earth, has withdrawn from its conquered territories, but in South Africa it stands intransigent upon its privileges against the terrible and majestic swell of black unrest. The Voortrekker Monument explains and expresses that intransigence: for it stands there so uncompromisingly on its *kopje*, seems to be socketed so deeply into the soil, is so buttressed with vaults, arches and ceremonial steps that it looks as though nothing short of cataclysm could ever destroy it.

On the face of it the monument commemorates the Great Trek, the legendary *hegira* of the Afrikaner people, the paramount whites of South Africa, away from the coast into these remote and tremendous uplands, where in the early 19th century they established their own independent republics and rooted their culture in the soil. But its real meaning is deeper. In withdrawing so far into Africa the Afrikaners were deliberately disavowing the values of the world outside, declaring their resolve to live in their own way in their own inviolate homeland: and in particular they were rejecting once and for all the thesis, pressed upon them by the pragmatic British on the coast, that all human beings were equal before God. It was basic to Afrikaner reasoning that all men were *not* equal, and in particular that the black indigenes of the country were divinely ordained to be inferiors, hewers of wood and drawers of water. The Great Trek of the Afrikaner zealots, lurching in the ox wagons ever further into the harsh hinterland, was a journey that led them and their little nation directly, against all hazards, with much splendor of spirit, toward the squalid racial impasse, whites balefully confronting blacks, which now engulfs their country.

The monument is an arcane edifice, like a place of pledge or sacrifice. The Afrikaner Volk, it proclaims, have overcome the forces of Evil to achieve this hefty consummation on the veld, and they alone have carried the torch of true civilization into these savage territories. There is an eternal flame burning in the crypt to prove it, and once a year, at midday on December 16th, a shaft of sunlight penetrates the high roof of the building and falls upon a great stone cenotaph which, like Napoleon's tomb at Les Invalides, stands somber in its subterranean chamber, mystically to illuminate the oath inscribed enormously upon its granite: ONS VIR JOU, SUID-AFRIKA—"We for Thee, South Africa."

December 16th: the day when, in 1838, an Afrikaner force of fewer than 500 men utterly defeated an army of 20,000 black Zulus at the Battle of Blood River in Natal. They had made a covenant with Providence, and December 16th is celebrated as a day not just of military victory, but of spiritual commitment—statistical procedures, we are assured by the Monument Handbook, show that there was only a one percent chance of Afrikaner success at Blood River, "supporting the belief that this victory was an Act of God." Over the years the historic meaning of Afrikanerdom itself came to be embodied in this divinely sponsored triumph over the Powers of Darkness, visibly and symbolically expressed in the black skins of the defeated adversaries, and the Voortrekker Monument was erected to perpetuate the message for posterity. The divine privilege of being white is demonstrated in a slaughter of blacks, achieved against all statistical odds by the direct intervention of God.

Standing inside this portentous structure, with the Lamp of Civilization burning steadily in its glass reliquary, the images of battle and dedication all around, the wind of the high veld moaning through the casements and the sun shaft imperceptibly moving through its high orifice, minute by minute toward the next anniversary, one begins to understand the almost occult reluctance of the Afrikaner government of South Africa to admit its black subjects to equality. The Voortrekker Monument is no place for conciliations or second thoughts. It is more like a setting for *Götterdämmerung*, and all around it there stands a barricade of sculpted ox wagons, encircling the shrine in perpetual watchful laager, as if to imply that the Battle of Blood River is not over yet.

Few countries in the world are more magnificent in scale, more richly stacked with resources, more naturally generous of character than the Republic of South Africa, probably the most generally detested state on earth. In area, it is twice the size of France; in temper, it ranges from the exquisite mountain valleys of the Cape, all mellow charm and intimacy, to the swart gold ridges of the Witwatersrand, the Drakensberg escarpment like a vast castellated rampart, or the wild, wooded coastline of Natal.

In this almost-paradise live some 24 million people. Seventeen million are black, divided into seven principal tribal groups speaking ten different languages. Some 4 million are white: 2.5 million Afrikaners, 1.5 million of British descent, plus communities of Jews, Italians, Portuguese and Greeks. There are 2 million Coloreds, as the South Africans call half-castes, and nearly a million Asians. Most of these peoples have lived in South Africa for generations, and there were times in the past when it seemed possible that they would be integrated into a harmonious, polychromatic whole: but during the 20th century the Afrikaners, achieving a position of political dominance over everyone else, have so imposed their own philosophies upon the country that black, white and brown have moved ever further apart, divided first by custom and habit, then by fear and prejudice, and since 1948, when the Afrikaner government instituted the policy of apartheid, legally enforced separation of the races, by a dense body of political and social legislation.

Today the white man is absolutely supreme, and the ideal of one South Africa is officially discounted. Not a single black or Colored man has a vote for the National Parliament in Cape Town, no non-European can rise high in business or in government, there are racial restrictions and discriminations so elaborate and so all-pervasive that they affect every facet of life, dividing the races absolutely and making it almost impossible for an ordinary black family to be friendly with an ordinary white. It is not a colonial arrangement, an elite of expatriates exploiting the natives. *All* these peoples are natives, and the racial order is something far more organic, deeply entrenched in history and religion, and supported paradoxically by the very riches of the country itself—riches which give the white man his power and make him so unwilling to change his style of life, or share these treasures more equitably among the other 20 million.

It is the most tantalizing of countries—a country permanently denied serenity, it seems, by the fact of race. Even now, when its antagonisms seem to be sliding toward catastrophe, there are parts of it where one may experience a melancholy sense of might-have-been—

especially in Cape Province where, not so long ago, blacks, browns and Coloreds seemed to have established a congenial equilibrium. Cape Town still feels like a civilized city in a civilized country—a touch of San Francisco, a slight tang of Sydney. People of all races walk its streets, and there are flower stalls about, and bookshops, and a symphony orchestra, and four daily papers of varying views. Above the city Table Mountain gloriously crouches, often swirled in cloud, frequented by nature ramblers and lugubrious baboons. Offshore the supertankers of the world steam by, never pausing on their long pilgrimage to the oil countries, but supplied with mails and medicines, like passing sadhus accepting offerings, by helicopters from this munificent shore.

And better still, you may glimpse the elusive idyll of South Africa in the delectable winelands to the northeast of Cape Town, where the Cape plain rises gently toward the summits of the Du Toit's Kloof. Here is the enchanting university town of Stellenbosch, the oldest seat of the Afrikaner culture, all Dutch gables, oaks, stinkwood furniture and musty, vinous smells. Here the fields of Riesling, Steen or Pinotage stretch away, meticulously tended, to plain white farmhouses at the mountain edge, and the very names on the map have an Arcadian ring —Bonfoi, Sir Lowery's Pass, the Jonkershook River or the Botterlary Hills.

Even here, though, up the winding dirt lanes, come rumors of riot, bloodshed and repression, for the inescapable reality of South Africa today, the truth around which all else revolves, is the suppression of the huge black majority by the whites, and the inescapable slow movement of the blacks toward revolution. The racial conflict dominates every conversation, as it dictates every political act and every economic decision. Every day its shadow grows more ominous, and every day its symptoms break into the newspapers—more deaths in the Cape Town black townships—another students' riot—a militant black paper is launched—a policeman is killed by a grenade—another batch of black protesters is charged under the Terrorism Act, or the Suppression of Communism Act, or the Internal Security Act, or they are detained incommunicado without charge, or placed under house arrest, or banned from public life indefinitely. The segregated black townships, on the edge of the white cities, are littered now with the wreckage of arson and communal violence, and the country is tense with apprehension, as though an enormous thunderstorm is brooding over it, sometimes spilling heavy raindrops on the sidewalk.

The blacks are angry, and this is something new to South Africa. After generations of slights and injuries, voteless, propertyless, underpaid, overworked, confined to vast monotonous ghettos with rotten houses and second-rate schools—after generations of all this the black masses of South Africa have remained, until now, astonishingly good-natured. It is only within the past year, as news of the black *Risorgimento* has filtered down from Angola and Mozambique, as Black Consciousness has at last fired the imagination of the African young, that the blacks have burst into open militancy and turned to violence. It is as though a monumental public patience has cracked at last, never to be soothed again.

The Grand Plan of Afrikanerdom does not allow for anger, for apartheid is essentially an intellectual conception, theologically tinged. It postulates that if the colored peoples of the country are allowed to integrate with the whites, they will presently take over the state and fundamentally alter its character. The alternative it proposes is the formal division of South Africa into separate, autonomous entities, one white, eight black, to be economically united but politically, socially and culturally distinct. This is a vision different in kind from the old American ideas of segregation, and when it was first defined by the academics of Stellenbosch there seemed a certain nobility to it.

But if the scholars devised it idealistically, the politicians interpreted it in expedience. For them it was a device of white supremacy. The delineated black "homelands" were small and poor, and anyway, more black people lived in the huge rich areas reserved for the whites, where their labor was indispensable: these people were to be deprived of all citizenship rights forever, remaining there as convenient helots. The Grand Plan was to be upheld too, when the politicians put it into practice, by a vast and preposterous edifice of racial discrimination, legalizing the basest instincts of the bigots, and ensuring that in death as in life, in urinating as in buying a postage stamp, in boarding a bus, in making love, in writing a sonnet on a bench, black and white were to be irrevocably kept apart. As the years passed the whole project became more obviously delusory. In 1948, when apartheid was born, the ratio of blacks to whites in the *white* areas was 2.3 to 1. By 1970, the the year of the last census, it was 2.9 to 1, and well under half the blacks lived in their own allotted territories. Today even some of the Stellenbosch theorists admit that the whole idea was an enormous miscalculation, almost a historical hoax.

Yet it is still being laboriously implemented, as though nobody knows how to stop it, while the resentment of the blacks surges toward an explosion. A few absurdities of petty apartheid have been abandoned, but the Grand Plan as a whole still stands. The first of the "homelands" has achieved its prescribed goal and has been declared an independent state—the Xhosa Republic of the Transkei, between Cape Province and Natal. There, displayed as it were in exhibition, one may see the final product of the Afrikaner political philosophy, the first graduate so to speak of apartheid's curriculum.

The western frontier of the new republic is everything a frontier ought to be—a deep river ravine, crossed by three parallel bridges, surrounded by open, rolling country and marked by the lonely flags, hutments and barriers of the frontier post. "One and All," says a handwritten announcement engagingly on the Transkei side, "Must Show Their Passports Here," and inside three or four black officials slowly, very slowly, perform the standard frontier rites. When I was there they gave me two documents. One bade me welcome to the new state, on payment of a two-rand entrance fee: the other declared me a Prohibited Person as defined in section 40 (1) (c) of Act 59, and warned me of frightful penalties if I ever set foot in the place. I took them at their kinder word, was waved in by a genial policeman at the barrier, and kept the anathema as a souvenir.

Not a single country in the world has recognized the independence of the Transkei, on the grounds that it is no more than a political fraud, a trick of apartheid. Yet in some ways it is *true*. Almost overnight, for instance, the degradations of social apartheid have been exuberantly abolished. Black men throng all the bars, ordering quarts where pints were once the measure, and a heady feeling of liberation really does brighten little Umtata, the new capital. National flags fly all over the place, Transkeian Army officers stump about in unexpected uniforms; from his fine new hilltop mansion, the Prime Minister, Paramount Chief Kaiser Matanzima, makes encouraging declarations about freedom, cooperation and South African generosity.

But in other ways it is a sham. Economically the Transkei is absolutely dependent upon South Africa—most of its young men go to work in the gold mines of the white Rand, and it cannot even feed itself. Politically it appears to be altogether subservient to Pretoria. Chief Matanzima—whose brother is finance minister—has already locked up most of the local skeptics, and while I was there I watched another group of his less joyously liberated subjects being tried in the High Court under the Suppression of Communism Act—prosecuted by white South African lawyers, judged by a white chief justice, charged under a South African law but arraigned there, as independence demanded, beneath the crest of the Republic of Transkei.

Yet independent they allegedly are: the flags fly bravely over Umtata, the flights from Cape Town land at Matanzima Airport, the smiling border officials stamp their prohibition orders and the South African government, in shiny brochure and policy broadcast, insistently declares it the True Way of racial progress.

Far away beyond the Drakensberg, beyond the wide pastoral uplands of the Orange Free State, so heartless in winter, so delicately flowered in spring, there stands a very different creation of apartheid: Soweto, Southwest Townships, the vast black ghetto, several segregated cities splotched into one, which supplies the labor force for Johannesburg and the gold mines of the Rand.

There is nowhere else in the world like Soweto. It is something like a disused exhibition, something like an open prison, something like a gypsy encampment, something like a construction camp and something like a slum. With a population of more than a million—twice the size of Johannesburg itself—Soweto is one of the great cities of Africa, but it does not feel like a city at all, for it has no center. Mile after mile, in interminable geometrical lines, curves and circles, the shabby little brick houses of the blacks extend across the treeless veld, linked by rutted mud roads, unkempt, unpainted, each section indistinguishable from the next, the whole seeming to possess no recognizable shape or limit. There is no focus to Soweto, no complex of stores and offices, no cathedral tower or television mast: it is like a haggard dream, in which one is always on the edge of somewhere, but never ever gets there.

In Soweto, in the summer of 1976, began the series of township riots which have already changed everything in South Africa, giving notice, so to speak, that the great black reactor was going critical. Here the whole structure of apartheid is seen as no more than a tyrannical device, and Matanzima and his kind are branded not merely as Uncle Toms, but as traitors. The black dynamic burns furiously in Soweto now. White people may enter the township only with special permits, prominently stamped AT OWN RISK, and the security forces watch the place almost as they might watch an enemy salient on a battlefront. Deep in that shabby maze the unknown revolutionaries are at work, and the place seethes with plots and rivalries and vendettas, and crawls with police informers.

A few years ago the Soweto blacks seemed like shadow people. They seemed to have no fervors of their own, except when they indulged in tribal dances, football matches or violent crime. In the daytime one saw them expressionless at their menial tasks in Johannesburg, at nighttime they vanished altogether. Now they seem very different. They swarm uninhibitedly through the shops of Jo'burg. They say very nearly seditious things at public meetings. They riot. They visibly grope out of their poverty toward a contemporary elegance, and have already achieved, in their command of the gaudy and the surprising, an excitement of bearing beyond the range of the whites. They are beginning to seem the salt of the place, the fizz of it, providing just those elements of brilliance, fun and response that white South Africans, on the whole the least vivacious people I know, so dispiritingly lack.

Nothing is more moving in Africa today than this spectacle, of the urban blacks suddenly finding their pride. It has been achieved, above all, by the young. It is a children's crusade. The 1976 riots, which told the world about it, were essentially a rebellion of children—children defying not only the terrifying sanctions of the state, the batons, the bullets and the detention cells, but the apprehensive disapproval of their parents too. Sometimes the students were undoubtedly exploited, by criminals and hooligans as by politicians, but the evidence seems to prove that their uprising was genuine and spontaneous, against the injustices and indignities of their young lives—"Now can we convince you that we are at the end of the road?"

The young people of the townships are the first blacks of South Africa to achieve a revolutionary cohesion. "We don't need any Communists to teach us," as one burning young activist told me in Soweto. "We know what we want, and we know what to do about it." They are as much like Puritans as they are like Maoists—contemptuous of their elders' servility, austere and earnest in their lifestyles. They have furiously attacked the township speakeasies, the "shebeens," which have been for generations the emblems of black degradation, and they have imposed upon the townships a macabre regime of mourning for the victims of the riots. Thousands of them have boycotted school, in protest against the educational system, thousands more have escaped from the country altogether, over the borders into the independent states of Lesotho, Botswana or Swaziland. They have been imprisoned by the hundreds, beaten up, reviled, herded about like animals, teargassed and snatched from their homes by security police: yet in all the years of apartheid theirs has been the first group of citizens to risk all in opposing the system, and to resist institutional violence by violence in the streets.

It is not all sublime idealism. It has often been vicious. Innocent blacks have been bullied and intimidated. Children have been frightened out of school. Above all, black racialism, which for so long seemed almost a contradiction in terms, has been given an ominous new impetus.

There was a moment in the 1930s when observers of the Indian scene realized that, though the British Empire still held all the guns, in a deeper sense the Indians had already won their struggle for independence. I think this is true in South Africa now. Though their oppressors are far more ruthless than the British ever were, already the black Africans feel like winners. They see Black Power supreme throughout the rest of Africa; they observe the world unanimous in their support; they realize at last that though the white South African looks powerful and important when he towers across the charge desk, bullies you from the prosecutor's stand or floods your school with poison gas, he is not important really, nor anything like omnipotent. The White Man's Magic has evaporated in this last segment of his empire.

There is no missing this new black assurance. It is everywhere, in the swagger of young men in the street, in the startling outspokenness of black leaders, in the progressive collapse, absurdity by insult, of petty apartheid. "We will take no more nonsense," one young black swore to me, assuring me that he no longer even bothered to carry his pass book, once the sine qua non of black existence in South Africa, "no more nonsense at all." Even the housemaid at my hotel in Johannesburg, when I asked her how she felt about her situation in life, answered me in one conclusive word: "*Angry.*"

The tables are turning. To the black militants the concessions already won are contemptible, and the slow relaxing of petty apartheid means nothing—it is not separate lavatories or demarcated bathing beaches that matter, but the realities of power. The blacks no longer wish merely to enter the white man's world, but actually to take it over. The papers are full of terrorist training camps, of schoolboys spirited away for Marxist indoctrination, of border infiltrations and secret armories. Sometimes casualty lists appear from the running conflict, misted in secrecy, being waged by the South African security forces on their northern borders, or heroes of the battle are honored with bands, medals and patriotic addresses. Gatsha Buthelezi, leader of the 4 million Zulus, openly and with impunity calls for mass civil disobedience, and says of himself, as a man speaking not out of weakness but of strength: "I am the hand that my people offer in friendship, but I am also the hand they will withdraw in their anger." Sometimes the rioters of the townships will let a white man pass if he gives the Black Power salute; and this seems proper enough, for the most profound recognition in South Africa today is the dawning realization, among blacks and whites alike, that *force majeure* works both ways.

There are still moderate, liberal blacks about, pro-white blacks even, but they begin to seem indecisive, dated people. The conviction of compromise lacks bite, and no fiery black evangelist has yet made the middle way, the conciliatory way, seem virile and exciting. A Christ might achieve it, but not even a Gandhi, I fear, could now convince the blacks of South Africa that moderation is the best policy. The very suggestion of cooperation with whites, even the most enlightened whites, is enough to blight a reputation among the fiercest of the young black patriots.

Now no black leader, at least in public, can demand anything less than majority rule—black rule, that is, for the entire nation. There is no concerted plan of black action—no black leader has published a reasoned manifesto of aims or ideology. The blacks of South Africa are far less homogenous than the whites, and Black Consciousness is flanked by a dozen other corporate impulses, old tribal ambitions, new ideological asperities, rivalries of leadership or inherited loyalty. Black power is diffused among many centers. There are the tribal leaders of the homelands, not always friendly to each other; there are the leaders of the banned African National Congress and Communist parties; there are the Maoists and Trotskyists, no doubt, and hosts of young militant organizers whose names we do not know. Nobody can foresee what kind of a South Africa will arise when the blacks achieve their ascendancy.

For it is not one of your planned revolutions, organized from some central cell. It is happening organically, almost seismically, as though Nature herself is restoring a balance. In twenty years, by current trends, there will be 37 million black people in South Africa, outnumbering the whites seven to one. "What will happen to us then?" replied a government official when I asked him the eternal South African question. "We'll be bred into the sea, that's what!"

Around the edges of the great predicament hover uncertainly the English-speaking South Africans. They are politically almost as impotent as the black men, the Afrikaner government being unassailably entrenched in power, and morally rather less decisive than the Afrikaners, being more liberal without being quite liberal enough. Seventy years ago, after their victory in the Anglo-Boer War, they were briefly the masters of South Africa, but in the peace that followed the Afrikaners gradually revenged themselves, year by year, until in 1948 Dr.

D. F. Malan's National party finally beat them at the polls. Since then the Afrikaners have increased their majority at every election, and have now so reorganized the constituencies that nothing short of a political convulsion could ever remove them from office.

The English still control most of the wealth of South Africa, sitting in palatial offices, supervising the gold output of the Rand or manipulating the commodity prices; they provide most of the fighting journalists who, more courageously perhaps than anyone else, maintain the struggle for human rights in South Africa; but generically they have rather an aimless air, a bemusement, as though they are absolutely at the mercy of events. Their own principal political party, the United party, has temporized with apartheid, opposing it in principle, accommodating it in practice, but by the standards of the Voortrekker Monument they are déclassé whites, whites outside the laager. Of the three major South African racial groups, their theoretical values are highest, their political performance weakest, and today one could almost write a political assessment of South Africa without mentioning them at all, so peripheral are their actions to the colossal drama of events.

Johannesburg is their chief creation, and it suits them. There it stands ringed by its yellow mine dumps, like stacks of its own excreta, the richest city in Africa but altogether without responsibility. It is the ultimate money city. Its only raison d'être is gold, and its pavements are literally impregnated with the stuff. The point of all its functions, the foundation of all its skyscrapers, is the presence of that bonanza beneath the soil of the Witwatersrand. The rich of Johannesburg are very rich indeed, and by their membership in the worldwide society of capitalists feel eerily detached from the racial antagonisms raging all around them. They are there simply to make money; air-conditioned in their downtown offices, couched among flamboyants and swimming pools in their suburban villas, often enough they remain staggeringly ignorant of life in the black townships a few miles down the road. Few of them have ever set eyes on Soweto. It is as though a totally separate black world exists somewhere over there, providing its uncomplaining domestics every morning, removing itself at night.

Apartheid has been very profitable to Johannesburg in the past, ensuring inexhaustible supplies of dirt-cheap labor, but things are changing, and the Randlords are beginning to wonder if it will be profitable much longer. Might it not be wise, they are reasoning now, to instill in the blacks some sense of capitalist values while the going is good? Money is the Jo'burg specialty, and money can surely solve the racial problem, as it solves all others. To a man like Harry Oppenheimer, the suave and scholarly chairman of Anglo-American Goldfields—the David Rockefeller of South Africa, perhaps—economics is the ultimate social weapon, and by its intelligent use the most enormous historic imponderables can be stayed or diverted.

A hundred of the richest businessmen, meeting in Johannesburg, have set up a body specifically to improve living conditions among the city blacks; the Association of Chambers of Commerce, hardly a liberal body by definition, has publicly demanded a better deal for blacks, in the interest not so much of justice as of dividends. "Why, the blacks are natural capitalists," said one supermarket tycoon enthusiastically. "Once you've got them into the system, they'll never destroy it"— and it is perfectly true that the most successful of the black businessmen, who like to drive very fast around the ghetto streets in spanking new BMWs, do look as though they would fit into the hierarchy of the multinationals.

The young blacks scoff, but at least it is an initiative. Otherwise the English-speakers, and especially the sizable contingent of English liberals, seem to have lost heart for the struggle. For thirty years they have, in a fairly gentlemanly way, argued against apartheid, at least its cruder aspects—not, as a general rule, so fiercely as to risk losing their jobs or going to prison, but still with an honorable consistency. But they have achieved nothing. They have been little more than irrelevances. Even their vote has counted for nothing: the United party is now a small and abject minority in Parliament, while the more frankly liberal party, the Progressive Reform party, has never achieved more than a handful of seats. History has proceeded anyway, ignoring the liberal truths, and now the English-speaking South African is left bewildered and afraid. "It is as though there is an avalanche waiting to fall upon us, and only a cough will dislodge it."

Among these unhappy people a sense of fatalism has developed. Their sense of urgency seems atrophied, and even their instinct of crisis slightly anesthetized. They, or their forebears, came to South Africa in the first place simply to better themselves, and ten years ago it seemed that they did in fact live better than most of us did elsewhere. Even now, I suppose, for certain temperaments there is an appeal to a country where you never have to make the beds, and where Mazda advertises their family cars as having "enough room for mom, dad, two kids and the maid." But the advantages are waning, and many an English South African must now be wondering if the sunshine and the servants are enough. The country is in perpetual emergency, the inflation rate is high, and even for the most apolitical white citizen life is uneasy and uncertain. His standard of living, once the highest in the world, is now about seventh, and he lives no more richly, for all his black helots, than a German or a Frenchman—besides being, so the statistics say, very much more likely to commit suicide.

What's the point? Even materially, Paradise is illusory. The apples are no rosier here—greener in fact, and more corrupting too. When I was in the Cape I often went down to Sea Point, the Malibu of Cape Town, to sit over a coffee at the Pavilion Cafe there, and watch the white indigenes at their leisure. They had come from many countries, though they would nearly all be numbered in the English camp, rather than the Afrikaner, and after a time, I found, they all began to look like so many refugees, here sheltering in their last haven. The business executives taking the sun with their families were refugees from socialism, obstreperous labor unions and 90 percent income taxes. The elderly military gentlemen, carrying sticks and trailing cardigans, were refugees from decadence and inadequate pensions. The Italians playing cards on the terrace were refugees from plain poverty who had made their small, easy fortunes with a cafe or two or an ice-cream factory. The Jewish ladies eating powerful ice-cream sundaes were refugees by upbringing or inheritance, gravitating here as they might to Miami Beach or Brighton. Colored servants waited on them all, reinforcing the effect of enclave, and there was a babel of languages in the morning sun—English, Italian, Portuguese, German—as there might have been (I could not help thinking) in the shuttered truckloads of concentration camp victims, shunted from siding to siding across Europe to a solution.

For even down here the light was fading, and their easy lives seemed

curiously unreal, like the lives of exiled monarchs in spas. How lonely
they looked, despite themselves! They did not look at all like the ex-
ploiters and racialists of popular conception, here in this last retreat of
their illusions, and indeed life among the English-speaking bourgeoisie
of South Africa is anything but dynamic. Responses are slow among
these escapists, jokes fail to ignite, faces are strangely flaccid and everyday life seems to move at half-speed, as though it has lost the joy of
locomotion, or is saving fuel for emergencies.

They are only supernumeraries, anyway. It is upon the Afrikaners,
they of the Sacred Flame, that the whole future of South Africa depends: they hold the power, they have the jets and the machine guns,
and they alone can dictate, by opting for conciliation with the blacks
or persevering with oppression, what becomes of this marvelous and
miserable country. The issue is gigantic—who is going to be boss, the
black man or the white?—and the Afrikaner understands it instinc-
tively, as part of his heritage.

Among all the tribes of Africa, the most formidable is this white
tribe of the Afrikaners—who have a right to be called Africans since
they have been indigenous to this soil almost as long as there have
been white men living in North America. They are truly tribal people.
They have their own atavistic version of the Christian god, their own
distinctive mores, their own colorful language—not a very old one, it
is true, having started life in the 18th century as a kind of kitchen
Dutch, but still recognizably a tongue of its own, with a lively, growing literature and a fine lexicon of phrases like *Foeitog* ("What a pity!")
or *Reddingsbaadjie Onder U Sitplek* ("Life Vest under Your Seat"). They
are bound by a rigid sense of kin and origin, and the concept of the
Volk, which enters so many of their usages, is more than just "the
people" in the American constitutional sense, but is something nearer
to cult or fraternity—the innermost society of Afrikanerdom is actually
called the Broederbond.

There are only 2.5 million Afrikaners. They form a very introspective community, and the development of their culture, the fostering of
their history, the formation of their national purpose, have all been
highly self-conscious processes. Little in Afrikaner history is hap-

hazard. It is a history of extremes and abruptness, a constant instinct toward separateness—no blurs, no blends, no overlaps. Until now the Volk have prospered by these uncompromising techniques, and have turned all their disadvantages into success. Having been defeated by the British in war, they used the subsequent peace to turn the tables. Being vastly outnumbered by the blacks, they subdued them by sheer arrogance. Every attempt to dominate or alter their society they have fought off or sidestepped—by trekking ever deeper into the African hinterland, by starting their own business enterprises, by the calculated instrument of apartheid. They have fought their battles all alone, and so far they have won through.

All is now at risk, because of the one great error in the Afrikaner creed. Those forces of darkness, so graphically conjured in the mysteries of the Voortrekker Monument, are *not* the black men after all. God did not mean it that way. The revelation is mistaken, and the conviction that Afrikaner society can survive only by the perpetual subjection of the black African is the one fatal flaw in the courageous outlook of the Volk. It has brought out the worst in them, the narrowness, the intolerance, the bigotry that goes with their patriotism and their religion. It has muddled their thinking and coarsened their merits. And though it has served them well enough during the first three hundred years of their history, it is almost inconceivable that it can succeed much longer.

They are in their last laager, symbolically represented in that circle of ox wagons around the monument. They have nowhere else to retreat, and they cannot fight on forever.

There is to South Africa a strong suggestion of the bull ring—the cruelty of it, the splendor, the mixed emotion of revulsion, loyalty and admiration, the absoluteness of sun and shade, the glare of the arena, the hissing, cheering crowd and, approaching all the time, dreaded but desired, the Moment of Truth to end it all. In this mise-en-scène the part of the bull is played by the Afrikaner traditionalist, the modern Voortrekker. One sees him bravely embattled, as always, but a little puzzled now by the course of the long fight—faltering perhaps but not yet stumbling, just as a brave fighting bull, toward the end of the *corrida*, stands baffled but undefeated by the taunts, trumpets and lance pricks of the afternoon.

The instinct of Blood River is still profound among the Afrikaners, and often in their minds they still hear the war cries of the impis, murderously loping down the mountainsides toward the ox wagons of the Volk. Compromise with the blacks, runs the old Afrikaner argument, is national suicide: unless they are kept forever subjugated, with their vast procreative powers they will soon overwhelm the whites by sheer numbers and the Afrikaner nation will disappear at last into an amorphous half-caste limbo, its identity submerged and all its generations of struggle betrayed. This is the cry of the *verkrampters*, the unyielding conservatives—still, it seems, dominant within the National party, and probably in the Volk at large.

They are the last last-ditchers, the final back-to-the-wallers, of the white empire which once spanned the world. They are the spirits who, pressed ever further into Africa by the interference of the British, lashed their ox wagons to these remote fastnesses beyond the Vaal. They are the guerrillas who, at the end of the Anglo-Boer War, adamantly refused either to surrender or to negotiate. They opposed South African entry into both world wars, and today they are inflexibly opposed to any concessions to the colored peoples, or any remission of white supremacy. They are perhaps the majority of the Afrikaner people, certainly of the ruling National party, and the race to save South Africa from catastrophe is really the race to save them from themselves.

But by their own lights they are right. Gone would be the mystic excitement of the sunbeam and the catafalque, if the blacks were master of the country; gone the pride of race and purity, if ever miscegenation became the practice. The abandonment of apartheid would be the abdication of Afrikanerdom as it exists today. So the *verkrampter* is ready to risk all, rather than submit to change. Perhaps, in some inner chamber of his psyche, he sees as the truest end to a shortish but always remarkable history the sacrificial massacre of his people—back to Blood River in the twilight of the gods. Yet for all his mystic urges, he is a realist—with the smoldering black militants of the townships, the earthiest realist in South Africa. He knows this is a struggle with no holds barred, a clash of brute forces.

Everything is *absolute* in such men's minds. Not only in matters of race but in every nuance of life, the Afrikaner society has traditionally closed itself against innovation or concession. Corporal punishment, sexual prudishness, Calvinistic Sundays, male privileges, the censorship of books—all these are familiar aspects of the culture, and have potently contributed to its strength and character. Anything leftish is necessarily Communist; anything permissive is clearly degenerate; anything original is probably heretical. Only in the last couple of years have the South Africans been permitted to run the moral risk of having a television service: but so muffled and modulated are its programs that already the TV companies are in severe difficulties, with many citizens understandably deciding that they can live without the miracle after all.

Like a monstrous earth-filled dam all these attitudes and prejudices obstruct the flow of progress in South Africa. To a *verkrampte* Afrikaner there is nothing evil to the notion of white supremacy—on the contrary, he has been brought up to think it an integral part of his Christian faith. The Afrikaners cannot grasp the time scale of the modern world—cannot believe that a man can be educated from the primitive to the sophisticated in a single generation—that the balance of the world can shift in a decade—that ideas acceptable to civilized people fifty years ago are repellant now. The disapproval of nations they interpret as Communist conspiracy. The remonstrances of visiting statesmen they put down to ignorance.

The apparatus of despotism in South Africa, constructed specifically to enforce apartheid and silence or overawe its opponents, is an ugly spectacle. Secrecy and conspiracy have always been elements of the Afrikaner ethos—the Broederbond, for half a century the inner caucus of Afrikanerdom, is publicly presented as a literary and cultural society —and the secret forces of the state are all-powerful. BOSS, the Bureau for State Security, is one of the most ruthless and uncompromising of Western security agencies: it learned a lot, it is said, from its study of the Gestapo (several ex-Nazis are supposed to have worked for it) and has professional links too with the CIA and British intelligence. From its offices in Pretoria it keeps a steely watch upon every political development concerned with Africa, anywhere in the world.

At its command it has a formidable roster of forces: a sizable and

well-equipped army, a ubiquitous constabulary, a vast network of secret agents and informers, a special force of riot police—paramilitary
thugs who, let loose on the black townships when rioting begins, pour
through the ghetto streets unkempt, obscene and violent, like beasts
released from their cages. More frighteningly still, behind these forces
the law itself has been mobilized for the enforcement of the dogma.
The law can do almost anything to you in South Africa. It can lock you
up indefinitely incommunicado without trial. It can place you instantly
under house arrest, or ban you from any public activities, or prevent
you meeting other people, or publishing your books, or even being
interviewed. It can prohibit any publication, expel you without explanation or appeal, confiscate your passport, imprison you for being a
Communist, or for sleeping with a black man, or for spending a night
in a white residential area, or failing to carry your pass book, or even
I dare say for writing an article like this. The law is all-powerful, but
powerless too, for even the fairest of its judges are caught in the web
of apartheid, and find themselves willy-nilly agents of its philosophy.

Your honest *verkrampter* is not antagonized when you mention these
matters. He is more pained, and puzzled, like the bull. Self-defense, he
explains courteously, is the first right of the human condition, and the
survival of racial identity is the top priority. Each almost impercep-
tible weakening of petty apartheid—a multiracial sports meeting, say,
or the desegregation of a post office—only confirms a few more of the
verkrampters in their inherited beliefs. The crescendo of events at home,
the clamor of the world outside, only make them more intractable.
Confused, wounded, now charging, now standing ground, noble but
debased, the Volk fight on, ready to die in their family cause and have
their communal carcass dragged out of the arena by mules.

But there is another aspect to the Afrikaner character. Side by side
with the sense of community there runs a hardly less forceful tradition
of individualism. It used to be the boast of the old Boers that from
their houses one could not see the smoke of the next man's chimney.
It was as so many mavericks, unamenable to orthodox discipline, that
the Afrikaners won their name for military dash and spirit—in their
time unquestionably the best guerrilla fighters in the world. And it
was as champions of political liberty, the rights of small nations, the

freedoms to choose, that they established their original and happier political reputation. They are a people of instinctive courtesy and hospitality: and when, as a princess is awakened from the sorcerer's trance by a knightly kiss, they are released from the more dour inhibitions of their heritage, they produce minds of wonderfully free and fanciful imagination, receptive to all ideas. Jan Smuts the statesman, Laurens van der Post the writer, Leo Marquard the historian, Christiaan Barnard the brain surgeon, the generous fighting generals of the Boer War, "the last of the gentlemen's wars"—these are the kind of the *verligte* Afrikaner, the liberated of the Volk.

Only their emergence to power and influence, in my view, can prevent the ultimate tragedy in South Africa—a permanent estrangement between the races, and perhaps a full-scale war. This is not a time for dogmatists. It needs subtle, modern, flexible minds to unravel the predicament of South Africa. The very scale of it all is stunning, and unprecedented—not merely the numbers of the powerless blacks, but the gigantic industrial and financial strength of the whites. South Africa is no Kenya of farming lands and game parks, no Rhodesia with a sprinkling of white settlers, no palm-fringed tropic colony, lightly to be passed to the easygoing indigenes. This is a great industrial power. Like no other country of Africa, it is clad in the whole massive complexity of a technological state, the steel mills and the car factories, the computers and the satellite networks, the tax structure, the shipyards, the stock exchanges, the mines.

The British South Africans, with their Jewish allies, built this machine, but gradually the Afrikaners have infiltrated it, founding their own corporations and finance houses, until now the old Volk of the ox wagons and the lonely farms are as committed to urban, industrial methods as any other people of the Western world. Your *verkrampter* argues that the very existence of the industrial structure is a guarantee of continued white supremacy—would the Americans really allow this powerhouse, strategically situated at the apex of Africa and built upon irreplaceable minerals, to fall into black and potentially Communist hands?

To the *verligter*, on the other hand, the growth of the industrial society, an amalgam of the races and the talents, is a token that the Volk can no longer live within themselves. Their trekking days are over. They have reached the last encampment, and there are other people about. Afrikanerdom must admit itself to be, not defeated indeed, but no longer sacramentally distinct. It must adapt, discard its outmoded articles of faith, and recognize in particular that the old relationship between black and white in Afrikaner thought, so close to the core of the tradition, can no longer be valid. It was *not* an act of God that beat the impis at Blood River, it was the courage of the Afrikaners; that courage must now be applied not to slaughter, but to reconciliation.

One senses poignantly the efforts of liberated Afrikaners to shift the vast mass of the national conviction. Some are trying to do it from within the National party itself, and voices that once would have been denounced as blasphemous are now to be heard calling for a new direction, a new definition of purpose perhaps. The bravest advocate of change within the Volk is perhaps Piet Cillie, the editor of *Die Burger* —a newspaper so deeply rooted in Afrikanerdom that even its shareholders have to satisfy rigid criteria of the Volk. A stocky, funny, rather goblinesque man, Cillie sees as South Africa's hope the revival of the old liberal tradition of Afrikanerdom—persuading the burghers that their truest vocation is not repression, however godly, but liberation, even of the blacks. He has made many enemies by daring to express these views, and when he explained them to me in his office, dominated by a huge bust of the inflexible Founder of Apartheid, Dr. Malan, I felt that he had to summon all his spiritual and intellectual strength, all his resolution, to break away from his own heritage and convictions.

Other *verligters* have abandoned the National party altogether, becoming in traditionalist eyes actually traitors to the Volk. Some have joined existing opposition parties, others hope to achieve some grand synthesis of all opposition to apartheid, black and white, and so break down the barricades of their own nationality. It is a traumatic moment for simple Afrikaners. It is as though their world is cracking—like a refutation of faith, or the discrediting of a prophet. I talked one day to an Afrikaner shopgirl at Bethlehem, in the Orange Free State, and found her cruelly bewildered by the times. Was it really possible, she wanted to know, that the entire Afrikaner canon of principles about race had been *mistaken*? Was it *conceivable*? How does it seem to a foreigner? she asked. Did anybody else in the world feel the same way as the Volk, or were the Afrikaners really all alone? Why not, I suggested, try making personal contact with some blacks—"Talk to them just as you're talking with me!" But no, she said, she just couldn't. She would like to, she really would, but she had been brought up to think of the Kaffir almost as a separate species, and to make friends with them would be, if not actually a biological impossibility, an experience too perverse to contemplate.

Yet even by thinking so, she was *verligte*. She was bending the old bars, looking beyond the laager. Everything in South Africa today is a matter of time. Can the Volk change their dogmas in time? Can the blacks be conciliated in time? Can the Bethlehem shopgirl make an African friend soon enough, or will it prove, by the time she steels herself to the experiment, that no African wants to make friends with her?

And while time passes, the whole towering edifice of white supremacy sways, and apartheid proves itself to have been one of the most terrible of all historical miscalculations. Its system is cracking anyway, by the momentum of history, and the blacks are forcing their way into the white man's world by plain force of circumstance. "Change," which Afrikaner last-ditchers call a Communist word, is nevertheless on every politician's lips, for it is evident that the apparatus of racialism is doomed. Three decades of apartheid have been a tragic waste of time and life and passion. It has not worked.

It is a fateful moment, a breathless moment, for nobody knows whether the Afrikaners will submit to history or defy it. Perhaps they are going to hang on after all, whatever happens elsewhere. They are unlikely to be toppled by internal revolution, however inflamed the blacks, and they may well be right when they claim that the capitalist West will save them from invasion. Besides, the spirit of laager still excites the Afrikaners, the urge to ultimate defiance, even to national self-immolation perhaps, holding the Eternal Flame while savagery, atheism, Communism and barbarism burn the wagons and storm the shrine.

But they will be defeated in the end anyway, if not by force then by the misery of it all, by the relentless threat of catastrophe which debilitates the life of the country, by the demoralizing boycott of the world, by the slow decay of their own certainties and the awful realization of error. Why, I asked an old black man once, did not Mr. Vorster, the Prime Minister of South Africa, frankly admit the misjudgment of apartheid and make a fresh start while there was still time? His answer, I suspect, came somewhere near the truth. "Because," he said, "it would make him look a fool."

It would make him look silly: more pertinently still, it would reveal the whole Afrikaner mystique, so full of pride and achievement, so inspired and so genuinely inspiring, to be fallible after all—as though that mystic sunshaft, one fine December noonday, were to miss the hole in the roof altogether, owing to an inaccuracy in the mathematics.

* * * * * * * * * * * *

II. War, Peace and Allegory in Rhodesia
[1977]

AWAY BEYOND the gray Limpopo, deeper into Africa than even the South African Voortrekkers ever whipped their oxen, the white men of Rhodesia man their armored cars and prepare their getaway plans, as the black Africans muster to displace, expel or overwhelm them. The peace of Africa, perhaps of the world, depends upon their actions, yet coming to Rhodesia from South Africa is like moving from Wagnerian tragedy to paperback thriller, for while to the south all is fearful apprehension, dark and brooding, in Rhodesia the battle has already started, and the 275,000 Europeans are fighting a shooting war in defense of their privileges. Within the country, the 6 million blacks, 95 percent of the population but politically utterly powerless, are poised to take over the government of the state: along a thousand miles of hostile frontier, with black Zambia and Marxist Mozambique, guerrillas armed, trained and financed abroad are fighting a murderous bush war, almost an invasion, in the black cause.

A few years ago Ian Smith, the Prime Minister of Rhodesia, declared that there would be no black government in his country for a thousand years. Now he has formally conceded, at least in principle, the right of the black majority to rule the place. In the meantime the whites fight on, some in the hope of maintaining the status quo anyway, some hoping that out of it all may emerge a stable black Rhodesia with room for the white man still. In chanceries and embassies around the world, statesmen and politicians desperately try to evolve a peaceful solution for the Rhodesian problem: here on the spot the shooting continues, and white Rhodesia is a community tautly mobilized for the worst. A warlike mixture of anxiety, exhilaration and comradeship sets the tone of this society. Army convoys rumble with plumes of dust down bush roads, uniforms and camouflage suits color the city streets, hitchhikers carry automatic rifles with their rucksacks; there are fund-raising campaigns for the Boys on the Border and frontline troop shows by patriotic entertainers (sample joke: "The Ugandan government has collapsed—the branch broke"). A stir of common cause inspirits this embattled handful of Europeans, cap-a-pie among the Africans, and since most are British by origin, the place reverberates with echoes of Dunkirk, the Battle of Britain, Winston Churchill and all that.

This is a different world from South Africa, besieged though the two countries are by the same predicament—the determination, that is, of a small and materially advanced white minority to maintain its own way of life by force against the resentment of the technically backward blacks. In Rhodesia, history has come to a head more waspishly. There is nothing epic or awesome in the posture of white Rhodesia today, as the future of the country hangs so precariously in the balance. One cannot imagine these people fighting to the last man, sacrificing their farms and factories, their very identity as a nation, rather than submit. Though the war is real enough, and there are men dying out there in the bush, somehow it feels like a kind of fantasy, and even those who have doubts about the cause often half relish the conflict. I lunched one day with a university law professor, graying, soft-spoken, learned and anything but racialist. Three weeks each month this scholarly citizen instructs his pupils in the juridical principles, but the fourth week he spends flying troops ("troopies" as they call them in Rhodesia) to the remote battle areas of the bush. He loves it. It is like a renewal of youth for him, an invigorating replay of his war years in the RAF. And so white Rhodesia as a whole, finding itself faced with the ultimate emergency, the emergency of survival, has developed a paradoxical verve and confidence, at once impressive and infuriating to observe.

Infuriating because it is an artificial emergency. Though it threatens the nations with a distinct possibility of a third world war, there is nothing inevitable to it, no sense of relentless destiny. The first white settlers came to this country less than a century ago—I have myself met an old lady, wizened but complacent, who claimed to have been born in an ox wagon of the original pioneer column. When white Rhodesians say, as they often petulantly do, "But don't you see, we are *Africans*?" it seldom rings true Their roots are shallow and their racial fervor has no real historical or spiritual excuse. Speculators and politicians created this autocracy of color, and there is an air of irresponsibility to the Rhodesian situation now. It is a bit cheap. The whites will doubtless lose the struggle, but most of them will simply go away and start life somewhere else, poorer but intact: white Rhodesia's beginnings were rather unsavory, and I suspect its end will be more ignominious than appalling.

The country was founded and eponymously named, at the end of the 1880s, by the enigmatic British financier Cecil Rhodes, who supplanted its native chiefs by persuasion, force and skulduggery, hoping to find the country rich in gold. For thirty years it was administered, on behalf of the British Crown, by his British South Africa Company: an enormous commercial estate, 150,000 square miles of it, with not much gold after all, but priceless deposits of chrome and asbestos, and rich farming country where maize and tobacco thrive. When company rule ended in 1923, government passed not to the generally progressive British Colonial Office, which ran Kenya, Ghana, Nigeria and half a dozen other African colonies, but to a regime of local white settlers who imposed upon Rhodesia an inflexible structure of white supremacy.

This is the key to its troubles now. While the other British possessions advanced gradually toward black rule, and eventually achieved their independence peacefully and with some grace, Rhodesian blacks were denied any true political progress at all. The whites clung tenaciously to all their comfortable perquisites, and when, in the 1960s, the British pressed them to share some slight proportion of power with the Africans, Smith's Rhodesian Front Government broke away from the British Empire altogether and in March 1970 declared the country an independent republic ("in humble submission to Almighty God," as the proclamation of independence unctuously put it, "who controls the destinies of nations").

Since then Smith and his colleagues, defying the exasperation of the British (who consider his regime illegal), the economic sanctions of the United Nations (who consider it wicked), the anathema of black Africa and even the growing coolness of the white South Africans, have maintained their grip on the country so completely that the black 95 percent it not only economically deprived and socially humiliated, but politically impotent still. The Republican constitution expressly prohibits a black majority in Parliament, however advanced the African becomes, and the only black leaders the government really recognizes are the traditional tribal chieftains, who remain conveniently detached from contemporary progress. Rhodesia is a last allegory of the colonial tradition: the whites, it sometimes seems, perpetually on the veranda, the blacks forever mowing the lawn or cleaning the swimming pool.

These Africans are far less inhibited than their fellows in South Africa. The Rhodesian despotism, though hardly less effective than the South African, is much less sinister in style. Apartheid has been less ruthlessly applied, and there is a livelier educated class—it is an irony that more than half the students at the University of Rhodesia are black, white parents often preferring to send their children to safely segregated universities in South Africa. But the blacks are fragmented. They are divided into two main tribal groups, the Matabele and the Mashona, and these two old enemies are subdivided into many lesser entities too, so that every political or ideological grouping is entangled in obscure antipathies and malevolences. The black leaders are viciously at odds with one another. Some are Marxist, some not, some within the country, some in exile. Some have their own guerrilla forces, or are supported by the black governments of neighboring states. All are fiercely hungry for power, after so many years of subjection, and are almost as hostile to their black rivals as they are to their white oppressors.

This, then, is the peculiar mess of Rhodesia—a fluid, not a solid mess. This is why negotiations for a settlement drag on so hopelessly; why the self-styled Frontline States—Tanzania, Zambia, Angola, Mozambique, Botswana—threaten to intervene by force; why the white Rhodesian soldier all too often finds it hard to explain what he is fighting for. Rhodesia is in limbo. Its white rulers are making no apparent preparations to hand over power. Its black politicians are so quarrelsome that there is no obvious candidate for national leadership, only the hideous prospect of civil war between the factions. The guerrillas in the bush, punctiliously described by the whites as "terrorists" ("*There are no, repeat no, guerrillas on Rhodesian soil*"), are armed with Communist-made weapons and are often fighting for Communist ends.

Dimly through the tangle, nevertheless, one may see the true outlines of the predicament. It has arisen solely because of the presence of the white man here, because of his reluctance to share his power or his prosperity, and because, here as in South Africa, he has misjudged the time scale of history. He has left it too late. For all his spirit he is a very lonely fellow, standing so firm but so confused amid the muddle. He has no true allies in the world—even the South Africans are prepared to abandon him if it suits their own policies. Those who help him, by smuggling materials through the sanctions, by buying his products or arguing his case, do so generally only for the basest motives: hardly anybody genuinely sympathizes with him in a struggle that seems purely selfish, in defense of values that are entirely materialistic.

One day recently I drove out of Umtali, on the road to Mozambique, toward the old frontier post on the Beira road, now closed and fortified. This is guerrilla country. All along this frontier ambushes are common, and farmers live with their guns at hand—even Umtali, the biggest town in eastern Rhodesia, has been shelled and rocketed. The empty road seemed awfully desolate as I wound my way around its curves to the east. Thick bush covered the rolling country all about, the last of the houses soon petered out and a hot, heavy silence hung disconcertingly over the landscape. "You'll be all right," said the driver of an army truck going the other way, whom I stopped to ask for reassurance. "You can only die once."

All alone there stood the border post, only a few miles from Umtali, but lifeless—festooned with wire and sandbags, like something on the Golan Heights, or a remoter outpost of the Iron Curtain. Nothing could epitomize more absolutely, I thought, the condition of Mr. Smith's republic today. The offices were shuttered, heavy iron gates barred the road, but perched high on the roof, surrounded by sandbags, a solitary white soldier crouched with his machine gun and his binoculars gazing steadily out across the bush. I could see no other sign of life. The interminable bush stretched away, dense and motionless in the heat. There was not a sound on the air, not a rustle, not a whisper. But ceaselessly the soldier peered about him, slumped in his observation post, looking as though he did not really know what he was searching for, or whether it would come upon him from the front, or behind, or suddenly up the concrete steps, with a savage rattle of automatic fire, from the disused customs offices below.

He might not know where his enemy was, but he certainly knew what he was defending, for the whites of Rhodesia have created for themselves one of the most comfortable societies on earth, and only a saint or a madman would want to abandon it. Even today nearly everyone arriving in Rhodesia from South Africa feels indefinably liberated and relieved, so easy is the pace of everyday life here, so amiable the temper. Physically, Rhodesia is a beautiful country, with its high highland veld and its forested, trout-streamed mountains, the evocative rock-strewn range of the Matopos, where Rhodes lies buried, the incomparable spectacle of the Victoria Falls, whose spray rises like a sheer wall of vapor from the deep chasm of the Zambezi. During their century in this place the Europeans have made a garden of it. Trim and inviting are the farms with their fat herds of Herefords, their plantations of coffee, maize or tobacco, their brightly painted homesteads up Kentucky drives. Clean and ordered are the country towns—main streets are wide for the turning of ox wagons, villas are set in English lawns, and outside the doors of small hotels black stewards hopefully stand, napkins on their arms, to catch the passing trade. Salisbury, the capital, seems to me on the whole the pleasantest city in southern Africa: the right size of city, verdant with parks and gardens, its central clump of office buildings sensibly restrained and its suburbs merging sensitively into the open country beyond.

It is a very provincial society, but rich, and with its underpinning of cheap domestic labor it often has an endearingly nostalgic air, as though life is being played onstage in a Noel Coward comedy. Tennis parties are often in progress, as one approaches Rhodesian homes, and black menservants in white cotton are encountered carrying trays of lemonade through rockeries. Probably no housewife in the world is more gently employed than the average Rhodesian matron, to whom women's lib is a faintly comic irrelevance, and whose life seems to progress in an almost Edwardian pattern from coffee morning to Good Works to luncheon at Mabel's to tennis at the country club and a quiet dinner served by Moses and young Joshua ("When *will* he remember to lay the cruet?") beneath the flowered pergola at home.

I went to a wedding party in Salisbury one day. It was held upstairs at Meikle's Hotel, the Ritz of Rhodesia, and took the form of a tea dance—a thé dansant, perhaps one ought to say, though long skirts were worn and champagne-type wine was served. It suggested to me a passage in a time machine, so insistently did it carry me back across the years. The eager tuxedoed band played waltzes and even fox trots; the girls were aflush with excitement and mostly wore pink; matronly hairdos were tightly permed and lacquer-glistened; corsages were worn, grandmothers danced quaintly with schoolboys in gray flannel, as at English nursery parties long ago. All around the room the black waiters stood in attendance, and sometimes there were shrill cries of recognition from table to table, and cork pops from the bar. It was rather touching. When I left the celebration and walked alone across Cecil Square to my own hotel, I could see silhouetted in that first floor window the whirling shapes of the dancers, as in a cruise advertisement of the 1930s, and hear pursuing me through the evening, as I sauntered back across the city, the drumbeat and saxophone of "Yessir, That's My Baby" jauntily in the African dusk.

I used to think these people singularly unattractive, and only now do such Rhodesian evocations please me. It seemed to me on previous visits that the whites had brought with them to this fresh, wide and splendid environment many of the more niggling defects of their British origins. They were snobbish, they were affected, they were self-satisfied

and they tended to treat their black servants with an insufferably nou-
veau riche insolence. There were many people, of course, especially those
of pioneer stock, who had made themselves prosperous by plain hard
work and guts, and had achieved marvels with the land: but by and large
the Rhodesians, especially the newer immigrants, had things all too easy.
At once defensively anti-British and more British *than* the British, they
sparked no empathy in me, and I was one of those who, when in 1965
Ian Smith declared the independence of the state, thought a Brigade of
Guards parachute force should instantly be dropped on Salisbury, to
whisk him away to the Tower of London as a traitor to the queen.

I still think so, as it happens, but I have to admit that time, adversity
and apprehension have matured the white Rhodesians. The old hands
have become a little less preposterously old-school-tie, less liable to talk
in a distorted parody of Oxford English, less likely to wear a British
regimental blazer or call each other "old boy." The new immigrants have
been mellowed by experience and setting and have adjusted more con-
vincingly to their anomalous role as members of a local aristocracy.

And all of them have most distinctly modified their attitudes toward
the black African. The worm turns! No longer does one hear that arrogant
sneer of contempt with which, ten or fifteen years ago, the young Salisbury housewife demanded her creature comforts from the servants. Black
people are still seldom to be seen on the streets of central Salisbury after
dark, but in the daytime, I observe, nobody now expects them to make
way on the sidewalk, or wait for madam to enter first. Foolish adolescents
may still refer to them as "wogs" or "munts," out of ignorance or
bravado, but few mature adults seem to reject in principle the idea of
majority rule. Except for lunatics of the far right, they admit the un-
fairness of the present system. Whatever their private thoughts, in public
they are seldom bigots.

This is remarkable, for one of the more dismal characteristics of Ian
Smith's Rhodesia is its stifling narrowness of information. No foreign
newspapers enter the country at all, even from South Africa. The local
daily press is cautiously subdued, the radio and television services are
government controlled and slavish. This is a queer sensation—a tiny
white community, no bigger than a middle-sized American municipality,
deliberately muffled within its own conceptions. The Rhodesian view

of the world is peculiarly myopic, and the Rhodesian view of Africa sees everything north of the Zambezi as plunged in irrevocable chaos or conspiracy—an illusion, heaven knows, not too difficult to sustain.

All the more creditable that so many white Rhodesians have evolved opinions of their own, and are responding fairly and rationally to the present crisis. Some, naturally, envisioning a future black Rhodesia at best corrupt, at next best communist, and at worst torn apart by civil war, have already packed their bags and gone—to England, to Australia, to America, wherever a somewhat begrudging world will accept them. Many more are undecided: they don't know what to expect, they don't know where to go, they have sons in the army perhaps, they have little capital and most of it they are forbidden to export. And a few of the more intrepid have already decided to stay whatever happens, hoping to find themselves welcome and wanted in Zimbabwe (as even the most dogged of the true-blue Europeans are sometimes betrayed into calling their homeland).

The future of the white Rhodesians is not one of history's more shattering problems (three times as many French people left Africa when Algeria became independent) but it offers anxiety enough for the Rhodesians themselves, to lose their all perhaps, to abandon their stakes so hopefully established, and to face the prospect of starting life afresh in some harsher, colder country, sans servants, sans swimming pool, sans sunshine, sans supremacy.

It hasn't happened yet, anyway, and in the meantime the war on the frontiers paradoxically inspirits them, and even gives to their community a curious sort of innocence. It is, of course, anything but an innocent war. Both sides fight it with an ugly savagery—priests and nuns are murdered, children are enticed into guerrilla service, villagers are intimidated first by one side, then the other. If the government forces are seldom so bestial as the guerrillas, they are certainly ruthless enough, and many of their operations are veiled in perpetual secrecy. Among the generality of the whites, though, there is something boyish to the belligerence. This is partly because universal male military service has rejuvenated them, made them a lithe and lively people. If they are to expire, at least they'll expire healthy. They used to look a flabby crew, and the Rhodesian Front gave its name to a paunchy condition too. Now it is as though every Rhodesian white man has been to some unusually demanding health farm, and I doubt if there is a fitter populace anywhere in the world. They eat lightly these days, go to bed early, get up with the light. They are a community of soldiers.

The young white Rhodesian is always under arms. When he has done his initial 18 months' conscription service he is held in perpetual reserve and is frequently mustered again, plucked from his office or farm, given a camouflage suit and an FN rifle and flown off by the professor of law to some almost invisible airstrip in the bush. The middle-aged are army reservists too, or spend time as auxiliary fliers, and anyone under 65 can serve with the auxiliary police, "Dad's Army," who are often to be encountered sternly but stertorously patrolling the suburbs after dark. Nearly every man does some war work or other—many women too—and everyday arrangements are subject always to Dad's call-up, the return of the assistant manager from police duty, or whether that nice Hudson boy is home from the bush yet.

All this makes for an unexpected sting, an almost Israeli punch and brilliance—not the quality one expects of a British colonial settlement on the verge of disbandment. In Umtali I was once visiting the local military headquarters, occupying the nice old Cecil Hotel in the middle of town, when the commander of the Rhodesian army, Lieutenant-General Peter Walls, happened to emerge from his operations room into the foyer—its reception desk now presided over by a brisk corporal, its floor littered with stacks of khaki gear. The immediate impression he gave me was very British—a clipped, gentlemanly sort of officer who exchanged a courteous greeting with me as he passed, just as though he were walking out of the War Office into Whitehall, en route to his Pall Mall club. Tightly at his heels, though, pushing urgently past the desk toward the street, a group of young aides of very different personality followed—without noticeable badges of rank, without immediately definable features, so that they might have been of any rank or nationality, wearing camouflage suits and jungle boots, heavily armed, and hastening their general along with a precipitous, almost violent speed, swiftly out of the hotel to the waiting line of Land Rovers outside. It only took a few seconds, but it left me with a sensation of buoyant excitement, so vital did those soldiers seem, so charged with immediate purpose.

I often had this feeling of a people mutated by events, turning these Europeans, in the last years of their imperial prerogatives, into some new subspecies. In Salisbury I sometimes used to take my lunch beside the swimming pool at my hotel, and there was generally a group of young officers on leave having a swim or a beer on the terrace. Stripped to their trunks and sun-bleached hair, they seemed to lose all ethnic identity. They might have been moon men. Some were probably mercenaries, Portuguese, German, Afrikaner; most were doubtless transplanted Britons, subtly changed in posture and physique; all seemed to me specific not simply to the place, but to the time, to the circumstance, to the prospect. I could seldom hear their voices, across the hubbub of the terrace, but I would never have been surprised to hear them conversing in some unintelligible tongue, an ad hoc vernacular evolved especially for white Rhodesia, 1977.

This anachronistic entity, this unrepublic, will almost certainly not survive the next decade. The first Rhodesia was an isolated fort in the pestilential country north of the Zambezi, of which not a trace remains, on the ground or on the map: and soon enough, we may be sure, the second Rhodesia too will be expunged from the gazetteers, and the little white state, 275,000 strong, will be no more than a bizarre historical footnote.

Official Rhodesia does not recognize this prospect, and behaves still as though the republic will last forever. While I was in Salisbury the president of Rhodesia held an investiture at Government House, honoring distinguished citizens on behalf of the state. No distinction could be more ephemeral, one would think, than the Order of the Rhodesian Legion of Merit, or the President's Medal for Chiefs, yet solemnly and reverently, as though they were being received at the White House, or winning Nobel Prizes, the recipients advanced to receive their medals— General Walls, naturally; Mr. Jack Mussett, the minister of internal affairs; Air Vice-Marshal Harold Hawkins, the accredited diplomatic representative to South Africa; Senior Assistant Commissioner Bradfield, the officer commanding Matabeleland Province of the British South Africa Police—functionaries of an almost extinct establishment whose very ranks and offices will soon be swept away, and whose Meritorious Conduct Medals and Independence Commemorative Decorations will be no more than historical curios, like billion-mark notes of the Weimar Republic.

A handful of blacks were honored that day too, but essentially the nation of Rhodesia is the *white* nation—no self-respecting black now calls it anything but Zimbabwe. It is self-reliant and, except of course for its black manual labor force, remarkably self-sufficient. Its only legitimate link with the rest of the world is by way of South Africa: and though a steady stream of essentials arrives from the south, and exporters in many countries ignore the UN sanctions, still the world's boycott has brought out the inventiveness and the resourcefulness in these settlers. The blockade is circumvented all the time, by routes defined by government spokesmen as "sensitive areas of information." A weird selection of foreign programs, for instance, somehow finds its way to the Rhodesian state television—old favorites from Britain and America, ancient Italian movies, documentaries mysteriously dubbed from unspecified tongues. Somehow or other the machine parts arrive for Rhodesian industry, and the foreign cars get assembled—Citroëns, Renaults, Peugeots and several Japanese makes are all assembled in Rhodesia.

In most consumer goods the country is now self-supporting, a prodigious accomplishment for so diminutive an economy—as though the city of Chattanooga, say, were suddenly to decide that in future it would make everything for itself, tires to toothpaste. The only shortage people complain about is of decent razor blades, and gasoline is rationed; otherwise, the world's indignant boycott has hardly affected ordinary life at all. It is true that Rhodesian Riesling leaves something to be desired ("Don't say it's nasty," an old-school Salisbury wine merchant counseled me, "say it's *too lively for your palate*"): but Rhodesian toothpaste is properly streaked with fluoride, Rhodesian newsprint is only moderately gray, and I seldom tasted a better cheese than Rhodesian Camembert. And for a birthday present for Mom or the kids this year, what better than the All-Rhodesian Rhogun Machine Carbine, 500 rounds per minute, $20 deposit secures—"The Ideal Weapon for Women or People Inexperienced with Weapons"?

The guerrilla war, too, the explosion of a long stalemate into frontier blood-and-thunder, has clearly sharpened the morale of the whites. The regime has been able to boast of a war in defense of civilized values, and the settlers have been given somebody tangible to fight—a ruthless enemy from across the borders, an intruder. "We don't mind fighting the war," soldiers often told me, "so long as a decent Rhodesia comes out of it." In their often ingenuous minds (the Rhodesian troopie, though very likable, is sometimes pretty thick) there is a clear distinction between the war on the frontiers, against alien and probably communist terrorists, and the political conflict with the indigenous blacks. Win the one, they seem to suppose, and you can somehow solve the other. "It's not a race war we're fighting," they repeatedly claim, "half our own soldiers are black anyway." This is perfectly true. The most glamorized of the fighting units, the semi-irregular Selous Scouts, is multiracial, and the army even has a few black commissioned officers—optimists maintain that the very tension of the border struggle, and this camaraderie among the ranks, is helping to unite the Rhodesian races.

That I doubt, but I do think that perhaps the intensity of the war, the stimulation of common purpose and peril, has sharpened the perceptions of the whites. Nothing concentrates the mind like the prospect of being hanged in the morning, and my guess is that few white Rhodesian soldiers out there in the bush are whole-hog white supremacists anymore. A new awareness has come out of the struggle, and a new dignity too: for most of those young soldiers, grinning at one so cheerfully from the backs of their bouncing trucks, or huddled watchfully over the weapons in their border gun pits, really do believe they are fighting in an honorable cause—to create a country fit for heroes, perhaps, even if most of them will have to be black.

Too late, that change of heart? Perhaps, for to ordinary Africans the war looks very different. For one thing, for them the conflict on the frontier is part and parcel of the political struggle at home. For another, whoever wins it their own future is terrifyingly in hazard—the whites

can always go away, but the blacks are here to stay. I wandered one morning into one of the Salisbury criminal courts, and there in progress was a
category of case hideously familiar to the black community. An elderly
black villager from the eastern frontier was accused of providing food
and shelter for guerrillas. He did not look at all like a revolutionary.
Frail, wispily bearded, his short curly hair gray and his eyes a little
watery, he was more like a very paradigm of the eternal victim. From
time to time, as the interpreter conveyed to him the evidence from the
young white policemen in the witness stand, he made helpless gestures
of resentment or indignation, but he was obviously beaten from the
start. What else could he have done? was the sole burden of his defense.
If he refused to help the guerrillas they would shoot him, or cut his ears
and nose off, or disembowel his wife, or burn his hut down. He was not
a political person—he held no political views—but what else, Mr. President, what else could he do? The court president had heard it all a hundred times before, and looked wearily sympathetic: but he sent the old
man away to prison all the same, *pour encourager*, as Voltaire bitterly put
it in another context, *les autres*.

The black people of Rhodesia are on the very brink of power. Their
right to it is admitted even by their own white masters, and it is only a
matter of time, negotiation or bloodshed. Yet in a disturbing way they do
not feel like winners, as the impotent South African blacks already do.
There seems no thrill of expectation to them, no ecstacy of black consciousness. For a taste of what I mean, come with me to the shopping
center at Highfields, the principal black township of Salisbury, on the
day when one of the most powerful of their political leaders, Bishop Abel
Muzorewa, returned to Rhodesia from abroad. Muzorewa, prelate of
one of the lesser sectarian churches, leads one faction of the African National Council, and is one of the four Rhodesian blacks who see themselves as first head of the Zimbabwe state—his party officials claim that
in a free vote he would easily win an election. For the blacks of Rhodesia,
his return on a Sunday morning from Europe was a great political event,
and the crowd that assembled at Highfields was said to be the biggest
ever seen in Rhodesia.

It was a very hot day, cloudless, and by noon, when I drove out there
with a carload of white reporters, the shopping center was already en-

gulfed in an ocean of blacks, jammed in a tight, shining phalanx, sometimes breaking into song, or chanting slogans, or waving sticks and
branches above their heads. "How many do you reckon?" said the party
officials who received us—the question party officials always ask of journalists—and when we wildly guessed 100,000 people their answer was
familiar too: "Oh no, far more than that—a million, we think—a million
at least." Through the good-natured multitude we made our way with
difficulty, periodically intercepted and frisked by party toughs, and frequently asked for our press credentials: until they unceremoniously
pushed us up a ladder to a parapet of the shopping center—a clutch of
white faces, rather whiter than usual perhaps, perched up there above
black Africa.

There we waited through the blazing hours. The crowd seemed cheerful but bemused. On the edge of it young men danced about with
fronds, in the middle of it women sometimes fainted and were passed
from hand to hand over the heads of the throng. Sometimes cheerleaders,
standing on boxes here and there, commanded the people into song or
slogan, like so many young prophets urging sinners to repent. A couple
of white police officers, in khaki shorts, hovered about self-consciously,
and a detective masquerading as a reporter was unmasked and asked to
leave, skulking away through a gap cleared for him in the crowd like a
figure of Shame in a morality play. Earnest officials buttonholed us now
and then: "You have had much experience in these matters—how many
people do you suppose are here? Oh no, madam, far more than that—
2 million is our official estimate, 2 million at least, from every corner
of Zimbabwe. . . ."

Then suddenly the crowd obscurely stirred—there was a mighty rustle
of attention, a kind of huge gasp across the township—and there on the
rooftop just above my head, silhouetted against the sky, half a dozen
young blacks burst suddenly and thrillingly into view. They were like
dancers out of the sun. They leapt into view with an animal vigor, some
with white scarves around their heads, some waving knobkerries, some
raising their two clenched hands above their heads in a gesture of triumph
and instigation. They were all quiver, all electricity, and instantly the
crowd broke into a gigantic roar, waving hands and sticks and handkerchiefs, singing, shouting, swaying, every face turned in astonishment

toward our roof. I looked above me again, and now, still and small among those prancing young bloods, the little black bishop stood there smiling, raising his clasped hands in greeting. It was a wonderful *coup de théâtre*. The crowd was amazed, the bishop himself looked rather like a member of the audience hauled onstage by some gregarious ballet group, and I myself was dazzled by the style of it—for nowhere else in southern Africa can one see the black genius exhibited with such contemporary flair.

And yet there was something missing—spontaneity perhaps, fire from the belly, exuberance. It felt a purely political occasion, not a great moment of popular celebration. I had no sensation of an immense collective will from the crowd down there. There was nothing elemental to it, I thought. When the bishop had gone and the people were dispersing I found my way to a local cafe, and there, over a bottle of tepid Fanta, talked about it with the flamboyant black patroness of the establishment ("Men and booze, darling, that's all there is to life"). Was she optimistic? I asked her. Did that kind, well-behaved, good-humored crowd presage a kind, well-behaved, good-humored Zimbabwe? To my surprise, discarding for a moment her pose of mindless bawdiness, she paused silently and gravely before she answered. "I'm frightened, love," she began. "There are too many men around here who . . ."—but at that moment one of her jollier customers, seizing her around the waist, swept her away behind the counter with screams and lusty laughter, out of my sight and hearing.

She had spoken sadly, and just for an instant, the anxiety I saw in her eyes was translated into those hundreds and thousands of faces in the crowd, singing and waving their branches in the sunshine. If the whites of Rhodesia are anomalously vivacious in their last months of authority, the blacks are sober on the threshold of power. Like the blacks of South Africa they remain astonishingly courteous and kindly. White though I was, not a hostile word, not a malicious glance did I feel that afternoon in Highfields, and nowhere in Rhodesia did I sense a single taunt of black racism. What Africans nearby always said to me was, in effect, this: "We want our rights, we have the right to rule this country; but we have nothing against white people, and hope they will stay and help."

Idealistic though it seems, naïve perhaps, still I believe this to be the true will of most articulate black Rhodesians, and I think if it were left to the people themselves, Zimbabwe could become the peaceful and prosperous multiracial state it ought to have been years ago.

"But there are too many. . . ." Too many scoundrels, she meant to say, too many cynics, too many Africans ready to exploit politician chances, tribal enmities, in the pursuit of power. Nobody really knows, least of all the ordinary black citizen, what their various leaders have in mind, what they stand for, who they represent. Muzorewa, Joshua Nkomo, Robert Mugabe, Ndabaningi Sithole—everybody knows their names, but nobody knows their true intentions. They often seem to fight each other as fiercely as they fight the whites, and none of them has made clear what *kind* of Zimbabwe they would create if they came to power. As for the guerrillas, fighting, so the people are told, for the freedom of Zimbabwe and the dignity of black Africa, most of the people they kill are Africans themselves, and hideous are the tales of murder and mutilation that reach the urban townships from the black villages of the bush. Nobody knows what to believe, or whom to trust, and if the people were excited by the moment out there at Highfields, I met few black Africans exhilarated by the times. As a satirist put it in the black *National Observer* the other day: "Some peoples is in very darkness. They is at seas bout knowledge. They says they supports a Nkomo, or a Muzorewa, or a Mugabe, or Ndabaningi, or even a Smith hizselfs, they just says so without ever knowing what it is all bout. . . ."

Very darkness it is, for it seems to me that whatever happens in Rhodesia will be wrong. If the whites hang on to power, come what may, there can only be more bloodshed, the guerrilla war developing perhaps into full-scale invasion from the neighboring black states, and erupting into urban terrorism within the country. If power is handed to the blacks, there is nobody to receive it—nobody with any clear ideological conviction, still less any experience of authority. If the West steps in to save the situation, the East will retaliate. The specters of the Congo, of Mozambique, of Angola haunt this pleasant countryside, and already one half-sees those homely country towns smoking with destruction, shattered tanks on the skyline and fine wide highways littered with the wreckages of war. "Angry" is what the Johannesburg chambermaid said, when I asked her how she felt about life, but the response of the Salisbury car park attendant was quite different: "All we want is peace."

"Should you not *help* us then," complained a member of the Salisbury white elite, "instead of criticizing us all the time?" A slight note of self-pity had entered her voice, but I was not much moved. South Africa I find truly heart-rending, a tragedy that has grown organically out of history, sweeping all its characters helplessly along with the plot. But Rhodesia is demonstrably the white man's fault—his recent fault, perfectly avoidable. It has been obvious to the world for years that if the white Rhodesians did not make a genuine start in the transfer of power, precisely this situation would arise—a restless, bewildered, increasingly rancorous black majority, without experienced political leadership, and powerful external agencies only too ready to help them. It was a historical prognosis so obvious as to be almost banal, and a succession of observers, statesmen, journalists, academics, delineated it in perfect accuracy for the Rhodesians.

But a regime of obdurate provincials, oblivious to wider realities, blindly supported by an ill-informed white electorate, inflated into absurd self-importance by absolute power, wantonly ignored the advice, and so threw away southern Africa's last chance for peaceful multiracial advance. Even now, it seems, the ruling elite of Rhodesia cannot grasp the truth that they are all alone in the world, at the very end of the line. They live in a dream, a last dream of empire. The only white people I saw at Highfields that day were the police and the press—not a single Salisbury private citizen had bothered to go and look, for even now the Rhodesian bourgeoisie do not take African aspirations seriously. "Most blacks simply aren't interested in that sort of thing," they habitually say, "my servants would never dream of going to a political meeting"— but in fact, if they only knew it, their servants are out there in the crowd with all the rest, waving sticks and shouting Shona slogans. The complacency of the Rhodesian right, as the republic slides month by month toward extinction, is almost eerie to contemplate. The business paper *Property and Finance* ("The White Voice of Rhodesia") considers Mr. Smith himself a cryptoleftist appeaser of the blacks, and calls for a Cromwell to declare independence all over again and assure white supremacy forever: "Nature," it decreed recently, "nurture, genetics or his Creator have made the African a second-rate citizen. . . ."

"Shouldn't you be helping us?" If it weren't for the fate of the hapless blacks, if it weren't for those thousands of guileless young white soldiers, if it weren't for the beauty of the place and the hard work of the pioneers, if it weren't for the looming nightmare of chaos, I would be tempted, were I some universal arbiter, to let the white Rhodesians stew in their own Rhodesian-made juice. But I see faces still, the puzzled ignorant faces of the Highfields blacks, the grins of the troopies in the backs of their trucks—innocent faces all, and condemned not by themselves, but by their elders and leaders, to have their lives embroiled in this unsolvable dilemma. For beyond happy solution I fear it is. I can just imagine South Africa, a different magnitude of society, somehow rescuing itself in the nick of time from its agonies, but Rhodesia has surely gone too far, or not far enough. The defiant spirit of the whites, fighting a war they were sure to lose, the premonitions of the blacks, supporting a cause that is bound to win—these seem to me the signals of catastrophe. Those faces haunt me terribly. How innocent will they look, I wonder, how boyish will their smiles be, when I come back to Zimbabwe?

. . . .

THE
STAGE-CITY

*Of all the cities I have written about over the
years, none has so persistently baffled me as London.
This essay, written in 1978 during one of Britain's periods of Socialist
Government, does not pretend to understand the place, or
even to probe very hard behind its peculiar appearances, but
merely expresses my mingled reactions to a capital that seems to me the
most theatrical, the most misleading, perhaps the least
likable and possibly the most resilient of them all.*

. . .

LONDON

. . . .

The Stage-City

[*1978*]

NE OF THE FLIGHT paths to London Airport, Heathrow, goes straight over the middle of the capital, east to west. The city does not look much at first: just a drab sprawling mass of housing estates, terraces and industrial plants, nibbled at its edges by a fairly grubby green—just mile after mile of the ordinary, splodged here and there with the sordid. ❡ Presently, though, the route picks up the River Thames, sinuously sliding between the eastern suburbs, and one by one landmarks appear that are part of the whole world's consciousness, images familiar to every one of us, reflecting the experience of half mankind. The Tower of London squats brownish at the water's edge. Buckingham Palace reclines in its great green garden. The Houses of Parliament, of all famous buildings the most toylike and intricate, stand like an instructional model beside Westminster Bridge. There are the swathes of London parks, too, and the huge Victorian roofs of the railway terminals, the cluttered hub of Piccadilly, the big new block of Scotland Yard, and always the river itself, twisting and turning through it all, out of the city center into the western purlieus, until the first of the country green appears again on the other side, with gravel pits and motorways. Windsor Castle appears tremendous on its hillock, and the aircraft, slightly changing its tone of voice, tilts a wing over Slough and begins the last descent to the airport.

It is the city of cities that we have flown over. Like it or loathe it, it is the daddy of them all. If New York is ethnically more interesting, Moscow or Peking ideologically more compelling, Paris or Rome more obviously beautiful, still as a historical phenomenon London beats them all. It has been itself, for better or for worse, for a thousand years, unconquered by a foreign army since William the Norman was crowned King of England in Westminster Abbey in 1066. It has spawned and abandoned the greatest empire known to history. It was the first great industrial capital, the first parliamentary capital, the arena of social and political experiments beyond number. It is a city of terrific murders and innumerable spies, of novelists, auctioneers, surgeons and rock stars. It is the city of Shakespeare, Sherlock Holmes, Dr. Johnson, Churchill, Dick Whittington, Henry VIII, Florence Nightingale, the Duke of Wellington, Queen Victoria, Gladstone and the two Olivers, Cromwell and Twist.

Mozart wrote his first symphony in London, and Karl Marx began *Das Kapital*. London has five great symphony orchestras, eleven daily newspapers, three cathedrals, the biggest subway on earth and the most celebrated broadcasting system. It is the original world capital of soccer, cricket, rugby, lawn tennis and squash. It is where Jack the Ripper worked. It is the home of the last great monarchy of all, the House of Windsor, likely to be outlived only, in the expert judgment of the late King Farouk of Egypt, by the Houses of Hearts, Diamonds, Clubs and

Spades. London is nearly everything. If you are tired of London, Dr. Johnson once remarked, you are tired of life.

It is a gift of London, or rather a technique, that through the dingy and the disagreeable, the fantastic habitually looms. Illusion breaks in! Its principal agency is that monarchy, whose heraldic lions, unicorns, crowns, roses, thistles and Norman mottoes are as inescapable in this city as Leninist quotations in Moscow.

Monarchy in London is part religion, part diplomacy, part make-believe; if the gleaming standards above the royal residences are like prayer flags or talismans, the ramrod soldiers stamping and strutting between their sentry boxes are pure Sigmund Romberg. The mystique of London's royal presence, the fetish feel, the mumbo jumbo, colors the sensations of this peculiar city, and often makes it feel like a place of pilgrimage, a Lourdes or a Jerusalem, or more exactly, perhaps, like one of those shrines where a familiar miracle is regularly reattested, the saintly blood is annually decongealed or the hawthorn blossoms each Christmas morning. The world flocks in to witness the mystery of London, enacted several times a year in the ceremonial thoroughfare called the Mall. The sidewalks then are thick with foreigners, and far away up Constitution Hill the tourist buses, emblazoned with the emblems and registration plates of all Europe, stand nose to nose in their shiny hundreds. The guardsmen lining the Mall are like acolytes at the shrine; the patrolling policemen, sacristans.

The beat of a drum is the start of the ritual, somewhere up there in the blur of gold, gray and green that is Buckingham Palace. The beat of a drum, the blare of a band, and presently a procession approaches slowly between the plane trees. A drum major leads, in a peaked jockey cap and gilded tunic, as impassive on his tall white horse as a time drummer on a slave galley. Then the jangling, clopping, creaking, panting cavalry, black horses, brass helmets, plumes, anxious young faces beneath their heavy helmet straps, the skid and spark of hoofs now and then, the shine of massive breastplates, sour smells of horse and leather. Three strange old gentlemen follow, weighed down beneath fat bearskin hats, with huge swords bouncing at their sides; they ride their chargers rheumatically stooped, as though they have been bent in the saddle like old leather.

Another plumed squadron . . . a pause . . . a hush over the crowd . . . and then, bobbing high above the people, almost on a level with the flags, the familiar strained and earnest face of the mystery itself, pale beneath its heavy makeup. It is like the Face on the Shroud, an image-face. Everybody in the world knows it. It is a lined and diligent face, not at all antique or aristocratic, but it is possessed by its own arcanum. The crowd hardly stirs as it passes, and the murmur that runs down the sidewalk is a tremor less of astonishment or admiration than of compassion. It is as though a martyr is passing by. She rides, she bleeds, for us!

There is something fatalistic about the spectacle. The ritual is so old, so very old, so frozen in so many conventions and shibboleths. The Queen bobs away with her guards, her captains and her bands toward whatever elaborate and long, meaningless ceremonial her major-domos have prepared for her beyond the trees, but she leaves behind something stale. Her martyrdom is the suffering of a tired tradition, and if the royal flummery is the saving fantasy of London, it is the city's penance too. London seems often to be laboring beneath the weight of its own heritage —year after year, century upon century, the same beat of the drum major's drum, the same jangle of the harnesses, the same bent old courtiers on their chargers lurching generation after generation down the Mall.

Like many another celebration of faith, it is an act, and this perpetual posturing around the royal palaces, like the swishing to and fro of surpliced priests around a reliquary, pervades the rest of the capital too.

More than any other city in Europe, London is a show, living by bluff and display. People have always remarked upon its theatrical nature. In Victorian time it was *Grand Guignol*, and the smoky blackness of the city streets, the rat-infested reaches of the river, coupled with the lively squalor of the poor, powerfully impressed susceptible visitors. In the blitz of the forties it was pure patriotic pageantry: the flames of war licking ineffectively around the mass of St. Paul's, Churchill in his boiler suit giving the V sign from the steps of 10 Downing Street, Noel Coward singing "London pride has been handed down to us" or "A Nightingale Sang in Berkeley Square. . . ."

Today we are between the great civic performances that have punc-
tuated London's history, but the greasepaint is always on, and the sensation of theater is still endemic to the place. It is a city of actors always,
as it has been since the days of Will Shakespeare and his troupers down
at the Globe. You can hardly spend a day in London without seeing a
face you recognize, and in this city, famous actors are not mere celebrities
or glorified pop stars, but great men. They are figures of authority, honored or ennobled. Laurence Olivier sits as a baron in the House of Lords.
Sir Ralph Richardson lives like a grandee in his splendid Regency house
by the park. Sir Alec Guinness, Sir Michael Redgrave, Sir John Gielgud—
these are the truest nobility of this capital: people who, like the admirals
of an earlier English age, frequently sail abroad to do their country honor,
fighting the Queen's battles in Rome or Hollywood, but who return
always, full of glory, to this their natural estate.

The histrionic art is the London art par excellence—the ability to
dazzle, mimic, deceive or stir. Look now, as you step from the restaurant
after dinner, across the blackness of St. James toward Westminster.
There is the floodlit Abbey, that recondite temple of Englishness; and
there is the cluster of the Whitehall pinnacles; and there, the flash of the
neons pinpoints Piccadilly and intermittently illuminates Nelson on his
pillar in Trafalgar Square; and riding above it all, high over the clockface
of Big Ben in the Palace of Westminster, high in the night sky, a still
small light, all alone, burns steadily above the city. It is the light that
announces the House of Commons, the mother of all parliaments, to be
in session below. There's theater for you! There's showmanship!

Or pay a visit to the High Court in the morning, and see the performers of London law present their daily matinee. No professional actors
ever played such unfathomable, judicial judges as the justices of Her
Majesty's bench, wrinkled like turtles beneath the layered carapaces of
their wigs, scratching away at their notes on their high seats, or inter-
vening sometimes with polysyllabical quips. No prime-time mimic
could outdo the sharpest of the London barristers, who play their briefs
like instruments, hold themselves whenever possible in profile and wrap
their robes around them in the ecstasy of their accomplishment, like so
many Brutuses assembling for the kill. Laughter in a London court is
frequent and often heartless; there is a regular audience of hags and lay-

abouts, and so infectious is the atmosphere of theater, that often the poor accused, momentarily hoisted into stardom, wanly smiles in appreciation.

With luck one may still see Cockneys in performance. The Cockney culture survives only precariously in the city of its origins, as the taxi drivers, marketmen and newspaper vendors move out to the suburbs, are rehoused in high-rise apartments, or find their accents, their loyalties and their humor swamped in the sameness of the age. It is many years since officialdom cleared the flower sellers from Piccadilly Circus, and even the buskers of the London tradition, the escape artists who used to entertain the theater queues, the pavement artists outside the National Gallery, are slowly being chivied on to oblivion. But the culture *does* survive, and remains among the most truly exhibitionist of all traditions.

Sometimes at fetes and functions, even today, you may see the pearly kings and queens, the hereditary folk monarchs of the Cockney vegetable-barrow trade, dressed in the curious livery, decked all over in thousands of mother-of-pearl buttons, which is their traditional prerogative. Better still, any Sunday morning, in the vast outdoor market of Petticoat Lane, among the shabby mesh of streets that lies to the north of the Tower, you may watch the Cockney salesmen exuberantly in action. Theirs is an art form straight from the music hall, or vice versa, perhaps; in their timing, in their sly wit, in their instinctive rebound from a failed joke, in their exhilarating air of grasping insouciance, the Cockney hustlers stand directly in the line of the gaslight comedians.

London is a stage! The big red buses of this city, moving with such ponderous geniality through the traffic, are like well-loved character actors. The beefeaters outside the Tower, holding halberds and dressed up like playing cards, are surely extras hired for the day. And most theatrical of all are those London functions which are not merely quaint or ornamental, but really integral to the status of this capital, close to the political power of it.

I went one day to the installation of a new member in the House of Lords, the upper chamber of the British Parliament. He was a prominent politician ennobled for his party services, and I was taken to the ceremony by another peer, of more literary distinction. We were late and hurried through the vast, florid halls of the Palace of Westminster, past multi-tudinous busts and forbidding portraits, "my great-great-great-grand-father," panted Lord J. as we passed William III, "illegitimately, of course," down interminable carpeted corridors, through chambers enigmatically labeled, between gigantic murals of swains, maidens, liege lords and war horses, until up a winding stone staircase, through a creaking oak door, he shoved me precipitately into the visitors' gallery.

Inside, a dream was in progress. The rest of the peers and peeresses indeed looked mundane enough on their benches below: thickset party reliables, jowly former ministers, a handful of flinty and talkative women, a bishop with heavy-rimmed spectacles and a resolutely ecumenical expression. But slumped eerily with his back to me, the Lord Chancellor of England sat like a dummy on his woolsack, the big woolen bag which has for 600 years and more sustained the Chancellorian rump. Dark robes blurred the shape of him, a black tricorn hat was perched on top of his judicial wig, and he suggested to me the presiding judge of some sinister hearing, with a hint of that magisterial caterpillar with his hookah, on top of the mushroom in *Alice*.

Just as I entered, the new peer, appearing silently out of nowhere, approached this daunting figure. He was dressed in red and ermine, escorted by two colleagues and preceded by a functionary in black knee breeches holding a silver wand. Spooky things ensued in the silence. The three peers sat down, but almost at once they rose again, in dead silence, and in unison bowed toward the woolsack, simultaneously removing their hats. The Lord High Chancellor removed his in return, adjusting his posture on his sack and bowing slightly, almost frigidly, in their direction. Twice more, without a sound, the ritual was repeated—down, up, hats off, bow, hats on, down—while we in the galleries, perhaps even the other peers and peeresses in their benches below, watched almost aghast, so arcane was the spectacle.

This was not a charade. This was a contemporary political occasion, London style. As soon as it ended I hastened out of the gallery and down the steps in time to bump into Lord J. emerging from the chamber below. "Good gracious me," I could not help saying, "however long have they been doing that?" "I believe it began," he replied quite seriously, "with the Druids."

Whether London is a success just at the moment or a failure, a rich

153

city or a poor one, nobody quite knows. It is, surprisingly, a very volatile capital: the U.S. ambassador recently diagnosed it as manic-depressive, on top of the world one day, all despondency the next. Sometimes the kingdom, of which it is not just the heart, but the mind, lung and belly too, is represented to us as almost bankrupt. At other times it stands on the brink of incalculable wealth, revivified by the promise of oil from the North Sea. One month its accounts are disastrously in debit, the next month it has an enormous surplus. The vaults of London burst with money, the gold reserves in the Bank of England are higher than ever, but much of it is foreign wealth, deposited there for security and quick returns, and easily withdrawable.

All this is nothing new. Despite its reputation for stability, calm and balance, London has always lived precariously. Dickens's Mr. Micawber, always confident that something would turn up, was a true son of the city. It is essentially a market for invisible commodities, services performed, expertise. Insuring, banking, auctioneering, valuing, analyzing— these are the archetypal functions of the place. They are fluid functions, hard to assess, and they are fragile too, since they depend upon the state of the world; so the prosperity of London is never certain, even in its euphoric periods, but seems to fluctuate, apparently dependent upon the weather, the news or the mood of Europe that day.

It is a neo-socialist city, its economy a mixture of state and free enterprise, and the one constant in its progress since the war has been the decline of the bourgeoisie, which in previous generations was its bulwark. This process is apparent always. Walk into a Whitehall pub, say, any sunny lunchtime, and you may observe it for yourself. Through the open door, the tide of the city flows busily by—the rumbling buses, the shirt-sleeved tourists reading to each other from guidebooks—but inside, the early drinkers are slumped heavily over their beers. They are businessmen and bureaucrats, senior enough to be able to slip out around twelve, not sufficiently successful to have a club round the corner in Pall Mall. They are all men, all middle-aged, and would be instantly recognized as English wherever they went in the world.

An aggrieved or embattled air attends them in the shadowy recesses of the front bar, as though they have retreated into this dim enclave off the streets to be among their own kind, to lick their wounds, perhaps. They do not talk much, but when they do it is generally to complain: about the state of the country, the beer, the young, the weather. Up the road their wives, in a break from shopping, are having their cups of coffee (or more exactly, the price of coffee being what it is, their cups of chicory extract). History has hit them harder still. Time was when a trip into town for a morning's shopping was a treat; they wore their best hats and coats and took a friend along. Now, all too often, they sit alone, and their clothes have lost their color. Their faces, though kind, look strained. They wear head scarves and solid shoes, and each year they seem to lose a little of their class identity, and it becomes harder to tell whether the lady opposite you is married to a factory hand or a schoolmaster.

Yet in those streets outside, there are signs of opulence wherever you look. Rolls-Royces are two a penny. Your cabdriver tells you about the holiday he is planning in Tunisia, the record shops are jammed with the free-spending young, up-and-coming executives in BMWs invariably beat you to the parking space. In the upper-crust restaurants the comfortable conventions of old London are sustained by the magic of the expense account, and businessmen who scarcely know a tithe from a ptarmigan are treated with all the homely respect once reserved for the landed gentry. "Certainly, my lady" is a stagey phrase that still drops easily from the lips of London lackeys, and if the English rich have been driven from their traditional haunts in Mayfair and Knightsbridge, they are still as snug as ever, with their nannies, their Filipino cooks and their Swedish *au pair* girls, in the villas of St. John's Wood or Little Venice.

All these contrasts and anomalies help to give London its febrile air. Between performances! Stripped of its enormous empire, neither quite a part of Europe nor altogether insular, socialist but capitalist too, hankering for its glory days, clinging to its ritual loyalties, London feels unsettled, unfulfilled, as though unsure which role to accept next. Is the old trouper "resting," reading scripts, past it or about to launch another smash hit? Nobody is sure. Radical decisions are always in the air but never quite happen. There is always an election impending, a strike threatened, a settlement in sight, a ring road about to be built, a demolition started.

Some of it is certainly loss of confidence. The thirty years since World War II have been rotten years for London. Rich or poor, this city is no longer the greatest capital of the world, as it could still claim to be before the war, just as the pound sterling is no longer the world's criterion of security. The consequence and authority of London, which are expressed in so many memorials and institutions, so many horseback statues, is half a dream now. Even the Scots and the Welsh challenge the primacy of this capital today, and a city that once decreed the destinies of a quarter of the earth is reduced to the somewhat testy direction of 50 million souls. The political style is accordingly rather wilted. When prime ministers emerge from their celebrated threshold, 10 Downing Street, with its attendant policemen like caryatids beside the door, they do so almost apologetically, or scuttle away into their waiting limousines as though they have just discovered their flies undone.

After dinner with friends one night, we wandered round the old market area of Covent Garden, now in the first pangs of rebirth, the vegetable stalls and fruit wagons having migrated south of the river. In London the removal of an old and beloved landmark is an especially traumatic experience, and the gap left by that most celebrated of markets, where opera rubbed shoulders so romantically with cabbages, and Eliza Doolittle was originally picked up by Professor Higgins, is now being tentatively filled in—to me a disturbing phenomenon, like a numb corner of the brain. We found a whimsical pottery shop, a very smart bookstore and the Rock Garden Cafe, through whose 17th-century arcade eponymous music thumped loudly through the night, suggesting to me less a corner of old London than a bit of some resuscitated ghost town living only by the summer trade.

The Opera House was being cleaned, and shone phosphorescent through its scaffolding, and to complete my sensation of dislocation, alienation perhaps, a solitary laser beam hung flickerless over London like a single wire of an imprisoning mesh. Didn't they feel it too, I asked my friends? Didn't they sense, in the condition of their city that night, some symptom of disintegration? It was like someone who had suffered a breakdown, I said, whose personality is split, splintered or possibly in abeyance.

"It's that damned laser beam," my host replied. "It's enough to give anyone the creeps. Anyway, people have been talking like that about

London for donkey's years. I remember a fellow a few years back describing London in menopause. Now you're on about schizophrenia. But we go on living here, you know! And all this," he swung his hand around the scene, "all this goes on just the same—same old buses down the Strand, same old Trafalgar Square, same old Nelson up there on his column, bless his blind eye!"

But actually it doesn't go on just the same. London has altered tremendously in the past twenty years. Once the robustly English capital of the English kingdom, among the most homogeneous of the great cities of the earth, London is now one of the most international of capitals. It is not international in a generous way, opening its arms to the hungry yearning to breathe free, but only under protest. Evelyn Waugh anathematized modern London as "a vulgar cosmopolitan city"; the alienation of London is not just an after-dinner fancy, but a sociological fact.

In the winter it may not particularly strike you. The West Indian and Pakistani bus conductors, the black inspectors on the Underground, have become so thoroughly Londonized by now that they seem an organic part of the scene, as indigenous as the buses themselves. It is no longer a surprise to be greeted with a cheery Cockney "hullo, ducks" by a jet-black functionary from Barbados, and London Airport would not be its familiar self without the melancholy commiserations of the Indian ladies sweeping the sandwich crumbs, or sometimes the sandwiches, from the coffee bar floors.

In the summer things feel very different. Then Londoners write letters to the editor of the *Times*, wryly complaining that they can't find another Englishman to talk to. Then, even to the most liberal mind, the foreigners seem to infest London like so many insects, and Waugh's definition becomes uncomfortably true. Across the ancient face of the city the strangers are inescapable, wherever a deal is to be struck, an old church inspected, a work permit obtained, a ceremony to be observed, a property acquired or (as Londoners would murmur) a queue to be jumped. On every double yellow line, it seems, a diplomatic car is imperviously parked. In every Marks and Spencer store, relays of Frenchwomen hold sweaters against each other's busts for size. Round the edges of Petticoat Lane, aged Oriental ladies sit in the backs of big black cars, watching the passing crowds as through *mashrabiya* windows, while their servants foray among the stalls for bargains.

All around Eros in Piccadilly Circus, the scruffy young of a dozen nationalities squat upon the statue's pedestal—its fountain spilling incontinently about their feet—or lie flat on the ground sustained by rucksacks, while a few yards away the visiting bourgeoisie wait in interminable lines for the open-topped tourist buses. Then the beefeaters stand like island bastions against the polyglot sea of sightseers, and the foreign bankers return purposefully to their offices from the steakhouses, carrying black fiber briefcases with combination locks and talking to each other in unknown tongues.

This is not just the usual internationalism, common to all great capitals and essential, of course, to immigrant cities like New York. This is something more. This has to it a strong feeling of takeover or possession, which is why, for the first time in many years, the average Londoner is showing symptoms of xenophobia. London used to be the most self-sufficient, the most proudly separate of all capital cities: as the celebrated London *Times* headline is supposed to have said, VIOLENT STORM IN THE ENGLISH CHANNEL; CONTINENT ISOLATED. Now the alien worms have turned, and at this particular juncture in its history, London depends upon foreigners more than ever to keep it solvent. It depends upon the pundits of the International Monetary Fund, upon the bankers of the European central banks, upon the tourist trade, and not least upon the Arabs, yesterday's wogs or Ayrabs, who now provide incalculable funds for the London money market and have actually bought large slabs of the capital itself.

London is momentarily in fee to the Arabs, and there are parts of the city that the Arabs actually seem to have colonized, thus turning the wheel of empire full cycle. In particular, Knightsbridge, that plush network of streets that lies between Kensington Gardens and Hyde Park Corner, has become a little Arabia. From Knightsbridge, the tracks of the London Bedouin crisscross the capital, linking the merchant banks of the city, the Oxford Street stores, the shoemakers of St. James, the shirtmakers of Jermyn Street and the antique dealers of Bond Street, with their lairs, pads and harems around Harrods department store.

Sardonic Londoners claim it is easy to differentiate them. The Kuwaitis, the Jordanians and the Palestinians, they say, are the charmers. Only the Saudis maintain the authentic plutocratic sneer in all circumstances. To most citizens, though, they seem a kind of dour unity, as Europeans once appeared to them, from the black-veiled ladies silent in the dentist's waiting room to the plump, small boys in expensive gray flannel ogling the shopgirls at Selfridges, or for that matter, the princelings, perfectly at ease in their beautiful tweeds, who offer, from time to time, slinky half-smiles in hotel lobbies.

By the standards of contemporary London, many of these foreigners are unimaginably rich, and many indeed seem to have no sense of money at all. They spend without thinking, without trying. And if this tide of alien opulence rankles Londoners, it also corrupts them. It breeds envy and resentment and brings out the lickspittles. The sycophancy directed by Londoners to English lords and knighted actors is now extended to Japanese industrialists and illiterate sheiks. Fawning and visibly fattened are the chauffeurs, sons of the stalwart Cockneys, seen handing white-gowned tribesmen from their Mercedes; bland are the faces of the bell-boys as they accept from yet another impassive primitive a gratuity beyond the remotest bounds of equity.

"You've been serving too many oil sheiks," my host observed mildly one day when he found his restaurant bill in flagrant error, but the waiter was not in the least offended; he merely smiled a sly, complaisant smile and corrected the figures without apology. For if money means so little to these convenient customers, why bother with details? "Make the most of it, son," one seems to hear old London saying. "It may not last! Besides, look at it this way, they'd do the same to you, wouldn't they? Know what I mean? They're nothing but a lot of wogs, really, after all. . . ."

London is in flux more than usual just now, and out of the uncertainty ugly things are sprouting. The slums have almost vanished, but they have been replaced by ill-constructed tower blocks, where the elevators are all too often out of order, the walls are habitually covered with obscene graffiti, and every apartment seems fortified against the rest. This is a state of affairs common in other cities, but new to London: and in these dislocated communities, where nobody need be destitute but nobody seems content, violence and prejudice fester. For the first time in London's history there are sizable segments of the city where foreign-born citizens are in a majority—and not just foreign-born, but actually black or brown, a different category of alien to the intensely race-conscious English. Racial bigotry thrives and indeed seems to fulfill some sort of psychological need; it is different in kind, I think, from the American variety and often seems not exactly a social attitude, even less a political conviction, but rather a category of sport.

I was walking with a friend one Saturday down Lewisham Way, a blighted thoroughfare south of the river, when we felt in the air some hint or tremor of trouble. The street indeed seemed built for trouble. As far as we could see it was lined with nothing in particular: apparently makeshift blocks of shops and offices, car parks that were mere extensions of ancient bomb sites, isolated terraces of Victorian houses left high and dry by social history, and occupied now by multitudinous tenants. Sure enough, that afternoon trouble approached. Far in the distance we descried a Union Jack, held high, crooked and bobbing, and we faintly heard above the Saturday traffic strains of that grand patriotic anthem, "Rule Britannia."

"You'd better watch it, mate," said a shopkeeper, standing in the door of a store that appeared to specialize in secondhand saucepans. "That's the National Front, that is. They're not funny, you know. They don't mind who they bash." But we walked gingerly on, and presently the flag disengaged itself from its dingy background, and the sensation of impending evil was embodied in a clutch of short-cropped youths in jeans, high boots and spangled leather jackets, holding the flag between two poles above their heads and striding northward toward the river with a certain jauntiness, like apprentice boys in Northern Ireland. Over and over again, as they drew nearer, they sang the same couplet of the old song, as though they knew no more:

Rule Britannia, Britannia rules the waves,

Britons never never never shall be slaves . . .

"What's happening?" we asked as they passed, and they stopped at once, without resentment, and clustered around us as though they had discovered some sidewalk curiosity, and were about to learn something themselves. They spoke a particular kind of debased Cockney and tended all to talk at once.

"Big rally dahn the High Street, innit? Us against the Socialist Revolutionaries, know what I mean? Coupla football games in tahn, too."

"What's it all about, then?"

"Well it's a bit of a punch-up, innit? Look, the coons and the reds give us a bit of aggro, know what I mean? The Paks and them, the nig-nogs and the football mobs, then we're in there, aren't we? Bit of violence, know what I mean? That's what it's all abaht, innit? Nig-nogs Saturday night!"

They laughed, but not maliciously—rather engagingly, as a matter of fact—and they clustered around us eagerly, as though we were visiting parents at a school match. There was a sort of chill innocence to their frankness. They were like moon children. "Wanna come and watch?" they kindly suggested. "You won't get no aggro. Just stand back, know what I mean?"

They laughed again, the laughter degenerating at the fringe of the posse into uncontrollable giggles, and for a moment we just stood and stared at them, and they at us. From the ear of one boy, I noticed, hung a small, golden cross, and it swung rhythmically while its owner tunelessly whistled, occasionally nudged a neighbor in the ribs when something comical occurred to him or tapped a booted foot upon the sidewalk. I smiled at him wanly, and he responded with an inept wink, as though he had not quite mastered the knack; and then abruptly, with the Queen's flag borne skewwhiff above their heads, off they swung again, raggle-taggle down the street.

They were pure riot fodder, a demagogue's dream, thick as potatoes, gullible as infants, aching for a fight, not without courage, not without gaiety, either. They were too slow to understand that the affray to which they were so boisterously heading—a clash between Right and Left, between the neo-Fascists of the National Front and the frank Communists of the Socialist Revolutionary party—was more than just a Saturday afternoon bust-up, but an ideological confrontation which might one day ravage the capital. Know what I mean?

The riot, deliberately planned, turned out to be the worst in London for many years. I watched it on television that evening. By the standards of Paris, Berlin, Calcutta or Detroit, it was a modest disturbance. Nobody was killed. Only a few cars were set on fire. But in London, the city of so many ordered centuries, it came as a nasty shock: the muddle of billboards and banners in the shabby streets; the knots of youths, black and white, lashing out at each other like tomcats; the occasional scream, the sudden bloodstained figures; the thick, blue lines of helmeted policemen, sheltered behind their transparent shields from the showers of stones and bottles; the mass chanting; the smoke of burning cars. And the horsemen—especially the horsemen, who, suddenly appearing upon our screens and advancing at a deliberate trot upon that terrified and infuriated crowd, were horribly evocative of more terrible events elsewhere in history.

It was as though that certain indefinable malaise of London, that laser beam across the evening sky, was erupting just for an hour or two into fulfillment, and in the middle of it all I noticed something odd. Three hatless policemen, ties askew, helmets half off, were struggling with a youth, whose ferocious writhings, kickings and mouthings made him look the very embodiment of a snarl. They dragged him off my screen in the end, but just before he disappeared, I saw, under the heavy arm of one constable, over the sweating forehead of another, a small gold cross in a horny ear, vigorously joggling.

A city between performances. Not The City—for that title, for so long the prerogative of Constantinople, must now go to New York, a world epitome—but still, to my mind, the most enthralling of them all.

I have described the neuroses I sometimes feel in London now, and the air of resignation which, to my mind, attends the pageantry of crown and state these days. But I know in fact that these are only on the surface, and do not reflect the real meaning of this city. Behind its shifts of fortune and history, London is impelled by a sharp expediency very different from the accepted images of the place. V.S. Pritchett, a Londoner himself, once wrote that the chief characteristic of London was *experience*. I am from Wales, a place of sea and mountains, and to me the unchanging essential of the capital is an eye for the main chance. London is hard as nails, and it is opportunism that has carried this city of moneymakers so brilliantly through revolution and holocaust, blitz and slump, in and out of empire, and through countless such periods of uncertainy as seem to blunt its assurance now.

It is a calculating city behind it all, a city of intelligence agents, a matchless center of political and military information. Its knowledge of the world is as exact and deliberate as ever it was in the days of empire. I was lunching one day with a chap from the foreign office, at Beoty's, the Greek place in St. Martin's Lane, when he happened to mention, as foreign office chaps do, a hotel in Canton called the Ding Sang—formerly, as I might perhaps remember, the Yang Cheng, Goat City, a name he personally preferred. What did the new name mean, I wondered? "Ding Sang? Oh, it means 'The East Is Red.'" It's actually the theme phrase, so to speak, of one of the best-loved Maoist patriotic songs, dear to every Chinese heart.

"At least," he then added thoughtfully, laying down his knife and fork, "at least I *think* it's the main theme"—and here a change came over his face, and for a moment he began to look oddly Oriental himself. His eyes were screwed up at the corners, and his cheekbones seemed curiously to rise. Faintly over the buzz of the restaurant I heard him, in a high, cracked tenor, softly singing to himself an eastern tune, quavery and halftoned. As he sang he mouthed the words. "Yes," he said presently in a satisfied voice, returning to the squids, "I felt sure it was. It provides the principal refrain of the song. But if I were you, I would forget about the melody."

This is the London expertise, to adapt deftly, if necessarily surreptitiously, to the changing times. Tradition in front, utter pragmatism behind. In the past ten years or so some of this inner steeliness has, so to speak, been revealed by the dispersion of London's smoke. Ever since the Industrial Revolution the nature of London has been masked by fog and murk. It has been a city of black suggestiveness, choked often in impenetrable mists off the river, against which the splendors of the kingdom were paraded in pungent contrast. The very name London used to sound echoing and foggy, and every Hollywood film about the place had it thick with murderous fog.

Now the smoke has gone, and with it some of the romantic mystery, the camouflage. The city has been steam cleaned all over. The river has been so brilliantly cleared of pollution that in 1977 the first salmon ran upstream through London from the sea. There is a new glint to London now, and its clarity tells a truer story than the swirls and opacities of old. The best place to look at London is not in the Mall after all, where the Queen rides by, and certainly not in Knightsbridge or Lewisham Way, but halfway across London Bridge—*new* London Bridge. The previous one now resides in Arizona, the one before that—the one with the shops, houses and turrets on it, and the malefactors' heads dripping blood at its gates—having been pulled down in 1832.

It is in fact the fourth London Bridge we are going to, completed only a few years ago, but still spanning the Thames in exactly the same spot as the ford by which, 2000 years ago, the Romans crossed to found their Londinium on the north bank. It is always, of course, an intensely busy place. The road is busy above, the river below. Distorted loudspeaker voices echo from beneath the bridge as the tourist launches chug their way to Greenwich or the Tower. Dirty squat tugs with lines of barges labor against the tide toward the Isle of Dogs. Downstream lies the super-annuated cruiser *Belfast*, speckled with the unseamanlike pinks and yellows of tourists, while upstream indistinct flotillas of small craft seem to be milling purposelessly about in the distant haze of Westminster. But when we reach the middle of the bridge, and discover the north bank spread there before us, the Thames seems hardly more than a country stream, a pleasure pond, beside the gleaming vulgarity, the harshness, the concentration of the new City of London, the square mile that is the financial heart of the capital and its true core of constancy.

It is new, because most of it has been rebuilt since World War II; only now are the last bomb sites being filled in, to complete its sense of packed intensity. It is a cramped, ugly, jostling, bitter, clever square mile, jammed there on the waterfront. Its buildings look as though they have been forcibly hammered into the landscape in successive stages, century by century, forcing less virile structures back from the river or into the ground. It is a terrific spectacle, to my mind the most startling urban view in Europe, and it is given touches of nobility by its hoary landmarks: the majestic dome of St. Paul's, the austere fortress turrets of the Tower, the fairy-tale silhouette of Tower Bridge, the spires of all the city churches squeezed in there among the concrete.

But it is not a nice scene, not a nice scene at all. There is something vicious to it. Every street you see down there is full to its attics with money-men, bankers, stockbrokers, agents, accountants, exchange specialists, economists, financial journalists and entrepreneurs. History does not much faze these adept Englishmen, and they are inhibited by no ideological qualms. Once the very champions of laissez faire, they have adapted with consummate flexibility to the advance of socialism, and would soon adjust again, I do not doubt, if communism ever took over this state. The City of London is the most intense, the most subtle and perhaps the most vehement of all the world's financial bazaars, even now, and it emanates a sense not of power, or responsibility, but of unremitting self-interest. It is chockablock full, one feels, of gentlemanly cunning.

The poet Wordsworth, surveying London in an earlier century from another of its river bridges, was moved to ecstasy by the sight. Earth, he exclaimed, had nothing to show more fair! One could not say the same, looking out from London Bridge in 1978, but I'll tell you this, for sure: earth has nowhere more capable of looking after itself, than this aged and incorrigible deceiver!

Cairo

. . . .

BEHIND
THE PYRAMIDS

*President Anwar el-Sadat of Egypt had become
a world figure in 1978 with his bold but risky initiatives
toward peace with Israel. I happened to go to Cairo, a city I have known
most of my life, in the spring of that year, and was
struck by ominous undercurrents of tension and discontent
in a city more crowded, vigorous, confident and disorganized than ever
before. The President evidently felt the same.*

. . .

CAIRO

· · · · · · · · · · · · · · · ·

Behind the Pyramids
[*1978*]

RESIDENT ANWAR EL-SADAT and I, separately considering the Egyptian capital city of Cairo, recently arrived at the same conclusion: it was about to explode. ❡ Our viewpoints were, of course, rather different. The President was seeing the place as the source of all his power, the city that had raised him from obscurity to international celebrity, and might with equal ease return him to ignominy: Sadat could do nothing—in the last resort could *be* nothing—without the acceptance of Cairo, and all his actions, however global in implication, were governed by the attitudes of that ancient capital. I, on the other hand, was seeing Cairo irresponsibly. I was on a sentimental journey of return to one of the cities that fascinates me most in the world, for which, at one time or another, I have felt the whole gamut of emotions—fear, hate, lust, love, despair, hope, disillusion—subsiding in the end into that all too frequent absolver of passion, disinterested affection. I care nothing for Cairo's opinion, and Cairo cares still less for mine.

Yet both the President and I, the one so burdened with the anxieties of office, the other so fancy-free, reached the same disturbing verdict on the capital: *combustible*. I do not mean seismically. Cairo is not a city of meteorological extremes. Its climate is brilliantly steady and preservative, which is why pharaonic artifacts last so long, and Cairo is spared all hurricanes, earthquakes, blizzards and humid torments. No, I am speaking of the metaphysical condition of the place, its political, social, historical state, which is never languid or lethargic, but which seems to me now to be almost lethally excitable.

Cairo is special. It is one of the half-dozen supercapitals—capitals that are bigger than themselves or their countries, and that are the focus of a whole culture, an ideology or a historical movement. Many places pass through a period of this pre-eminence, to be left forlorn when history passes on. Cairo remains Grand Cairo, as they called it in the Middle Ages, not because of political power or economic strength—on paper it is only the metropolis of a ramshackle, hopelessly congested and cripplingly poor republic of 40 million souls—but because it is the supreme physical manifestation of an idea. Here Islam, a complete system of law, society and moral conduct, found its first grand fulfillment. The pharaohs had their cities, of course, near the site of Cairo, but it was the zealots of Islam, having burst out of Arabian deserts in the 7th century, who later named it al-Qahirah, the Victorious, and made it what it is: the supreme city to all the Arabs, and to countless millions of Moslems beyond.

Power of a kind, then, is endemic to Cairo. This is unquestionably, unmistakably the Big Time. Though you can see the surrounding wilderness from many parts of town, though the green of the fecund Delta nibbles away at the suburbs, though bright and speckled country birds bob through city gardens, and angular egrets dig for worms, still there is nothing remotely provincial to Cairo. With a metropolitan population of at least 6 million, it is much the largest city in Africa, and much the most compelling of the entire Mediterranean basin. It is not power, though, of the monolithic sort—not the power of dead weight or material authority, like the power of Washington or Moscow, but that of catalyst. Though the Arabs look to Cairo for leadership in matters of war and statesmanship, the real point of the place is this: that here Islam, whose holy land is Arabia, is translated into worldly terms, into the languages of art, politics, showmanship and economics, into the dialectics of thinkers and the formulas of science.

Such a function makes for ferment in a city, but never in my experience has Cairo been so fermenting as now. The longer I walked the downtown streets, the more urgent I felt the mood to be. Especially in the sultry evenings, a tenseness hangs in the air now, a kind of combination, if you can imagine it, of tumult and hush. The ceaseless traffic jostles and honks its way across the bridges, the numberless evening crowds press their way into the city center, clinging to the sides of swaying trams or pouring like a migration out of the railway station. But at the same time, gentle but oddly persuasive above the hubbub, you may hear the loudspeaker cries of muezzins from their distant minarets, calling the faithful to their evening prayers, and sometimes on the great river you may see the lateen sails of old feluccas, impervious to it all, magnificently proceeding toward Nubia.

Hush and tumult: the ancient and majestic streaked indefinably, somewhere among the city lights, with the ominous.

Last time I was in Cairo it was a socialist capital, presided over by the autocrat Gamal Abdel Nasser, and sustained by the money, arms and advice of Soviet Russia. It was disciplined, drab and a bit scary. Now the very opposite is true. President Anwar el-Sadat is an eager advocate of free enterprise and competition. All the new energies of the Moslem world, the energies of political clout, of oil wealth, of growing sophistication and cosmopolitan awareness, are coming to a head in Cairo, hyped up by powerful injections of capitalist stimulant.

Wherever you look now there are the signs of private money at work—foreign money nearly all of it, Egypt itself being virtually destitute—and especially Arab money from the oil states to the east. Financiers, investors, entrepreneurs, speculators of every kind and every nationality, pour in and out of Cairo by every flight. The big new hotels beside the Nile are booked, apparently, to perpetuity. Wherever you look, foreign banks are sprouting, foreign cranes are swinging and the familiar names of foreign capitalism are being polished up on new brass plates, from German construction firms to classy London realtors. This is Sadat's open door, the policy on which he has based his good relations with the West, and it is more than just economic. It is political, social, moral, historical, sexual. There is a libidinous, hedonist feel to it.

The veil has almost vanished from the streets of Sadat's Cairo, and the students of Cairo's secular universities, who used to look so unmistakably like the children of the Levantine bourgeoisie, now look like the students of any southern European university, free in their dress and easy in their relationships. The young women interviewers of Egyptian television might well commute between Cairo, Paris and New York. The guests at Mena House Hotel, once served exclusively by shuffling lackeys in tarbooshes and long white galabias, now find themselves attended by girls in jeans and denim jackets. As night falls over Cairo the Saudis, the Kuwaitis, the Americans, the West Germans and the Egyptian *bon ton* swarm in their big cars to the nightclubs along the Pyramids Road, or stand to their tables and their petro-dollars in the plush casinos of the Cairo Sheraton. Cairo has a dazzle to it now: a fairground dazzle, perhaps, with hustlers and red lights.

Like it or not, this creates fizz. I have never known Cairo to be so alive. The poverty of this city remains insoluble, the unemployment rate is terrifying, inflation is running over 35 percent a year; nothing works properly, whether it is a bus, a telephone or a sewer, and the municipal services seem to be perpetually on the edge of breakdown; and yet I swear this is a more cheerful population than any in Europe or America. The Egyptians, the young Egyptians especially, have moved on to a new plane of consciousness, have acquired a new corporate personality. There was a particular moment, it seems, when they acquired their poise and panache: the moment of the 1973 war, when the Egyptian army stormed the Israeli position on the east bank of the Suez Canal, and in one stroke transformed the self-opinion of this nation. Though in some strategists' eyes the victory turned into at least a semi-defeat, and though subsequent exercises in national machismo have not always been so gratifying, still the Egyptians have never looked back. They are not a martial people, but that martial moment remade them.

Until our times, Cairo survived largely by reacting against the world. Besides being inhibited by the supposed superiority of the Israelis along the coast, the Cairenes have been dominated in one way or another, during the last half-century, by British, French, American and Russian influences, all apparently more virile than their own. They were never quite themselves. Sometimes they cringed, sometimes they rioted, and one of the revelatory experiences of my life was seeing Cairo on the morning after Black Saturday, 1962, when a mob ranged through the streets burning and looting every symbol of foreignness, from the cinemas to the Turf Club, leaving the half-wrecked downtown city sullen and aghast beneath a pall of smoke.

Today the foreigner in Cairo is no more than a foreigner, as he is any-where else, and this makes for an altogether new freshness and clarity of intercourse. The real heart of this immense city is not the downtown quarter, where the financiers fiddle and the oil sheiks play, but the few square miles of medieval Cairo that lie beneath the ramparts of Saladin's Citadel, to the east. This is Grand Cairo proper, the magnificent walled city of antiquity. It is the crux of Cairo, Islam in stone. Here is Al-Azhar, the supreme theological university of the Moslem world, where dogmas have been defined, mysticisms dreamed or denounced, for more than a thousand years; here is the world's richest concentration of me-dieval Moslem architecture.

Tremendous stand the gates of Cairo, like castles, but in Islam strength is nothing without faith, and beside each city portal—sometimes phys-ically amalgamated—a mosque stands sentry too. Within the walls, along the tortuous thoroughfares that thread the place, the towers, turrets and great doorways of holy buildings are never out of sight—mosques, col-leges, mausoleums, places of charity, through whose squint doors one may see the faithful meditating on grass mats beneath dark arcades or washing their feet in plashy fountains. A patina of age, dirt, habit and sanctity clothes the whole, and all among these prodigious derelictions (for half the mosques look as though they are slowly crumbling into dust) the commercial life of the quarter imperturbably proceeds.

It is archaic—city life lived, in many ways, just as it was lived in the Europe of the Black Death. Yet it possesses a metropolitan presence. Think what is happening in these streets! The finest instrument makers in the Arab world are making their exquisite flutes and viols. The most eminent theologians are instructing their students, from every part of the East, in the ancient lecture halls of Al-Azhar. The weavers are busy making the Noble Garment which, every year, is carried from Cairo to Hijaz to be placed upon the Islamic holy of holies, the Kaaba at Mecca. And everything else too, all the life of shops and factories, schools and marketplaces, is heightened by the living presence of the city's very raison d'être, Islam itself. Cairo is an intensely religious city still, and Islam, that old regulator of all existence, still disciplines the lives, or at least the consciences, of ordinary Cairo citizens.

Once the inner strength of this society was a kind of secret from the world. Cairo's foreign masters seldom understood it, did not *want* to understand it. European bureaucrats and managers never did realize, for instance, that one of the most powerful of all Sufi sects thrived among the middle-class clerks and functionaries of this city; the writers, artists, performers and thinkers of Islamic Cairo were unknown to those thousands of foreigners who, from their comfortable apartments along the Nile, ventured into the old quarters of town only for an occasional excursion to the bazaars of Muski and Khan al-Kalili. Cairo's native intellectualism was a mystery to Westerners, and to generations of foreign visitors the true grandeur of the city went unperceived.

Now the truth is out. The inhibitions are gone on both sides. There was a time when three archetypal buildings stood almost as a barricade, or a *cordon sanitaire*, between indigenous Cairo and the encroaching West: Abdin Palace, the town house of the alienated monarchy; the original Shepheard's Hotel, the principal resort of Europeans; and the Royal Opera House, the focus of everything speciously westernized in Cairo society. Now the barrier has vanished. The Opera House was burned. Shepheard's was destroyed by a mob. The royal palace is now partly a museum and partly an official place of entertainment for the republic. The crowds swirl heedlessly over all these sites and memories, and one hardly notices the transition at all when one walks from the Parisian symmetry of the downtown boulevards into the vivid crookedness of Grand Cairo.

The old culture has proved astonishingly resilient, and has held its own against all alien incursions. Even television, the great leveler, far from overwhelming the mores of this capital with Western junk and juju, has only served to give the native culture a new sheen or flamboyance. Television is not always very good, relying as it does on officially emasculated news bulletins, anecdotal drama and somewhat prolonged and fulsome interviews, and it has its inevitable share of westerns and sleazy British crime. But it has successfully transposed the civilization of Grand Cairo into modern keys, so that the great Arab singers and musicians are seen as truly contemporary figures, stars like the Hollywood champions and rock heroes of the West.

Cairo feels *released* by all this, like a personality finding itself after decades of neurosis. The British embassy, once the true center of power in this capital, is now hardly more than an agreeable museum, which Egyptians cherish as a historical monument and speak of with wry affection. The Soviet embassy, once aswarm with commissars, agents and technicians, now looks half-populated in its incongruous site almost next door to the Sheraton (and almost next door too to the President's mansion —his conversations, I am told, could easily be overheard with electronic devices). The huge Protestant cathedral is being demolished to make way for a new bridge and when I passed by one morning I saw two workmen at that moment knocking down the big Christian cross on top of it.

I chanced to see the President of Aghanistan, Mohammad Daud Khan —who almost immediately afterward, as it happened, was shot dead during a coup in Kabul—arriving at Cairo Airport for an official visit. He was welcomed by Sadat and a guard of honor, and the occasion was a revealing palimpsest of passing styles and influences. The guards' uniforms seemed to be based on the U.S. Marines, and the arms drill on the British Brigade of Guards. The rifles were Russian, the official limousine, West German. The band played a fairly lumpish waltz. The guard commander preceded the inspecting dignitaries in a grotesque kind of semi-goosestep, sword at the salute, polished jackboots flashing, pausing, stamping, moving on, with an arrogant dandyism that seemed almost fin de siècle, as though Franz Josef were the visiting ruler, or the Kaiser in his winged-eagle helmet.

What a jumble of history, I thought as I watched! What an image of Egypt's varying interferers, Ottoman to Soviet! But then President Sadat escorted his guest to the inspection in a manner that was quintessentially Cairene and altogether indigenous: with his hand not quite touching the Afghan's shoulder, he shepherded his visitor gently, almost lovingly, perhaps a little humorously, down the ranks, while that coxcomb captain pranced in front, and "Tales from the Vienna Woods" resounded across the Tarmac into the desert beyond.

Which brings me back to the ominous streak: for all my life the sight of that desert below, when the aircraft has dipped its wing for the descent to Cairo Airport, has given me a queasy feeling in the stomach—accentuated when I have glimpsed, sprawled in the heat below and apparently dusted all over with sand, the unimaginable brown mesh of the capital. Egypt has habitually frightened me, and if this is partly my timidity, it is chiefly historical circumstance. For twenty years Egypt and I were, so to speak, out of sync.

Egypt is the only country where I have been stoned, sworn at by vicious beggars or had my legs smeared with boot polish by disaffected urchins. Here I have been chased by rioters, shot at by terrorists, unnerved by the broken limbs of political prisoners. One of my acquaintances was imprisoned here for years as a spy; one of my best friends was shot dead in the back on his way into town from Cairo Airport. For half my life, Egypt and my own country apparently were irreconcilable, and innocent as I was of imperial prejudices, I could not escape the old antipathies.

All that was long ago. The Egyptians are marvelously free of grudge or rancor; violence is not really their style, and there is no need nowadays for that qualm in my stomach. The retreat of the West from the Arab world, the end of the imperial idea, has changed all that forever, and few capitals offer a more agreeable welcome to the foreigner than Cairo. Yet there remains for me still that sediment of the sinister, a suggestion of stealth, secrecy and subversion. I sense it always in that immensity of desert, so empty, so close and somehow so threatening. I feel it in the detestable folds of the Egyptian bank notes, with a smell all their own and evocations of slum and bordel; in the postures of the silent, long-robed watchmen, sleepless in the night streets; in the tall presences of the minarets, elegant but always watchful; and most palpably of all, in those terrible monuments of egoism and enigma, the pyramids of Giza.

I could see the pyramids from the balcony on which I prepared this essay, and even from that comfortable distance, I could sense a miasma of horror that attended them, swirling down to the Sphinx in its bunker over the ridge. I have hated that plateau of the pyramids always: when I climbed to the top of the Great Pyramid once, its evil influence debilitated me there and then, and I was violently ill upon the summit.

Every morning platoons of Egyptian soldiers run in formation up the hill to the pyramids, shouting rhythmic war chants that echo off the sand like pharaonic curses. Every hour of every day the tourist buses drive up there too, and from my balcony I could see unhappy newcomers fallen upon by those immemorial pests of Giza, the touts and guides, swirling showily about on their camels and ponies, smiling the ancient smile of mendacity which visitors have received with a shudder since the beginnings of tourism. Goats scavenge about up there, flies swarm around the camel dung, ominous dragomans stalk here and there with tall sticks in the sunshine, spouting spurious reminiscences.

Sometimes one sees, as in horror movies, groups of hapless tourists being shepherded into the bowels of the Great Pyramid. In the gully below the hill, all day long, off-duty attendants squat among their animals, crouching over open fires like guerrillas in some bitter campaign, the camels vacuously munching, the ponies whisking the flies from their encrusted rumps, the men in small, shrouded groups, huddled in the sand, as though after a thousand years of successful marauding they are plotting new methods of extortion.

It has always been so. It is a living memory of what was there, even before Islam arrived. Son follows father in the Giza war of attrition, and many families have prospered for centuries by the presence of the pyramids, like tomb robbers of another kind. Above them all the eerie monuments themselves stand mute and lifeless, always and forever, so immoderately old, so feverishly big, that they seem always like emblems of some tormented folk-memory, a dream of bad beginnings.

The strain persists. Rumors, and rumors of rumors, whisper their way through Cairo always. It is a city of undercurrents. Sadat himself, his portrait now all over the city above slogans like SADAT THE PEACEMAKER or SADAT IS WORTHY TO NOBEL PRIZE, was a German collaborator during World War II and first gained power by conspiracy in the Officers' Revolution of 1952.

This is a capital of conspirators. As absolutely as Moscow in the 1920s, it is ruled by men who plotted and clawed their way out of political impotence, and social obscurity, to absolute authority. Many of the activists of 1952 have vanished now, dead, discredited or simply superseded. But there are some, like Sadat himself, who have survived all the shifts of fortune and intrigue to remain apparently unperturbed in their hard-won seats of consequence. Take for example Colonel X, who was active in the revolutionary movement from the very start and is still a respected figure in the hierarchy.

He was only a young lieutenant at the time of the revolution, but he was plumpish already, and now that he is a graying senior colonel he seems to have much the same build. He wears plain clothes—military uniforms being rather out of fashion—and rises from his desk most courteously to receive you. He talks with a bland conviction about the last time we met (which he has forgotten all about), and seems altogether serene, confident and certain of his values. He is like an English gentleman transmuted, brought up (one would suppose) to an absolute sureness of faith and conduct in a society to which he was naturally attuned.

Don't you believe it. He is a sort of patrician now, but he was born into the indigent household of a petty civil servant in Upper Egypt and took to the army as the traditional means of escape from the lower middle class. The society of his youth he loathed, with its fawning devotion to a shameless monarchy, its subservience to arrogant foreigners, its fatalistic dependence upon venal moneylenders and obscurantist men of religion. His politics, far from being preordained, fluctuated wildly from democratic to fascist to communist to Moslem extremist. The only consistent theme of his youth was an emotional patriotism, expressed often with a tear in the eye and a blend of the maudlin and the fanatic.

Even that has since wobbled, the loyalties that seemed so immovable in the epic days of revolution having proved more tractable later. Gamal

Abdel Nasser, the idol of the Egyptian masses and the cynosure of his adjutants, turned out to be less than perfect after all. The masses themselves, seen now through the eyes of experience, inspire in Colonel X rather less compassion than they used to, and rather more irritation. And patriotism has taken his beloved Egypt, even under revolutionary masters, along some curious paths with some strange friends: he remembers fugitive Nazis and emissaries of the CIA, powerful dialecticians from Moscow, Arab chieftains sleek with cash, furious guerrillas from Palestine, persuasive West German plutocrats, Libyans, Yugoslavs, Algerian exiles—all collaborators of one kind or another, at some period of his career.

His bosses, too, have come and gone, and perhaps before long there will be further changes still in the grander offices upstairs. . . . Never mind: Colonel X, smiling charmingly, shows you to the door and wishes you luck with every sign of thoughtful concern, as though it is you who are traveling hazardous paths merely by braving the traffic outside, while he, like any other servant of the state, steadily works his way, through well-graded ranks of secure responsibility, toward an honored retirement. Yet just as Colonel X once plotted the humiliation of the old pashas, so I felt every day that there were plotters arranging to overthrow him and his kind. I felt in my bones, as old reporters do—as Colonel X does himself, I dare say—that in this caldron of a city some fresh revolutionary substance was simmering.

I felt it particularly, in an almost symbolic way, in a cafe called El Fashawi's, which has always suggested to me a plotters' rendezvous. The tables and frayed sofas of this establishment straddle the public highway, a narrow pedestrian alley. The street traffic of old Cairo thus flows perpetually through the cafe. Bootblacks saunter here and there among the customers, cats scrounge and children scrutinize. Occasionally tourists discover it, and foreigners of the more adaptable kind are among its habitués. Traditionally, though, it has been a meeting place of the Moslem intelligentsia, who like to sit and drink their mint tea there almost within sight of Al-Azhar. Often enough, when I see three or four of them in earnest conversation on a sofa, laughing cabalistic laughs, scribbling agendas or comparing passages in what look like ideological manuals, I am reminded of student plotters in the boulevard cafes of

Paris, or even of the Russian exiles one reads about in novels, arranging the future of the world at the lakeside tables of Geneva.

The young men at El Fashawi's now are far less secretive and huddled than they were in King Farouk's or Nasser's day, but I suspect they are hardly less dissatisfied. Glorious though it is, and marvelous to visit, politically Cairo is not a healthy place. Something tells me its febrile excitement has gone too far, is reaching the boiling point. It is like one of those illusory mornings, when the light seems almost preternaturally bright, every tree delineated, every mountain etched, which nearly always ends in a thunderstorm. There is too much vigor in the air, sustained by the animal instincts, the exuberance, the good humor, the initiative, the discontent and the subterfuge of too many Egyptians. Over Tahrir Square, the main downtown plaza of the capital, there is a pedestrian walkway from one side to the other. So absolutely unremitting is the flow of people over this track, at any hour of the day, that at first I thought it must be the crowd leaving a cinema, or the flow of commuters to their daily train; but no, it is only the ordinary pedestrian coming and going of Cairo, a city almost overwhelmed by its own fertility.

It is not a squalid or a dismal congestion, such as freezes one's heart in Calcutta, for Cairenes are high-spirited people, and carry themselves with blithe dignity; but it felt to me out of hand and dangerous. Winners take all in Cairo now, the city seems unable to cope, and there is a suppressed frenzy in the air.

I smelled corruption, too, and corruption entered almost every conversation, whether it was with the student theorists at El Fashawi's, or with old effendis, respectable to the last bootlace, remembering the old days in the riverside gardens of the Zamalek. Egypt generally has been corrupt, and corruption indeed has often lubricated the gears of its government or society. But it was one of the great claims of Nasser's regime, which swept the beggars off the streets, that it had kicked the crooks and extortionists out of power too. The notoriously rapacious pashas were dispossessed of their great country estates; big business was mostly nationalized, not to say socialized; the awful old political parties, plunged in endless graft, were dissolved and discredited. Socialist aims, it seemed, demanded honesty in government, just as Nasser's junta really did seem to be concerned with the problems and the progress of the poor.

Now capitalism is back again, and even the pashas, older now but still vigorous, are riding the tide. Many of the old hierarchy are rich again, too. Urban property was not affected by land reforms; in a socialist totalitarian state, such property was worthless anyway. Now, as free enterprise surges back, it is becoming immensely valuable, and the old ruling classes, or at least their sons and daughters, are correspondingly enriched.

Every kind of peculation appears with the vast sums of Arabian money that are subsidizing the transformation of Cairo. Sadat's ministry is said to be disturbingly venal, and everyone with capital to spare, land to develop, friends at court or credit to gamble is at least aware of temptations to corruption. The rich in Cairo are visibly getting richer, and while the poor may not actually be getting poorer, they are distinctly further removed each year from the plush villas and apartments of Zamalek or Heliopolis, the speeding Mercedes of the corniche along the Nile, or the roulette tables along the road to the pyramids. That bitter old Egyptian gulf, between the complacently affluent and the almost destitute, is visible in the land again, nasty and ominous as ever.

I went one evening to a salon presided over by one of the younger, richer and more cosmopolitan of the Cairo society ladies, allied to the government by marriage, and so close to the sources of power and patronage. The purpose was to present to the Cairo *grand monde* a wise woman, of indeterminate Levantine origins, named, well, let me say Ethel. Ethel would judge character, tell fortunes, give semi-occult advice and accept confidences. The attendance was *soignée* and international; a couple of ambassadors' wives, an Indian, a German, a few bangled Egyptian patricians. We were served coffee in very fragile cups, by a Berber in a tarboosh, and we sat on squashy sofas at spindly tables in a room above the Nile furnished in a mixture of Scandinavian modern and authentic Parke Bernet.

Ethel was closeted on a balcony (she did look pretty wise, I must admit, in an unexpectedly schoolmistressly way), and one by one her clients disappeared for consultations, taking their coffee cups with them—her divinatory system made use of the coffeegrounds. In the meantime, the rest of us chatted, and a very suggestive chat I found it. Did we know that G was almost certainly going to St. Tropez with A? Was it really true that B was getting Omani money for his new hotel? Had we tried the chopped liver at the Hilton? What about F selling that awful house of his for a quarter of a million?

From time to time another lady left for the confessional, but the returning devotees, I noticed, never seemed much dismayed by Ethel's perceptions, and returned instantly, without so much as a reference to their brush with the occult, into our distinctly worldly exchange. But then Ethel, my hostess told me beforehand, seldom had unhappy premonitions. "Well, one would hardly expect her to, would one, actually in one's own drawing room?"

During my stay in Cairo there was an international conference of ulema, Islamic holy men, at Al-Azhar, and I often observed these saintly persons, in their turbans and long gray gowns, deep in discussion at the college gates, or stalking meditatively home to their lodgings after seminars. One in particular I repeatedly encountered. He was evidently a man of particular distinction, and was preceded at a distance by a sort of herald or acolyte, holding a stave. The sage himself was lame, and hobbled down the alleys of the old city as though in pain, his face slightly grimaced with the effort. But he moved swiftly nonetheless, purposefully, his eyes flashing, as though he were always on the track of some visionary thought or pursuing traces of the inner way.

What could such a devoted Moslem think, I could not help wondering, of fashionable Cairo today, so ostentatious, so grasping, its women unveiled and its whiskey freely flowing? Not much, I fear, and the more I thought about it, the more I came to feel that the explosive feeling of Cairo now came chiefly from the arsenals of Islam. Puritans of all extremes are probably gunning for Sadat, but it was the shock of the Moslem Right that I could sense. The peculation, the high life, the emancipation of women, the moral permissiveness, the influx of foreign notions —all are asking for trouble in this, the legal and dogmatic capital of the faith. The Saudis have actually been pressing Sadat to reintroduce Shari'ah Law, the Islamic code which is enforced in their own country: public hangings, penal amputations, seclusion of women and all.

It was odd that I should feel some sympathy for these zealots, and feel oddly drawn toward that holy man of the alleyways. I am, after all, a born hedonist, a happy citizen of the permissive age, dedicated normally to the right of everyone to do anything, providing it harms nobody else. But in Cairo it is different. Partly, no doubt, it is the brainwashing of our times, which makes unbridled enterprise in such a city feel uncomfortably anomalous. We have been too often disillusioned, perhaps, by the Johannesburgs and the Saigons, so that the very fun of capitalism, the very vigor and variety, has come to seem vulgar against the immensities of Africa and Asia.

But more to the point, the brash new liberty of manners defies the origins of Cairo, and is thus in a sense inorganic. The truest meaning of Cairo is the conviction, resolute and austere, that brought Amr Ibn al As and his soldiers of Allah here in the first place, and has since flowered with such magnificence. The site of Amr's original settlement, founded over a thousand years ago, is recognizable still in a patch of rather dowdy desert called Fustat, on the southern edge of the city. Amr's own mosque, the first Moslem construction in Egypt, still stands there, but nobody has presumed to build on the historic site since, and when I went out there to think about things one afternoon, I thought its desolation uncomfortably like a reminder to the Cairenes of their original values— almost a reproach.

It was as though the spirit of old Islam were watching there and waiting. The revolution I find easiest to envisage in Cairo now would be neither communist nor militarist nor xenophobic. It would be a coup of Islam—the sons of Amr demanding their heritage back. Islamic fundamentalism, after all, is resurgent these days. In Iran, the Shah's most virulent opposition came from the Mullahs. In Pakistan, Shari'ah Law has been restored in full. It is hard to see Egypt itself, so indulgent, good-natured and open-minded, willingly reverting to these fanatic codes, but it is easy enough to imagine the puritan extremists of the faith, all the same, riding in from Fustat to sweep the money-changers from the mosques and the belly dancers from the nightclubs.

The explosion hasn't happened yet, and this perhaps is because, while I was foreseeing the future in this theatrical way, the President of Egypt was taking a harderheaded look at his capital. He, too, evidently felt it to be approaching some perilous climax, and he knew that all the mounting pressures, the pressures of envy, ambition, Moslem resentment and opportunist greed, spelled danger for his regime. Before I left Cairo, he had decided to close that open door a little. He dropped a few unmistakable hints that the secret police were still there for the unleashing, and that the whole apparatus of despotism could easily be reactivated. He saw to it that newspaper criticism was practically silenced. He prompted two opposition parties to dissolve themselves. He canceled a vast free-enterprise project near the pyramids, where the magic of foreign investment was to bring into being a gaudy complex of hotels, casinos, swimming pools and other adjuncts of the materialist way.

The Egyptians were not much surprised, and as an old Cairo hand, neither was I. I knew the symptoms. Cairo has always been too big for its leaders, too volatile for its ideologues, and no history repeats itself like Egyptian history. Chilled though I had been by my forebodings, and easy though I found it to see Cairo given over once more to riot and rebellion, still they were not pictures of dismay that were uppermost in my mind when I completed my pilgrimage. I found I was able to forget the unimaginable crowds, the hapless telephone system, the lurking sense of danger or the spectacle of that harassed leader clamping down upon his capital. It was the inviolate images that remained with me, the hush behind the tumult, the old sailing boats creaking and swishing their passages upstream, the baleful mass of the pyramids, and the speckled brown minarets, like phalli and pepper pots in the sand, silent in their hundreds above the City of the Dead.

Istanbul

· · · · · · · ·

CITY OF
YOK

*By the end of 1978 the discontent of traditional
Islam, which I had detected earlier in the year in Cairo,
was coming to a head in the Iranian revolution, and powerfully affecting
all the countries of the Middle East. Turkey, still
largely Moslem, was no exception, and this portrait of Istanbul is colored
by the sensations of unrest and uncertainty which
dogged my explorations of old Byzantium.*

· · ·

ISTANBUL

· · · · · · · · · · · ·

City of Yok

[*1978*]

THE FAVOR-
ite epithet
of Istan-
bul seems to
be *yok*. I don't speak Turkish, but *yok* appears to be a
sort of general-purpose dis-
couragement, to imply that
(for instance) it can't be done,
she isn't home, the shop's
shut, the train's left, take it
or leave it, you can't come
this way or there's no good
making a fuss about it,
that's the way it is. ¶ *Yok* (at least in my interpretation) is
like *nyet* in Moscow, "Sorry luv" in London or "Have a
good day" in New York. It expresses at once the good and
the bad of Istanbul civic philosophy: the bad, a certain
prohibitive attitude to life, a lack of fizz or obvious hope-

fulness, a forbidding fatalism and an underlying sense of menace; the good, an immense latent strength, an accumulated toughness and stubbornness, which has enabled Istanbul to keep its personality intact, if not its fabric, through 1600 years of viciously variable fortune.

Istanbul is a traumatic kind of city. Standing as it does on the frontier between Europe and Asia, it is like a man with a squint, looking east and west at the same time; it is also a northern and a southern city, for immediately above it is the Black Sea, a cold Soviet lake, while almost in sight to the south are the warm waters of the Mediterranean, waters of Homeric myth and yearning.

Contemplating all this one evening, wondering about the meaning of *yok* and looking at the famous view from a high vantage on Galata hill, I found myself peculiarly disturbed by my thoughts. Morbid fancies assailed me, and wherever I looked I seemed to see threatening images. Up the Bosporus toward Russia, a mass of water traffic steamed or loitered between the green, villa-lined shores of the strait, but the ships did not have a cheerful air—they seemed balefully assembled, I thought, like a ragtag invasion fleet. To the south, the Sea of Marmara, which ought to have looked wine dark and heroic, seemed instead bland, pallid, almost accusatory. Across the inlet of the Golden Horn the ridge of Stamboul, the original core of the city, was crowned in sunset with a splendid nimbus of domes, towers and minarets, but its flanks of hills below seemed to be festering in the shadows, like a maggot heap beneath a throne.

I shook myself free of the obsession, and hurried down the hill for a late tea; but *yok, yok, yok,* the birds seemed to be squawking, as they whirled beady-eyed above my head.

Istanbul leaves many of its visitors similarly unsettled, for it is not an easy place. It is one of the most obsessively fascinating of all cities, but indefinably deadening too; a gorgeous city, but unlovely; courteous, but chill. If you came to it by sea from the south, the classic way to come, you may sense these paradoxes almost from the start. The view from the Marmara is an unforgettable first prospect of a city, but its beauty is somehow unwelcoming. The tremendous skyline stands there, high above the sea, like a covey of watchtowers: one after another along the high

Stamboul ridge, the pinnacles seem to be eyeing your approach suspiciously.

For Istanbul does possess, as you can feel from the deck of your ship, the arrogance of the very old: like the rudeness of an aged actor whose prime was long ago, whose powers have failed him but who struts about still in cloak and carnationed buttonhole, snubbing his inferiors. Seen from the sea, Istanbul seems to be sneering from across the confluence of waters, the junction of the Marmara, Bosporus and Golden Horn, which is its raison d'être, and all the caiques and motorboats and ferries seem to scuttle past it as though afraid of wounding comments.

It is only when you get closer that you realize the illusion of it, just as you observe, if he leans too close to you on the sofa, the creases of despair around the actor's mouth. Then that proud mass above the water dissolves into something crumblier and shabbier; the watchtowers lose some of their haughty command, the great sea wall of Stamboul is no more than a ruin, and it turns out that the passing boats are taking no notice of the city at all, but are simply impelled to and fro across the waterways, up and down the Golden Horn, zigzagging across the Bosporus, like so many mindless water insects.

For half the civilized world this was once *the* City, the ultimate—Byzantium, Constantinople, the stronghold and repository of all that civilization had retrieved from the wreck of Rome. For the Turks it still is. It is no longer the political capital of Turkey, but it is much the greatest Turkish city: the place where the money is made, the books are written, the place, above all, where the Turks see their own national character most faithfully mirrored or fulfilled. When I put myself into Istanbul's shoes that evening, I felt only some inkling of schizophrenia: when Turks do so, I am told, by immersing their imaginations in the history and spirit of the place, they feel most completely themselves.

I know of no other city that is so impregnated with a sense of fatefulness, and this is partly because few cities have been so important for so long. Constantine founded his capital, the New Rome, in 330 A.D., and there has not been a moment since when Istanbul was not conscious of its own mighty meaning. The successive dynasties that ruled the place competed with each other to proclaim its consequence. The Romans built their showy Hippodrome, adorning it with captured trophies and staging terrific chariot races beneath the golden horses of its tribune. The Greeks of Byzantium raised their marvelous cathedral, decorating it with precious frescoes and genuflecting in dazzling ritual before its jeweled reliquaries. The conquering Moslems of the Middle Ages commemorated themselves with mosques, schools and caravansaries across the city, each larger, more pious and more philanthropic than the last. The Ottomans built their vast Topkapi Palace, crammed with vulgar jewelry, where the ladies and eunuchs of the Seraglio gossiped life away in marble chambers, and the Sultans eyed their odalisques in exquisite pleasure kiosks above the sea. The mound of old Stamboul, the original Byzantium, is studded all over with monuments, so that every alleyway seems to lead to the courtyard of a stately mosque, a blackened obelisk or a triumphal column, a casket church of Byzantium or at least a magnificent city wall.

But in between them all, under the walls, behind the churches, like a hideous carpet spreads the squalor of the centuries. It is as though these famous buildings were built upon a foundation of undisturbed muck—as though every scrap of rubbish, every gob of spittle, every bucket-load of ordure, has been stamped into the very substance of the place, never to be cleaned or scraped. When it rains, which it often does, the lanes are soon mucky: but it is not just mud that cakes your shoes, not plain earth liquefied, but actually a glaucous composition of immemorial city excreta. The market streets of Istanbul are not exactly picturesque, if only because the citizenry is so drably dressed, in browns, grays and grubby blacks, but they are vividly suggestive of unbroken continuity. The dark, cluttered mass of the covered bazaars—the clamor of the market men—the agonizing jams of trucks, cars, horses and carts in the back streets—the clatter of looms in half-derelict tenements—scuttling dogs and scavenging cats—bent-backed porters carrying beds or crates or carcasses—the click-clack of the man selling plastic clothes pegs, the toot-toot of the man selling wooden whistles, the ting-ting of the water seller with his tin cups—listless detachment of coffee-shop men, oblivious over their cups and dominoes—stern attention of policemen strutting through the shops—the shouts of itinerant greengrocers—the blare of pop music from the record stores—the glowering stone walls, the high towers above—the tumultuous odors of spice, coffee, raw meat, gasoline, sweat, mud—the sheer swell and flow and muddle of humanity there, seething through that urban labyrinth, makes one feel that nobody has ever left Istanbul, that nothing has ever been discarded, that every century has simply added its shambled quota to the uncountable whole, and made these streets a perpetual exhibition of what Istanbul was, is and always will be.

Just as decomposing matter makes for fertile vegetation, so from the compost of Istanbul a timeless vigor emanates. Few cities move with such an intensity of effort, such straining virility. The generations of the dead are risen, to prod the living into life.

For yes, this is a vigor of the grave. These are bones rustling, and the restless ferryboats of Istanbul are so many funeral craft, carrying their complements of dead men to and fro between the railway stations. Though Istanbul is home to some 3 million souls, though its suburbs stretch far along the Marmara shore, deep into Thrace, up the Bosporus almost to the Black Sea, though there are few towns on earth so agitated and congested, still it sometimes feels like a tomb-city.

Of all the great Turkish despots, only Kemal Ataturk, the latest, rejected Constantinople as his capital. It was Ataturk who renamed the city Istanbul, and he had no sympathy, it seems, for its sedimented pride—he visited the city reluctantly during his years in office, though he died there in 1938. He was a futurist, a reformer, a secularist, and old Byzantium must have seemed the very negation of his aspirations. To this day Istanbul has never really absorbed his visionary ideas, or become a natural part of the Turkey he created.

Of course it has lost much of the Oriental quaintness that the great man so resented. No longer do the gaily skirted peasants swirl into the covered markets; gone are the tumbled wooden houses of tradition, and only a few of the old Ottoman love nests along the Bosporus, those tottering clapboard mansions that the romantic travelers used to relish, still stand frail and reproachful among the apartment blocks. Ring roads and flyovers have cut their statutory swaths through the slums and city ramparts. The obligatory international hotels ornament the best sites. Here and there one sees blighted enclaves of contemporary planning, blown by litter, stuck all over with peeling posters, invested with car parks and sad gardens.

But it is not really a modern city at all, not modern by taste or instinct, and it seems to reject transplants from our century. In the Municipal Museum (housed in a former mosque in the shadow of the Emperor Valens's great aqueduct) there is dimly displayed an American plan for a new bridge over the Golden Horn, with ceremonial approaches at either end. It is a lavish conception of spotless plazas and gigantic avenues, but it was doomed from the start, and survives only in an old brown frame upon a musty wall; even if it had been built, I do not doubt, long ago the mold of old Stamboul would have encroached upon its symmetries and rotted its high pretensions.

There can never be a fresh start in Istanbul. It is too late. Its successive pasts are ineradicable and inescapable. I always stay at the Pera Palas Hotel on the Galata hill, almost the last of the old-school grand hotels to survive the invasion of the multinationals—a haven of potted plants, iron-cage elevators, ample baths with eagle feet. It has been halfheartedly modernized once or twice, but like Istanbul itself, it really ignores improvements and is settled complacently into its own florid heritage. My bedroom this time was Number 205, overlooking the Golden Horn. It was clean, fresh and very comfortable—I love the hotel—but when, on my first morning, I lay flat on the floor to do my yoga, lo, from the deep recess beneath my double bed an authentic fragrance of the Ottomans reached me, dismissing the years and the vacuum cleaners alike: an antique smell of omelets and cigars, slightly sweetened with what I took to be attar of roses.

Something fibrous and stringy, like the inherited characteristics of a patrician clan, links the ages of Istanbul, and is as recognizable in its people today as a six-toed foot or albinism. For all its distracted air, in small matters at least Istanbul is a surprisingly reliable city. I never feel vulnerable to assault or robbery here, I seldom feel the need to check the bill, and even the most pestiferous of the local bravoes generally prove, if approached with sufficient firmness, dependable guides and advisers. *Yok* stands for rigidity, but for staunchness, too.

Istanbul has had to be staunch, to withstand the corrosions of time and retain its stature in the world. It has outlasted most of its rivals, after all, and generally wins its battles in the end. Scattered around Pera, the old foreigners' quarter of the city, are the former embassies of the powers, the nations of Europe that have periodically foreclosed Turkey as the bankrupt invalid of the Golden Horn. Nowadays, with the government in Ankara, they are mere consulates, but in their very postures you can still recognize the contempt with which their envoys and ambassadors, not so long ago, surveyed the pretensions of the Sublime Porte: the Russian embassy, like Tolstoy's estate behind its forecourt; the British a huge classical villa by the architect of the Houses of Parliament; the French with its private chapel in the garden; the Italian (once the Venetian) like a stately retreat upon the Brenta. They are still functioning, but they are half buried all the same in the debris of history, forlorn down messy cobbled alleyways or peering hangdog through their railings across the turmoil of the old Grand Rue.

Or take the Greek quarter across the Golden Horn. Here there stands the Patriarchate of the Greek Orthodox Church, the Vatican of Orthodox Christianity. Once it was an organization of immense power, attended by pilgrims and plenipotentiaries, surrounded by acolyte institutions, defying even the dominion of the Moslem caliphs down the road. Now it is pitifully diminished, an unobtrusive little enclave in a semi-slum, its ceremonial gateway symbolically painted black and welded shut forever: while on the hill behind it the huge Greek *lycée*, once aswarm with aspirants, now stands empty, shuttered and despised.

Istanbul outlives all its challengers, reduced of course in worldly influence since the days of the Ottoman Empire, but hardly at all in self-esteem. Those powers and principalities have risen and fallen, some humiliated, some exalted, but the matter of Istanbul outlasts them all. This is a survivor city, essentially aloof to victory or defeat. The nearest a foreign enemy has come to assaulting Istanbul in our century was in 1915, when the armies of the Western alliance in the Great War, landing on the Gallipoli Peninsula some 150 miles to the south, tried to march north to the city. Supported by the guns of the most powerful battle fleet ever seen in the Mediterranean, they threw half a million of the world's finest infantry ashore on Turkish soil and expected to be at the Golden Horn within the month.

Though Istanbul was rigidly blockaded, though British and Australian submarines roamed the Marmara and bombarded the roads to the city, though a warship was torpedoed within sight of the sultan's palace, though the rumble of the battle shivered the minarets on the heights of Stamboul—still the enemy armies never advanced more than five miles from their beachheads.

Istanbul had said *yok*.

In theory this is a secular city, just as Turkey is a secular state. Ataturk decreed it so. In practice the voice of the muezzin rings out across the city, electronically amplified nowadays, almost as insistently as it did in the days of the caliphs, when this was the formal capital of all Islam. Like everything else in Istanbul, the faith proves irrepressible, and it remains the most potent single element, I suppose, in the personality of the place. I went one day to the Blue Mosque at the time of Friday prayers and positioned myself inside its great doorway—discreetly I hoped—to watch the faithful at their devotions. Not for long. A young man of distinctly unecumenical aspect rose from the back row of worshipers and approached me darkly. "Beat it," he said, and without a moment's hesitation, beat it I did.

The muezzin voices are voices from the glorious past, never silenced, calling Istanbul always back again, home again to itself—back to the great days of the caliphs, the noble Ahmets and the munificent Mehmets, back to the times when the princes of this city could build incomparable monuments of belief and generosity, high on their seven hills above the sea. Nobody has built in Istanbul like that since the end of the caliphate and its empire, just as nobody has given Istanbul a faith or a pride to call its own. Even the name of the place has lost its majesty. "Why did Constantinople get the works?" a popular song used to ask. "That's nobody's business but the Turks' ": but the new name lacks the grand hubris of the old, and sends a frisson, I am afraid, down almost nobody's spine.

So many a patriot of this city looks back to Islam. The mosques are busy, the fanatics are aflame, regressive religion is one of the fiercest political movements in Istanbul. Though it used to be postulated that Turkish Islam, like capitalism, would wither away in time, the average age of that Blue Mosque congregation looked strikingly young to me. And though the veil has been officially forbidden for half a century now, women are going to the university these days with black scarves drawn

pointedly around their faces. The activist Moslems of Istanbul look outside their own country for inspiration—to Iran, to Pakistan, to the Arab
states, where militant Islam is on the march or already in power: and
when they take to the streets, as they recently did, or engage in student
skirmishes, or burn cars, or break windows, the newspapers are unable
to define this heady amalgam of nostalgia and zealotry, and cautiously
describe them as Idealists.

On the other side, now as always, are the leftists, by which the press
means the heterogeneous mass of liberals, anarchists, hooligans and real
Communists, which roughly stands for change in an opposite direction.
The longest graffito in the world is surely the one that somebody has
painted along the whole expanse of the mole at the Kadiköy ferry station,
containing in its message almost the entire idiom of the international
Left, and leaving those with strong feelings about neo-Fascist hyenas
with nothing much more to add. The leftists think of themselves as pro-
gressives, modernists, but they are really honoring a tradition older even
than Islam: for long before the caliphate was invented, the city crowd
was a force in Byzantium. In those days the rival factions of the Blues and
the Greens, originally supporters of competing charioteers in the Hippodrome, were infinitely more riotous than any soccer crowd today, and
the great circuit of the race track, around whose purlieus the backpack
nomads now drink their mint tea in The Pub or the Pudding Shop, was
the supreme arena of anarchy, the place where the frustration of the
people found its ferocious release in bloodshed and insurrection.

Even now, I think, the quality of mercy is fairly strained in Istanbul,
and the threat of public violence is always present. It is not so long since
the mob, in its inherited and ineradicable suspicion of Greece, burned
down half the covered bazaars of the city and destroyed everything Greek
they could find. Step even now from a bus in Beyazit Square, on the
Stamboul ridge, and you may find yourself looking straight down the gun
barrel of a military patrol. Hang around long enough in Eminönü, by the
waterfront, and you are sure to see somebody frog-marched off the scene
by plainclothes toughs or clapped into handcuffs by the implacable
military police. This is the country of *Midnight Express*, and it has a
heavy touch.

But you feel these antagonisms, this touch of the sinister, only so to speak by osmosis. The Turks are a courteous people, very kind to harmless strangers, and the ruthless side of their nature is generally masked. For that matter, nearly everything in Istanbul is blurred by its own congealment and delay. Cairo, Calcutta, Istanbul—these are the three great cities of the world where you may observe the prophecies of the doomwatch specialists apparently coming true. Chaos has not arrived yet, but it feels imminent enough. The ferry steamers seem to swirl around in a perpetual state of near collision. There is hardly room on the sidewalks for the press of people. Ever and again the city traffic, balked by some unseen mishap far away along the system, comes helplessly to a halt. The festering rubbish dumps of Stamboul seem to heave with incipient disease.

It has not happened yet. The ferryboats generally evade each other in the end. The traffic does move again. The plague rats have not yet emerged from their garbage. But the suggestion is always there, the shadow of breakdown and anarchy: incubating, one feels, in the day-to-day confusion.

"Tell me, lady," said the youth, falling into step with me as I walked down Alemdar Caddesi past the ridiculous ceremonial gateway that gave its name to the Sublime Porte—"Tell me, lady," he said, as we skirted the high wall of Topkapi, "was the movie *Midnight Express* true?"

Was it true? Is it real? The sense of foreboding that characterizes Istanbul does have a half-illusory quality, and seems to bewilder its citizens as it does its visitors. It is a city of theatrical hazards. Fires and earthquakes have periodically ravaged it. Empires have risen and fallen within its boundaries. There is a humped island called Yassiada, ten or so miles from Istanbul in the Marmara, which was pointed out to me one day as the place where Prime Minister Menderes was imprisoned after a military coup in 1960. It looked a nice enough place to me: a companionable little island, not at all remote, which looked as though it might have some agreeable bathing beaches. And what became of Menderes? I ignorantly asked my companion as our ship sailed by. "They killed him," he replied.

Now *that* hardly seemed real, on a blue and sunny day, on the deck of a pleasure steamer, on a trip around the islands. Half fictional, half fact, a nebulous sense of menace informs the conversations of Istanbul. The foreign businessman has chill presentiments as he leans with his gin and tonic over his balcony by the Bosporus, watching a Russian cruise ship sliding by, cabin lights ablaze and hammer-and-sickle floodlit, toward Odessa and the Motherland. "Something's going to happen. Something's going to crack. . . ." The Turkish bank official, pausing didactically with your traveler's checks beneath his thumb, attributes the malaise to strategy. "Strategy is the curse of Istanbul—it's where we live; we can never be left in peace." The army colonel, over a drink at the Hilton, talks apocalyptically through his mustache of conspiracies and conflicts. "I'll tell you quite frankly—and the Americans know this well enough—the Greeks don't simply want Cyprus for themselves, they don't simply want to make the Aegean a Greek lake—*they want Istanbul itself!* They want to restore Byzantium!"

And the youth in the street beside the Sublime Porte cannot put his worries into words, for he has no standards of comparison, and does not know if that grim movie was allegory or reportage, whether the world is all like that or whether these hints and horrors are specific to his own country. It is easy to feel perturbed in Istanbul. Every evening at the Pera Palas a string trio plays, attentively listened to by the German package tourists at their communal tables, and gives the place a comfortable, palm-court air. Two elderly gentlemen in gypsy outfits are on piano and accordion, and they are led by a romantic fiddler, adept at waltzes and polkas.

I was sitting there one evening when suddenly there burst into the room, driving the trio from its podium and severely disconcerting the hausfraus, a team of ferocious Anatolian folk dancers, accompanied by a young man with a reedy trumpet and an apparently half-crazed drummer. The dancers were fairly crazed themselves. Apparently welded together into a multicolored phalanx, they shrieked, they roared with laughter, they leaped, they whirled, they waved handkerchiefs—a performance of furious bravura, leaving us all breathless and aghast. They were like so many houris, come to dance over the corpses on a battlefield.

They withdrew as abruptly as they had arrived, and in the stunned hush that ensued I turned to the Americans at the next table. "My God," I said, "I'm glad they're on our side!" But a knowing look crossed the man's face. "Ah, but *are* they?" he replied.

You can never be quite sure, with the Turks. They are nobody's satellites, and they habitually leave the world guessing. This does not make for serenity, and Istanbul is not a blithe city. For foreigners it is a city, all too often, of homesickness and bafflement, for Turks a city where life gets tougher every day. I saw a protest demonstration one day clambering its way up the hill toward the Hippodrome, on the Stamboul ridge, and never did I see a demonstration so lacking in the fire of indignation. The hill is very steep there, and the cheerleaders, men and women in antiphony, found it hard to raise a response among their panting protégés: while flanking the procession on either side, guns across their bellies, helmets low over their foreheads, an escort of soldiers did their chesty best to keep up. An armored car brought up the rear, flashing blue and white lights, but even it found the progress heavy going.

More telling still perhaps, one day I walked up a hill on the Pera side (every walk in Istanbul is up or down a hill) in the wake of a big brown bear, chained to the staff of a lanky man in black. It was a distinguished-looking bear, lean and handsome, but it walked through Istanbul in movements of infinite melancholy and weariness, as though the day, the walk up the hill, life itself would never end. I overtook it presently, and prodded by its master it stood on its hind legs for a moment to salute me as I passed: but it did so disdainfully, I thought, and somewhat *grandly*.

Istanbul indeed is nothing if not grand. It may not be exuberant, it is seldom funny, its humor running characteristically to not very prurient posters and bawdy badinage. It is hardly uplifting: sometimes, when I take the old funicular from Galata hill to the Golden Horn, I feel that its carriages, sliding into their narrow black tunnels, are plunging me into perpetual night. It is never optimistic: one feels that dire things may happen at any moment, and all too often they do, arrests, accidents, collapses, unidentified gunshots and screaming sirens in the night being commonplaces of the city.

But grand, unquestionably. For all my unease in Istanbul, I greatly admire the place, and it is the grandeur that does it: not the grandeur of history or monument, but the grandeur of *yok*, the ornery strength and vigor that gives a living dignity to its affairs. There is one incomparable vantage from which to observe this ironic vitality—the deck of one of the restaurant boats which are moored beside the Galata Bridge; and there at a typical Istanbul lunchtime—grayish, that is, with a warm breeze off the Bosporus to flutter the canvases—I will end my essay.

The setting down there is terrific. The bulk of Stamboul rises magnificently behind our backs, the iron-brown Galata hill is stacked across the Golden Horn, and to the east the ships pass to and fro along the wide expanse of the Bosporus. Everything is a little hazed, though: not merely by the cloud of spiced smoke in which the restaurateur is cooking our fish, on the open quayside by the boat, but by a kind of permanent opacity of life and light along the Golden Horn, through which everything moves powerfully but inexactly.

Those inescapable ferryboats, for instance, twist and scuttle in a dreamlike frenzy, and across the bridge the traffic seems to lurch without pattern or priority. Peddlers, defying the massed tide of pedestrians like Californians wading into the surf, offer balloons, cutlery, incomprehensible household gadgets and sizzling corn on the cob. Military policemen saunter watchfully by, eyes darting right and left for deserters or unsoldierly conduct. From their boats below the quay smoke-shrouded fishermen hand up chunks of grilled fish to their customers above, who sprinkle rough salt upon them from pots tied to the railings and wander off munching into the crowd. Lines of indistinguishable youths hang over their fishing rods beneath the bridge, and sometimes clouds of pigeons, suddenly emerging from their roosts in the dusty façade of the mosque at the end of the bridge, swoop across the scene like huge gray raindrops.

It is a wonderfully animated scene, but animated it seems by habit: numbly animated, passively animated, like a huge mechanical theater worked by the engines of history. Presently our food comes, with a chopped tomato salad on the side, a glass of beer and some fine rough Turkish bread. "Oh," we may perhaps murmur, in our foreign way, "excuse me, but I wonder if we could possibly have some butter?" The waiter smiles, faintly but not unkindly. "*Yok*," he says, and leaves us to our victuals.

WHAT BECAME
OF WARING

I am strongly biased in favor of Trieste,
the first city I lived in as an adult, but tried in this
piece nevertheless to capture a civic flavor which combines the genial with
the melancholy, the bourgeois with the conspiratorial,
plushness with seediness, back street with crossroad.
Nothing particular was developing in Trieste in 1979. At the same time,
in the way of the place, nothing was exactly
settled, either.

. . .

TRIESTE

· · · · · · · · · · · · · · · · · · ·

What Became of Waring

[1979]

WHAT'S BE-
come of Waring?"
asks Robert
Browning (in
verse) of an errant
friend, and he an-
swers the question
memorably in the
last stanza of the
poem. Deep in the
stern of a lateen-
rigged boat Waring is discovered, in the distant harbor
of Trieste—just a glimpse of his smile we see, just
a flash, before the boat turns like a leaping fish and
disappears, "as with a bound, into the rosy and golden half
of the sky...." ❡ At the northeast corner of the Adriatic
Sea, where capitalist Italy meets Communist Yugoslavia,
Trieste has always been the kind of place where wanderers
and exiles turn up, once-familiar faces are transiently recog-

nized, or famous figures briefly show themselves. James Joyce teaching English at the Berlitz School, Freud dissecting eels at the Zoological Station, Richard Burton the scholar-pornographer translating *The Arabian Nights* at the British Consulate, Mahler complaining about the noise of the trains outside the Hotel de Ville, the Archduke Ferdinand returning as a flowered corpse from his recent visit to Sarajevo—all these are characters of Trieste, briefly displayed upon this narrow stage beneath the golden half of the sky.

Trieste is a fulcrum of nothing, but an extension of much more, and here are two local images to illustrate the point. The first is an early morning image. The sun is warmly rising as we step onto our hotel balcony over the harbor. A couple of fishing boats are bustling off into the bay, a couple of anglers are already settled against their bollards on the quay. It is a shining morning, and across the water down the coast the romantic little castle of Miramare is already caught in the sunlight. But below us along the quayside a long, long freight train is laboriously moving among the parked cars, its engine out of sight along the waterfront, and all its wagons are crusted with snow. *Snow!* Snow from Vienna? Snow from Carpathia? Snow from some distant steppe or forest of Asia? Trieste snow: momentary snow: snow passing by.

The second is an evening image. Near the street corner beside the church of St. Antonio Nuovo, as the streetlamps come on, a five-story house of genteel architectural aspect stands already ablaze with neon. Diffidently between its doors we pass, as though entering a house of dubious repute, and inside all is a dazzle of lights, rock music and jewelry, like a pop star's ambition, or an emporium in old Port Said. Through its blinding salons a multitude of thick-set Slavic-looking men mutters and wanders, inspecting lockets through eyeglasses, stashing away watches in briefcases, having gold chains weighed in infinitesimal scales. We are in Darwil's, the Trieste jewelers famous to gold speculators throughout eastern Europe, where you buy your bracelets by the gram, where any currency goes, and the trail of intricate transactions leads far away to Bucharest, Sofia, Prague, Warsaw and for all I know Moscow itself.

From time to time through life I fetch up in Trieste, obscurely attracted there by such inklings and allusions. It never seems to change much, but that does not mean that it is always the same: for it is a place of shift, chance and opportunity, never settled, never sure.

Some would say never satisfied, for recent history has been churlish to Trieste. In the Middle Ages it was always overshadowed, and sometimes assaulted, by its neighbor Venice, a hundred miles along the coast, but under the Austro-Hungarian Empire it prospered mightily. It became the only great port of the empire, the port of Budapest and Vienna, serving a vast hinterland of inner Europe, and assuming all the airs of consequence.

Everything flowered then. Lloyd Triestino, the great shipping company, rose to power—the very first steamship to pass through the (still uncompleted) Suez Canal flew the Trieste colors—and Trieste became the headquarters of the Austrian fleet, a fancy flotilla of aristocratic admirals and geriatric ships. Austrian and Jewish bankers thrived, merchant dynasties were founded. From the Slavic east, the German north, the Italian west, financiers and entrepreneurs of every kind came to settle on the bay, followed by many a remittance man, indigent artist, Joyce and Waring. For two or three generations Trieste was organically fulfilled. It was the sea outlet of Austria-Hungary, the promenade of Vienna, and one of the great ports of the Mediterranean.

The empire disintegrated in the First World War, and things have never been the same since. Trieste fell into a kind of limbo. Handed to Italy in 1919, it was claimed almost immediately by the new Yugoslavia (where they called it, somewhat sibilantly, Trst), and for the next half-century it was endlessly disputed. It is said that in the Second World War, when the Russians and the Yugoslavs were still brothers-in-Marxism, Stalin and Tito stood together on the heights above this city, and decided that its destiny was to be the chief warm-water port of the Communist world, enabling the Russians to reach the Mediterranean without passing through either the Bosporus or the Strait of Gibraltar: but the Western Allies had their eyes no less specifically upon the place, and they got it instead.

They succeeded in keeping it on the capitalist side of the fence, but they never found a role for it. The status of Trieste was finally determined only in 1975: the city became permanently Italian, the countryside around, including the Istrian peninsula which had seemed almost integral to the place, became definitively Yugoslav. But it is a makeshift kind of status still, leaving Trieste always out on a limb—geographically, economically, ideologically, culturally.

Tightly packed around its splendid bay, its villas and apartments rising tight-packed on the hills behind, its riviera running away westward toward Venice, the city is overlooked everywhere by the grim limestone heights called the Carso—proud, decayed-looking ridges, clad only in scrub and thicket, riddled with potholes. Nearly all this high ground is Yugoslav: so is the Istrian coastline, speckled with Italian campaniles and pretty Venetian ports, which runs away so delightfully from the eastern suburbs of the port. Only a narrow corridor along the coast to the west connects Trieste with Italy, like the most fragile of umbilicals.

No wonder the place has an uneasy feel. There is a monstrous Trieste wind called the Bora which, suddenly screaming across the city out of those stern and sterile ridges, knocks pedestrians off their feet and sometimes sweeps railway wagons into the harbor. So potently does it figure in the lives and mythologies of the Triestini that they have actually called a street after it—Via della Bora. Well, the 20th century has had such an effect on Trieste itself, and has left the city buffeted, bruised and clutching the wall.

It is a grand old city, mind you, a city of great character, an *original* among cities. If Stalin and Tito had achieved their aims, it would now be one of the most important places on earth. As things are, it is not really an important place at all, but like a writer always on the brink of bestsellerdom, like an actress perpetually about to achieve a comeback, Trieste remains a thwarted excitement, wistful and affronted.

To some people it is an outpost, to others a dead end. Whichever it is, here worlds meet: Communist and capitalist, Latin, German and Slav, Catholic and Orthodox, Christian and atheist. Trieste is an Italian city, but only just—*faute de mieux*, perhaps. It has a big Slav minority, its personality is strongly Austrianized, and it is willy-nilly conscious of its differences from the rest of Italy—the fleur-de-lys of Trieste flies always beside the Italian tricolor on the gigantic ceremonial flagposts in Piazza dell'Unita, and when Trieste soccer teams play elsewhere in Italy they are often sneered at as Slavs or Germans.

"Hostages of our culture," is how literary Triestini sometimes describe themselves, and they have a point, for their city is really a cat's-paw of Europe, someone else's stake in the Great Game. A trace of petulance, laced perceptibly with self-pity, is understandably part of the ambiance. The crowds who pour into the streets after the midday siesta, strolling arm-in-arm down the waterfront, chatting in clusters on the pavements of the Piazza della Borsa, decorously fur-wrapped in squashy cafes or radically sprawled on the enormous Fascist steps of the University—the Trieste street crowds are courteous, and mostly comfortable-looking, and well dressed, but seldom exuberant. They do not smile too easily. They never whistle. They seem almost to be waiting for something to happen—nothing specific perhaps, nothing actually foreseeable, just *something*.

Something does happen at the weekends. Then the Yugoslavs pour over the frontier to do their capitalistic shopping—there are several thousand crossings of the Trieste frontier posts every day. In the days of the Communist innocence they used to come in broken-down Skodas, now they often come in Mercedes or BMWs, and they make for two places in particular: Darwil's the jewelers, where the Gold Road into eastern Europe begins, and the open-air market on the Ponte Rosso, where the Jeans Road starts.

If Trieste never became the warm-water port of Russia, it does have a part of sorts to play in the economies of eastern Europe. Because Yugoslavia provides a kind of de-pressurizing chamber, a halfway house which Hungarians, Poles, Czechs and Romanians find it relatively easy to visit, for millions of east European citizens Trieste is the most accessible of capitalist entrepôts. If they cannot come in person, they can fix it through Yugoslav agents, and the one commodity they want above all else, it seems, the object of all their thwarted desires, is a pair of genuine all-American blue jeans.

In Trieste supply meets demand, and on weekends the Ponte Rosso market is the busiest place in town. It is the very first thing, actually, that Triestini tell you to see these days, for at least it is an international function, a distorted but sufficiently vigorous reflection of Trieste's great days. It is true that most of the jeans are fake, made in Italy anyway, and stamped with comically solecistical brand-marks (of which my favorite is "Best for Hammering, Pressing and Screwing"). True too that the trade is said to have been heavily infiltrated by the Mafia, and that before very long, when the American jeans manufacturers open their promised factories behind the Iron Curtain, it will presumably be expunged.

But for the moment the Saturday market, the start of the Blue Jeans Road, is Trieste's liveliest reminder of its place on the map. The haughty Hapsburgs may have gone, the boat trains no longer spill their passengers on the Molo for Egypt and the East, but at least at Ponte Rosso there is no mistaking the international nature of this city. Everywhere Balkan voices, Balkan faces, stocky Balkan figures remind you of it, and if you walk through the car parks every other number plate is from Split, Dubrovnik or Belgrade. A sweet old lady does a roaring trade in illicit currency exchanges; flashy young men stalk the market stalls looking for easy pickings; across the city the satisfied customers spill out, clutching their brown paper parcels or plastic shopping bags, and laughing gold-toothed comradely laughs.

"We are the furthest limit of Latinity," the Mayor of Trieste exclaimed to me one day, "the southern extremity of Germanness." Triestini love this sort of hyperbole, and it is true that nothing in their city, even now, is parochial. It is a microcosmic city, even in its doldrums, whose anxieties are all too often the world's worries in small. Take the matter currently most taxing the city's politicians, the so-called Asimo Agreement which proposes a Free Industrial Zone to be built high on the open Carso above the city. The Zone is intended to straddle the frontier between Italy and Yugoslavia, and the Triestini fear that it will shift the ethnic balance of the region, wreck the ecology and spoil the environment. But the implications are far deeper really: for one thing the agreement is part of a general quid pro quo between Rome and Belgrade, and for another the Americans want it because they hope it will help to bind post-Tito Yugoslavia to the West rather than the East.

Or take the supposed agreement with the Chinese that Trieste is to be the European terminal of the developing Chinese merchant marine, with ships supplied by Lloyd Triestino. This sounds fine on the spot, but what of its wider meanings? How will Italy's EEC partners view it? How will it affect détente? Will the Italian Euro-Communists sanction it? Strategy, regionalism, ecology, minority problems, the Chinese emergence, the oil problem—all these generalized preoccupations of Europe and the world have their particular demonstrations in Trieste.

The people of Trieste, too, powerless though their city is these days, can never be provincial. History has touched them once and for all. They are a mixture—not a heady mixture, certainly not that, but more a stew-like mélange of origins, thick and sustaining. If the culture of the city is overwhelmingly Italian, it is an Italianness laced with less volatile strains —nowhere could be much less Neapolitan, or even Mediterranean. There are the thousands of Slavs of course—perhaps 10 percent of the population, and still speaking their own languages. There are hundreds of people of Austrian descent. There are many Greeks. There are 800 Jews, survivors of the great community of 6000 which flourished here before World War II.

All these peoples have been tossed around by the two world wars: such have been the vagaries of Triestino fortune that it is hard to remember sometimes which side the city was on in which conflict, or which cause its many memorials honor. The gaunt statue of a naval officer, for instance, which stands outside the Marine Terminal represents an Italian submarine commander from Istria who fought for Italy in the First World War, was captured by the Austrians who then ruled these parts, and was accordingly shot for treason: his effigy originally stood in Istria, but was moved to Trieste when the Yugoslavs took over the peninsula. As for the big World War I memorial on the castle walls, I am honestly not sure which alliance was served by the men who are commemorated upon it, and their names certainly do not help, for they include not only Borgello, Silvestro and Zanetti, but Bednawski, Brunner, Liebmann, Slocovich, Xydias, Zottig and Blotz.

But out of this jumbled past Trieste has acquired a tolerance and awareness unexpected in so solidly mercantile a city. It is as though the cosmopolitan ethos of the old empire survives despite all setbacks—more pungently perhaps in this abandoned outpost than in Vienna itself, let alone poor stifled Budapest. Trieste indeed is often nostalgic for the double-eagle of the empire. A traditionally popular way of spending New

Year's Day is to take an excursion by Pullman train to Vienna, and every year groups of Triestini go out to a village on the Isonzo River, the old imperial frontier, to celebrate the birthday of Franz Josef.

Nobody could embody these several strains much more exactly than does Maestro Barone Rafaelle Douglas de Banfield-Tripcovich—Rafaelle de Banfield as he is generally known—composer, businessman, director of the Trieste Opera (and of the Spoleto Festival), active politician and Honorary French Consul in Trieste. De Banfield is the son of a famous Triestino war hero—on the Austrian side—an ace naval flier who became the most highly decorated officer in the entire Austro-Hungarian forces, and was made Baron of Trieste for it. His more distant forebears were Irish, his mother was a Slav countess, he himself was born in England and studied law in Bologna before turning to music.

He is a worldly, elegant, hand-kissing kind of man, very gentlemanly: and he sits in his office at the Opera House with an air of commanding but civilized amplitude, sometimes responding to a telephone call from a colleague of the opera circuit—"Of course, Maestro, of course, see you in Paris!"—sometimes dealing with petty problems of score, orchestra or repertoire—assuring his secretary that he will be at the consular luncheon party later that morning—parrying inquiries concerning his attitude, as an independent Christian Democratic member of the City Council toward the Asimo Agreement.

How exquisitely a man of the world, I thought to myself as we talked—but *what* world? He fits into no category, a modish bachelor of deep religious fervor, a fierce politician who creates sensitive ballets, a rich rentier known in all the opera houses of the world, a French Consul of Irish-Austrian-Slav blood who uses a title granted by a long-disintegrated empire in an Italy against which his father became famous by fighting! I revised my opinion hastily, before the syntax became too much for me: not a man of the world after all perhaps, but pre-eminently a Man of Trieste.

The Baron noticed my pensive expression presently, and took me over to the window of his office. "There goes one of my boats," he said, pointing out to me a stocky little vessel hastening across the harbor toward the mooring berths: for as it happens he owns all the Trieste tugs, too.

Rafaelle de Banfield is a bachelor, living handsomely with his now aged father, and come to think of it in this too he is somehow emblematic of Trieste. The style of this city is rather club-like—like the period itself perhaps, the ornate late decades of the Hapsburgs, which brought the port to fruition, and which strikes me not as celibate indeed, and certainly not infertile, but distinctly unfamilial. Expect no Italian jollity in this Adriatic seaport. No hearty family parties sing and laugh over their Sunday pastas in its restaurants. No tremulous tenors resound. The most characteristic Trieste entertainment is not a boisterous soccer game, or a folk dance in a piazza, but that *spindliest* of spectator sports, trotting.

All the robustness, one feels, went to the making of money, and the Trieste style is essentially a glorification of commercial opportunity: a plump and optimistic style, whose banks and office blocks express as devout a faith in the comforting power of Cash as did the great Victorian railway stations in the fructifying force of Steam. The vast neo-Renaissance palace of Lloyd Triestino faces in absolute equality the Prefect's Palace across the square, while most visitors to Trieste mistake the Borsa for the Opera House.

It is the nostalgic glory of Trieste, for better or for worse, that it remains half rigid in the postures of its prime. There are modern buildings in the city, but they do not show much: there are high-rise blocks, but they certainly do not dominate the bay. The magnificent business houses of the imperial heyday, emblazoned with symbolisms explicit or implied, have seldom been tarted-up with air conditioning or curtain-wall, but remain inviolate monuments of another era. Take your traveler's checks to one of these terrific old clearinghouses, and you will find all around you still the opulent bric-a-brac of fin de siècle: the heavy marble or mahogany counters, the mosaic floors of goddesses or mercantile virtues, the daunting statuary at the foot of the grand staircase, the big silver bells you bang with the palm of your hand for attention, the rubber stamps with carved wooden handles, the great brass pipes, like ships' fittings, by which at last your money is discharged with a masterly hiss into the cashier's hand.

There are scores of such institutions in Trieste, prodigies of conservatism, inherited certainty or perhaps lost will, towering in Teutonic classicism above narrow downtown streets, supported by giant caryatids or mammoth Corinthian columns, approached by monumental staircases, sustained by elderly well-greased elevators. The City Hall seems to be built in several different styles all at once, and is capped by a bell tower vaguely suggestive of 19th-century battleships. The synagogue is the largest in Europe, and is dramatically Oriental-looking, Assyrian perhaps, like a gloriously extravagant movie set.

The most telling Trieste building of all, though, is the sombre Revoltella palace, a portentous structure which overlooks, as a despot's headquarters might, the Piazza Venezia off the waterfront. This was the home, pride and eventual justification of Baron Pasquale Revoltella, a local worthy of astute but wobbly business practices who made his fortune in timber and grain. After expiating some of his misdemeanors by a short spell in jail, Revoltella made up for the rest by building this tremendous home, stuffing it with works of art and bequeathing it to the city.

It is a museum now, but is still wonderfully evocative of resplendent evenings long ago, when the *beau monde* (and the *nouveaux riches*) of Austrian Trieste swept up that velvet-railed staircase with their fans, ribbons and orders, pausing for a moment perhaps at the emblematic sculpture called *Cutting the Isthmus of Suez*, which is illuminated by a red electric bulb held between the fangs of a wrought-iron snake—dutifully admiring no doubt Cesare Dell'Acqua's painting, commissioned for the house, entitled *The Proclamation of the Free Port of Trieste*—wondering I expect how it was that Baron Revoltella, who lived with his mother and lots of servants, managed to stay unmarried—"lucky devil" breathed the husbands, "what a waste," murmured the wives.

You can almost hear them now, in the immensity of the deserted palace: but even more suggestive than their echoes, I think, even more illustrative of Trieste's prime than the uncautionary tale of the Baron's majestic rise to respectability, is a small gilt-framed picture that hangs in a corner of one of the upstairs rooms. At least it *looks* like a picture, a precious small street scene perhaps by one of the lesser Impressionists, until peering at it more closely one discovers that it *moves*. The painting is alive! That object in the foreground is a 1977 Fiat, not a Montmartre dray, and a distinctly realist Trieste housewife is seen to be entering the shop over the way.

Baron Revoltella, denied the closed-circuit television which sounds just his style, had made a virtue out of necessity, and to keep an eye on events outside his palace doors, I suppose, besides adding charm and curiosity to his salon, had installed a camera obscura among the canvases.

There are many rich men in Trieste still—thirty declared millionaires, they say. But though this is a well-policed city, where crime is low and the kidnap craze has never caught on, here as in the rest of Italy the law of inconspicuous consumption applies. Why take risks? the rich ask themselves, in this city of insurers, and so you find men of enormous means living in restrained upstairs apartments, and women with the undisguisable inflection of great wealth being driven about in fairly poky limousines. Trieste is a cautious place, and calculating too, determined to live comfortably whatever the foolish world does.

In this it succeeds pretty well. For a very epitome of an ordered bourgeois society I recommend a visit to the Caffe degli Specchi, the cafe of the mirrors, the city's most famous, which stands sun-awninged in sunshine, window-steamed in cold, next door to the Prefecture in the Piazza dell'Unita. It is much more Central Europe than Mediterranean. Clutches of middle-aged women in check coats and felt hats talk in undertones over their cream cakes, sometimes holding listless dogs, and occasionally breaking into low cynical laughter. Gaunt men with pinched faces, like Magyar nobles, smoke small cigars and read the financial news with camel coats slung over their shoulders. The waiter knows everyone, and when some obvious stranger comes in, a figure too obviously flamboyant, too cheerfully at large, heads discreetly turn, chatter momentarily pauses, cakes are temporarily reprieved in the chewing, and all the Caffe degli Specchi seems, just for a few seconds, to stare.

The average age is rather high, in such a bastion of the moneyed classes, and this is because many people like to retire to this socially dependable city. The standard of living is perfectly adequate; the quality of life is discreetly agreeable; the setting is lovely; the climate is generally benign. The magazine *Europa* recently concluded that Trieste was the best place to live in the whole of northern Italy, and it is true that most strangers who come here, posted by company or diplomatic service, grow very affectionate toward the city—a familiar hazard of the U.S. Foreign Service, I am told, is the predisposition of consuls toward the causes of Trieste.

But there is poignancy to this affection, for somehow all efforts to restore the grandeur of Trieste seem to come to nothing. It really is the natural port of eastern Europe, as a cursory glance at the map will show, but so long as ideology splits Europe it can never regain the role. When I am in Trieste I stay at the handsome old Savoia Excelsior Palace Hotel, on the waterfront, and in the mornings I like to take my breakfast coffee to my window, and survey the wide sweep of the port below me. Every morning the view seems slightly different. Perhaps a gleaming flotilla of Yugoslav tourist buses is drawn up on the quay. Perhaps the fishing boats are streaming home. Perhaps an Italian warship has docked during the night and is moored directly across the street, its marine guards swaggering around the gangplank, its liberty men surreptitiously slicking their hair in the reflections of porthole glass.

What I seldom discover, when I draw the curtains back, is an honest-to-goodness merchant ship. Baron de Banfield's tugs must sometimes be short of work, for the port of Trieste visibly stagnates. Its traffic has been lured away to Genoa in the west, Hamburg in the north, the flourishing Yugoslav port of Rijeka in the east. Its equipment is old, its labor force is prone to strikes, communications with its hinterland are obsolescent. Only in the handling of Brazilian coffee is it pre-eminent—half the Honorary Consuls are coffee-men—and of the thirty ships that still fly the Lloyd Triestino flag, only six are actually based in Trieste. The trains clanking sporadically to and fro along the waterfront, and so irritating Mahler long ago, hardly represent the flair of a great port: and even they are sometimes pulled, with pantings and heavy breathings, by a very old steam engine.

Once the fourth port of the Mediterranean, now the twelfth port of Italy! No wonder Trieste is sometimes fretful, even bitter. Is this all being Italian has meant to the city—purpose gone, prosperity suspended, even that beloved Istrian coastline snatched away? It is not surprising that a separatist instinct has found political expression lately. The Mayor himself is head of a regionalist party, called Lista per Trieste, which gives angry expression to this frustration. The first Trieste-born mayor for ages, he is wry, ironic and loving about his city, simultaneously, and discusses its condition with urgent reproach.

Talking to such a man makes one feel one is back in the era of the City-States, and the half-embittered patriotism of the Triestini is certainly far more than mere civic pride. On Sunday this winter volunteers have been turning out to sweep the city streets, inadequately cleaned these days by the sanitary department ("What do you expect of this damned Italian bureaucracy?"). They have been doing so with a defiant gusto, as citizens of an ancient autonomous entity. The Mayor will assure you that he is not separatist in the least, that he is deeply loyal to the Italian culture and civilization: but if you ask the average Triestino patriot what the city gets out of the Italian connection, he is likely to give you a dusty if not blasphemous reply.

The trouble with Trieste is not lack of interest in the city, but interest for the wrong reasons. It is a negative kind of pawn on the chessboard. The Western Powers, when they ensured its incorporation in Italy, only wanted to stop the Communists' getting it. The Communists only coveted it as an outlet for their own power. It suits the Germans to see Trieste languish, because it helps the port of Hamburg. It suits the Yugoslavs, because it helps Rijeka. It even, say the Triestini, suits the Italians, because Trieste competes against a dozen other Italian ports, all clamoring for subsidies and preferences, and all closer to the sources of patronage.

Nobody seems to care about the city for its own sake: only the somewhat skeptical but never despondent Triestini, always looking hopefully forward, always glancing wistfully back.

The best-known event in Trieste's history, I suppose, was the departure of the artistic, imaginative but evidently gullible Archduke Maximilian, younger brother of Franz Josef, from his beloved castle of Miramare to become Emperor of Mexico. He never came back, for he was shot by a Mexican firing squad within three years, and his story has haunted the city's memory ever since. With its mingling of the charming, the tragic and the unfair, it provides a proper text for the place, through whose solid streets and pleasant parks, especially in the winter, a mist of melancholy habitually drifts. "And trieste, ah trieste ate I my liver," wrote James Joyce, and for once I think I know what he meant. Trieste is just the place for the introspective, the melancholic, the solitary, the deserter and the unrecognized genius.

I see them sometimes in the evenings, silent young men in office windows, gazing at the traffic and composing never-to-be-published elegiacs; or slumped thoughtfully over their calculators in the back premises of Lloyd Triestino, long after the office is closed; or even dressed up as policemen, long hair, dangling moustaches and sad poetic eyes beneath their white Keystone Kop helmets. And I sense the same indeterminate, unfulfilled longing in the museum rooms of Maximilian's Miramare—a sweet and modest castle above the water, with its own little harbor below the garden, from whose drawing-room windows one can look across the lovely bay, in the pale gray light of an Adriatic evening, to where the city spills somewhat featureless above its docks from the high Carso—a view somehow without a fulcrum, a waiting view, a wish.

Every public clock in Trieste seems to tell a different time, and this is appropriate to a city where time past is exact enough, but time present is a little evasive. In this city, I often feel, one could lose a year or two without anyone noticing, without affecting the calendar at all. It is, in its piquant way, a beguiling illusion. It eats one's liver. If ever you hear them saying "What's become of Morris?", tell them to come to Trieste, and look for me loitering with my adjectives along the waterfront, where the trains go by, or laughing in the stern-sheets of one of the Baron's tugs.

· · · · · · · ·

THE
ISLANDERS

*Manhattan is always different but always
the same—shifting from day to day in fashion, trend or
bigotry, constant in the fascination and excitement of its presence. When
I went to New York in 1979 to write this essay I had
been there every year for twenty-five years—it was
my Silver Jubilee of Manhattan: but I found it fresh and fathomless as
ever, and went home to Wales, as usual, in a condition of slightly
intoxicated, and perceptibly sentimental, enthrallment.*

· · ·

MANHATTAN

· · · · · · · · · · · ·

The Islanders

[1979]

OMETIMES, FROM THE HIGH OFfice windows of the *Rolling Stone* offices in Manhattan, you can make out a faint white blob in the green of Central Park far below. It is like the unresolved blur of a nebula in the night sky: and just as through a telescope the fuzz in Andromeda resolves itself into M31, so that whitish object in the park, defined through binoculars, becomes a phenomenon hardly less spectacular. It is the polar bear in the Central Park Zoo, and even as you focus your lenses, bringing his indistinct physique into clarity, with a shaggy shake of his head he swings his great form vigorously from one extremity of his cage to the other. ❡ The bear lives alone in his compound down there, and I am told that he is a character of weird and forceful originality—sadly neurotic, some informants suggested, genuinely imaginative, others thought. He is a bear like no other, and it is not the fact of his captivity that makes him so, I am sure, but its remarkable location. Destiny has deposited that animal plumb in the middle of Manhattan: you might say he is the central New Yorker. He affects me profoundly, whenever I see him, and when I put my binoculars down, and only the suggestion of him remains, apparently inanimate among the trees, all around him in my mind's eye the marvelous and terrible island of Manhattan concentrically extends, ring after ring of cage, ditch or rampart, precinct limit and electoral boundary, Hudson, East River and Atlantic itself—the greatest of all the zoos, whose inhabitants prowl up and down, like victims of some terrific spell, for ever and ever within it.

For Manhattan really is an island, even now, separated from the mainland still by a channel just wide enough for the Circle Line boats to continue their pleasure circuits, and it is this condition of enclave that gives the place its sting. Like the bear, its citizens are heightened, one way or another, by their confinement. If they are unhappier than most populaces, they are merrier too. If they are trapped in some ways, they are brilliantly liberated in others. Sometimes their endless pacing to and fro is sad to see, but when the weather is right and the sap is rising, then it assumes an exhilarating rhythm, and the people of Manhattan seem to dance along their avenues, round and round the city squares, in and out the sepulchral subway.

Images of confinement certainly haunt me in Manhattan but the first thing that always strikes me, when I land once more on the island, is its fearful and mysterious beauty. Other cities have built higher now, or sprawl more boisterously over their landscapes, but there is still nothing like the looming thicket of the Manhattan skyscrapers, jumbled and overbearing. Le Corbusier hated this ill-disciplined spectacle, and conceived his own Radiant City, an antiseptic hybrid of art and ideology, in direct antithesis to it. His ideas, though, mostly bounced off this vast mass of vanity. Tempered though it has been from time to time by zoning law and social trend, Manhattan remains a mammoth mess, a stupendous clashing of light and dark and illusory perspective, splotched here and there by wastelands of slum or demolition, wanly patterned by the grid of its street system, but essentially, whatever the improvers do to it, whatever economy decrees or architectural fashion advises, the supreme monument to that elemental human instinct, Free-For-All.

But the glowering ecstasy of it! No other city, not even Venice, projects for me a more orgiastic kind of allure. I do not mean the popular phallic symbolism of the place, its charged erections thrusting always into the sky. I am thinking of more veiled seductions, the shadows in its deep streets, the watchfulness, the ever-present hint of concealment or allusion. The clarity of Manhattan is what the picture postcards emphasize, but I prefer Manhattan hazed, Manhattan reticent and heavy-eyed.

I like it, for instance, on a very, very hot day, a day when emerging into the streets from the air conditioning is like changing continents. Then a film of chemical vapor seems to drift around the city, fudging every edge, gauzing every vista. Exhausted, half-deserted, the island seems to stand stupefied in the haze: but sometimes flashes of sunlight, piercing the humidity, are reflected momentarily off windows or metal roofs, and then I am reminded of those uncertain but resplendent cities, vaporous but diamond-twinkling, which stand in the backgrounds of all the best fairy tales.

Conversely on a gray lowering day it is like some darkling forest. The tops of the buildings are lost in fog, and only their massive bases, like the trunks of so many gigantic oaks, are to be seen beneath the cloud base. I feel a mushroom feeling in Manhattan then, and the huddled scurry of the people on the sidewalks, the shifting patterns of their umbrellas, the swish of cars through pothole puddles, the blinking of the traffic lights one after another through the slanting rain, the plumes of steam which, like geysers from the subterranean, spout into the streets—all this speaks fancifully to me, here in *urbanissimus,* of clearing, glade and woodland market.

But best of all, for this reluctant and secretive beauty of the island, I like to walk very early in the morning down to Battery Park, the southernmost tip of it, its gazebo on the world, looking out across the great bay towards the Narrows and the open sea. This is a melancholy pleasure, for the shipping which used to make this the busiest basin on earth has mostly been dispersed now. Most of the Atlantic liners sail no more, the freighters mostly berth elsewhere around the bay, and of the myriad public ferries which used to bustle like so many water insects to and from Manhattan, only the old faithful to Staten Island survives.

So early in the morning, the scene down at the Battery is not likely to be bustling. If it is misty, it is likely to be a little spooky, in fact. The mist lies heavy over the grayish water, muffled sirens sound, somewhere a sound-buoy intermittently hoots. Perhaps a solitary tanker treads cautiously toward Brooklyn, or a pilot boat, its crew collars-up against the dank, chugs out toward the Narrows. Early commuters emerge blearily from the ferry station; two or three layabouts are stretched on park benches, covered in rags and newspaper; a police car sometimes wanders by, its policemen slumped in their seats dispassionately, like men at the end of a shift.

It seems eerily isolated and exposed, and you feel as though the few of you are all alone, there at the water's edge. But as the morning draws on and the mist clears, something wonderful happens. It is like the printing of a Polaroid picture. The wide sweep of the bay gradually reveals its outlines, the Statue of Liberty appears unforeseen upon her plinth, lesser islands show themselves, and as you turn your back upon the water, glistening now in the freshening breeze, it turns out that the tremendous presence of Manhattan itself, its serried buildings rank on rank, has been looking over your shoulder all the time.

I was walking one day down Sixth Avenue (as New Yorkers still sensibly prefer to call the Avenue of the Americas) when I saw a lady taking a bath, fully clothed, in the pool outside the Time-Life Building. This struck me as a good idea, for it was a hot and sticky day, and I approached her to express my admiration for her initiative. I did not get far. When she saw me step her way she sat bolt upright in the pool, water streaming off her lank hair and down the clinging blue fabric of her dress, and screamed obscenities at me. It was unnerving. Shrill, wild and dreadfully penetrating, her voice pursued me like an eldritch curse, and everyone looked accusingly at me, as though I had insulted the poor soul, and deserved all the imprecations she could command (and her repertoire, I must say, was impressive).

Nobody, I noticed, looked accusingly at *her*. She was evidently mad, and so unaccusable. Confined like that bear on their own rock, the people of Manhattan are the most neurotic community on earth. The twitch, the mutter, the meaningless shriek, the foul-mouthed mumble, the disjointed shuffle—these are native gestures of the island. Pale and ghostly, violently made up or sunk in despair are thousands of its faces—clowns' faces, chalk white and crimson, or haunted faces that have survived concentration camps, or faces alive with a crazy innocence, like those of murderous infants.

Every great city has its bewildered minority—the confused are always with us. Manhattan, though, is the only one I know that sometimes seems on the brink of general nervous breakdown. Intensely clever, cynical, introspective, feverishly tireless, it has all the febrile brightness, alternating with despondency, that sometimes attends insomnia, together with the utter self-absorption of the schizophrenic. Few residents of Manhattan really much care what happens anywhere else. Backs to the sea and the waterways east and west, theirs is a crosstown outlook, focusing ever closer, ever more preoccupied, upon the vortex of the place—which is to say, themselves. "Does dyslexia," I heard an interviewer say in all seriousness on television one day, "crop up in other parts of the country, or is it pertinent only to Manhattan?"

Lord Melbourne, when he was Queen Victoria's Prime Minister, was once asked by an anxious acquaintance for his advice on how best to cope with the problems of life. "Be easy," was all the statesman said. "I like an easy man." He would have to look hard for one in Manhattan, where the old gamblers' precept "Let it ride" has long been rejected. Analysis, I sometimes think, is the principal occupation of Manhattan—analysis of trends, analysis of options, analysis of style, analysis of statistics, analysis above all of self. Freud has much to answer for, in this island of tangled dreams, and the women's movement has evidently liberated all too many women only into agonized doubt and self-questioning.

But actually, like most people New Yorkers like to be thought a bit crazy. When they had a poll in New York and Los Angeles, each city complacently claimed its own population to be madder than the other. I know a business corporation in Manhattan—I dare not mention its name—which seems to me to be run entirely, top to bottom, by people off their balance. The minute I enter its offices, an uneasy suggestion of collective therapy assails me. Concealed and unapproachable behind his monumental mahogany doors sits the president of this corporation of nuts, mad as a hatter himself, and in hierarchy of psychosis his sub-ordinates hiss and fiddle their days away below. Sometimes a whole de-partment is fired: sometimes a surprised and hitherto unnoticed employee is plucked from obscurity and made the head of a division for a month or two; sometimes the company, which deals (let us say) in commodity shares, suddenly invests a few million dollars in a Chattanooga umbrella factory, or a grocery chain in Nicaragua.

They have all been driven off their heads, I suppose, by the needling and hallucinatory pressures of Manhattan, the prick of ambition, the fear of failure: and in their eyes I see, as they contemplate the future of their lunatic careers, just the same fierce but loveless passion that one sees in the eyes of brainwashed cultists—a blend of alarm and mindless dedica-tion, dimly tinged with tranquilizers.

I say hallucinatory pressures, because to the outsider there is much to Manhattan that seems surreal. This is not a place of natural fantasy, like Los Angeles—its spirit is fundamentally logical and rationalist, as befits a city of merchants, bankers and stockbrokers. But its daily life is spat-tered with aspects and episodes of an unhinged sensibility, of which I record here, from a recent two-weeks' stay on the island, a few by no means extraordinary examples:

Item: An eminent, kind and cultivated actress, beautifully dressed, is taking a cab to an address on Second Avenue. Cabdriver: *Whereabouts is that on Second Avenue, lady?* Actress, without a flicker in her equanimity: *Don't ask me, bud. You're the fucking cabdriver.*

Item: Sign at a Front Street garage: NO GAS. DEALTH IN FAMILY.

Item: At the headquarters of the New York police, which is at Police Plaza, and is approached along the Avenue of the Finest, there is a func-tionary called the Chief of Organized Crime. I heard an administrator say to a colleague on the telephone there: *You're going sick today? Adminis-trative sick or regular sick?*

Item: A young man talks about his experiences in a levitation group: *Nobody's hovering yet but we're lifting up and down again. We're hopping. I've* seen a guy hop fifteen feet from the lotus position, and no one could do that on the level of trying.

Item: Coming down in the hotel elevator at the New York Hilton is a delegate to the American Urological Association convention. He is on his way to a presentation on Pre-Lymphadenectomy Staging of Testicular Tumors, and his name, I see from his lapel card, is Dr. Portnoy.

Item: An aged court-appointed lawyer, down at the state courts, histrionically convinces the judge, with a florid wealth of legal jargon and gesture, that an adjournment is necessary, but spotting a row of hostile witnesses as he passes through the courtroom on his way out, loudly offers them a comment: *Too bad, assholes.*

Item: Graffito in Washington Square. YIPPIES, JESUS FREAKS AND MOONIES ARE GOVERNMENT OPERATED.

Item: Four angry ladies are trying to enter St. Patrick's Cathedral by the wrong entrance for the celebration of the cathedral's centenary, to be attended by three cardinals and eight archbishops. Their way is barred, but as the chanting of the mass sounds through the half-closed door, I hear them responding with a genuine *cri du cœur: We must get in! We must! We're tourists from Israel!*

Item: The terrifyingly ambitious, inexhaustible girl supervisor at one of the downtown McDonalds. Over the serving counter one may see the glazed and vacant faces of the cooks, a black man and a couple of Puerto Ricans, who appear to speak no English: in front that small tyrant strides peremptorily up and down, yelling orders, angrily correcting errors, and constantly falling back upon an exhortatory slogan of her own: *C'mon, guys, today guys, today . . . !* The cooks look back in pained incomprehension.

Item: I feel a sort of furry clutch at my right leg, and peering down, find that it is being bitten by a chow. *Oh Goochy you naughty thing,* says its owner, who is following behind with a brush and shovel for clearing up its excrement, *you don't know that person.*

Item: At nine in the morning, on a smart street in the East Seventies, a highly respectable middle-aged lady leans against the hood of a black Mercedes, meditatively scratching her crotch.

Item: It is night, and drizzling. I am crossing Park Avenue on my way home, and looking to my left to the mass of the Grand Central Terminal, see a sort of vision: piled on top of the New York General Building, and silhouetted floodlit against the monstrous Pan Am tower behind, the pinnacled cupola of the structure looks, just for a moment, like a shrine— a stupa, perhaps. I pause in astonishment, half expecting to hear mystical prayer bells sounding, until a passing cab, hooting its horn and showering me with mud from an adjacent gutter, scuttles me back to realism.

How small it is! Thirteen miles long from tip to tip, two and a half miles across at its widest point—at Eighty-sixth Street, I believe. It would be hard to be anonymous for long in Manhattan, if anyone well known ever wanted to be. When I was here last I went to see Mr. Woody Allen's masterpiece *Manhattan*, the truest contemporary work of art I know about the island: after the show I went next door for a cup of tea at the Russian Tea Room, and there, large as life, toying with what I assume to have been a blini, was Mr. Allen himself.

Sometimes it is hard to remember that this is one of the earth's most powerful cities, for in some ways it is oddly parochial. The *New York Times* is half a newspaper of international record, and half a parish magazine, with full obituaries of respected local insurance managers, and blow-by-blow accounts of the engagement of Miss Henrietta Zlyman to Edward Twistletoe III. Like all great metropolises, Manhattan is divided into lesser enclaves, each with its own personality and purpose, but the skinny shape of the island, the rigidity of its grid and the flatness of it all, make it impossible for any district to feel remote from any other. You can easily walk from Central Park to Battery Park in a gentle morning stroll; I boarded a bus recently with an acquaintance in the very heart of Harlem, all dingy tenements and apparently abandoned stores, and before he had finished telling me his war experiences we had arrived outside the Plaza Hotel. Besides, the great landmarks of the place, the Empire State Building, the twin towers of the World Trade Center, are so enormous that they are visible almost everywhere, and give the island a foreshortened sort of intimacy.

All crammed in like this, it is no wonder that the inhabitants of Manhattan sway to and fro, as though with minds linked, to the shifting tunes of fashion. No city in the world, I think, is so subject to the *Diktats* of critics, snobs and arbiters of taste. Manhattan feeds upon itself—intravenously, perhaps. A very public elite dominates its gossip columns and decors, the same faces over and over, seen at the same currently fashionable clubs and restaurants, Stork Club in one generation, Studio 54 another, drinking the statutory drinks, *kir* yesterday, Perrier today, using the same ephemeral "in" words—when I was here last, for example, "schlep," "supportive," "copacetic," "significant others."

I was taken one evening, at my own request, to the saloon currently the trendiest in town, Elaine's on Second Avenue. Everyone knows Elaine's. Secretaries hang about its bar, in the hope of being adopted by wild celebrities, young executives talk about it the morning after, and even the most intelligent of public people, it seems, literate directors and scholarly critics, unaccountably think it worth while to be seen there. No such phenomenon exists in Europe, for Elaine's is neither very expensive nor exactly exclusive—anyone can go and prop up the bar. I detested it, though: the noise, the jam-packed tables, the showing-off, the gush, the unwritten protocol which gives the best-known faces the most prominent tables, and banishes unknowns to the room next door. The beautiful people looked less than beautiful shouting their heads off in the din. The waiter resisted my attempts to have scampis without garlic (not liking garlic is *infra dig* in Manhattan).

I felt fascinated and appalled, both at the same time: but more surprising, I felt a bit patronizing—for all of a sudden, as I observed those bobbing faces there, wreathed in display or goggled in sycophancy, fresh as I was from my little village on the northwest coast of Wales, I felt myself to be among provincials.

Not a sensation I often get in New York. More often, when I am at large in this incomparable city, I feel myself to be among ultimates. *How're they gonna get me back on the farm?* This is, after all, The City of our times, as Rome was in classical days, as Constantinople was through centuries of Mediterranean history. This is everyone's metropolis, for there is no nation that has not contributed something to Manhattan, if only a turn of phrase or a category of bun. I went one day to the street festival which is held each May on Ninth Avenue, one of the most vividly

cosmopolitan thoroughfares on the island, and realized almost too piqu-
antly what it means to be a city of all peoples: smell clashing with smell,
from a mile of sidewalk food stalls, sesame oil at odds with curry powder,
Arabic drifting into Ukrainian among the almost impenetrable crowds,
Yiddish colliding with Portuguese, and all the way down the avenue the
discordant blending of folk-music, be it from Polish flageolet, Mexican
harmonica or balalaika from Sofia.

Nothing provincial there! And if over the past 300 years the clambering upon this huge raft of refugees, adventurers, idealists and crooks from
every land has given Manhattan always a quality of paradigm or fulcrum,
so when it comes to the end of the world, I think, most people can most
easily imagine the cataclysm in the context of this island. The great
towers crumpling and sagging into themselves, the fires raging up the
ravaged boulevards, the panicked rush of the people, like rats or lem-
mings, desperately into the boiling water—these are 20th-century man's
standard images of Doomsday: and in my own view, if God is truly going
to sit one day in judgment upon the doings of mankind, he is likely to
set up court on the corner of Broadway and Forty-second Street, where
he can deal first (and leniently I am sure) with the purveyors of Sextacular
Acts Live on Stage.

We live in baleful times, and it is a pity that Manhattan, that temple
of human hope and ingenuity, should be obliged to fill this particular role
of parable. There is no denying, though, that there often passes across the
face of this city, like a shudder, a sense of ominous portent. I read one
morning in the *Times* that a woman, walking the previous day down a
street near City Hall, had been attacked by a pack of rats "as big as
rabbits." I leapt into a cab at once, but Manhattan had beaten me to it:
already a small crowd was peering with evident satisfaction into the
festering abandoned lot from which the rodents had sprung. Already one
of your archetypal New Yorkers had appointed himself resident expert,
and was pointing out to enthralled office workers one of your actual rats,
almost as big as a rabbit, which was sitting morosely in a wire trap among
the piled rubbish. What became of the original victim, I asked? "I guess
she was some kind of screwball. She just drove off screaming. . . ."

I would have driven off screaming too, if those rabbit-rats had attached
themselves to me, but around the corner, almost within excretion dis-

tance of the rat pit, business was brisk as ever at the neighborhood takeout food store. New Yorkers are hardened to horror, I suppose, and perhaps it is this acclimatization that gives their island its sense of fated obliteration. It might be designed for nemesis, and suggests to me sometimes an amphitheater of pagan times, in which ladies and rats, like gladiators and wild beasts, are pitted against each other for the rude entertainment of the gods.

Everything comes onto the island: nothing much goes off, even by evaporation. Once it was a gateway to a New World, now it is a portal chiefly to itself. Manhattan long ago abandoned its melting-pot function. Nobody even tries to Americanize the Lebanese or the Lithuanians now, and indeed the ethnic enclaves of the island seem to me to become more potently ethnic each time I visit the place. Nothing could be much more Italian than the Festival of St. Anthony of Padua down on Mulberry Street, when the families of Little Italy stroll here and there through their estate, pausing often to greet volatile contemporaries and sometimes munching the soft-shelled crabs which, spread-eagled on slices of bread like zoological specimens, are offered loudly for sale by street vendors. Harlem has become almost a private city in itself, no longer to be slummed through by whities after dinner, while Manhattan's Chinatown is as good a place as anywhere in the world to test your skill at that universal challenge, trying to make a Chinese waiter smile.

So the lights blaze down fiercely upon a tumultuous arena: but its millions of gladiators (and wild beasts) are not in the least disconcerted by the glare of it, or daunted by the symbolic battles in which they are engaged, but are concerned chiefly to have swords of the fashionable length, to be seen to advantage from the more expensive seats, and preferably to face the lions at the same time as Jackie Onassis, say, or Dick Cavett if you like.

Back to the park. At the center of the world's present preoccupation with Manhattan, for one reason and another, stands Central Park. "Don't go walking in that Park," they will warn you from China to Peru, or "Tell me frankly," they ask, "is it true what they say about Central Park?"

The Park is the center of the island too, no man's land amid the surrounding conflict of masonry—on the postal map it forms a big oblong blank, the only portion of Manhattan without a zip code. To the north is Harlem, to the south is Rockefeller Center, on one flank is the opulence of the Upper East Side, to the west are the newly burgeoning streets that sprout, teeming with artists, agents, Polish grocers and music students, right and left off Columbus Avenue. It is like a big rectangular scoop in the city, shoveled out and stacked with green. It covers 840 acres, and it is almost everything, to my mind, that a park should not be.

This is a heretical view. Central Park is enormously admired by specialists in planning and urban design. The architectural critic of the *New York Times* calls it the city's greatest single work of architecture. It was laid out in 1856 by Frederick Law Olmsted and Calvert Vaux, and ever since everybody has been saying how marvelous it is. "One of the most beautiful parks in the world," thought Baedeker, 1904. "This great work of art," says the AIA *Guide to New York City, 1978*.

Not me. With its gloomy hillocks obstructing the view, with its threadbare and desolate prairies, with its consciously contrived variety of landscapes, with its baleful lake and brownish foliage, with the sickly carillon which, hourly from the gates of its appalling zoo, reminds me horribly of the memorial chimes at Hiroshima, Central Park seems to me the very antithesis of the fresh and natural open space, the slice of country-side, that a city park should ideally be.

Nevertheless the world is right when, invited to think of Manhattan, it is likely to think first these days of Central Park. If I deny its ethereal beauty, I do not for a moment dispute its interest. It is one of the most interesting places on earth. "It is inadvisable," warns the Michelin guide, 1968, "to wander alone through the more deserted parts of the park": but wandering alone nevertheless through this extraordinary retreat, dominated on all sides by the towering cliffs of Manhattan, is to enjoy one of the greatest of all human shows, in perpetual performance from dawn through midnight.

You want tradition? There go the lumbering barouches, their horse smells hanging pungent in the air long after they have left their stands outside the Plaza, their Dutch trade delegates, their Urological Association conventioneers, or even their honeymooners from Iowa, somewhat self-consciously sunk in their cushions, and their coachmen leaning back, as they have leant for a century or more, whip in hand to ask their customers where they're from.

You want irony? Consider the layabouts encouched apparently permanently on their benches along the East Side, beyond the open-air bookstalls, prickly and raggedy, bony and malodorous, camped there almost in the shadow of the sumptuous Fifth Avenue apartment houses, and more tellingly still perhaps, actually within earshot of the feebly growling lions, the cackling birds and funereal carillon of the zoo.

You want vaudeville? Try the joggers on their daily exercise. Dogged they lope in their hundreds around the ring road, generally cleared of traffic on their behalf, like migrating animals homed in upon some inexplicable instinct, or numbed survivors from some catastrophe out of sight. Some are worn lean as rakes by their addiction, some drop the sweat of repentant obesity. Some flap with huge ungainly breasts. Some tread with a predatory menace, wolflike in the half-hour before they must present that memo about ongoing supportive expenditures to Mr. Cawkwell at the office. Sometimes you may hear snatches of very Manhattan conversations, as the enthusiasts labor by—*So you're saying* (gasp) *that since 1951* (pant) *there's been no meaningful change whatever* (puff) *in our society?* Sometimes you may observe a jogger who has taken his dog with him on a leash, and who, obliged to pause while the animal defecates behind a bush, compromises by maintaining a standing run, on the spot, looking consequently for all the world as though he is dying for a pee himself.

But no, it is the sinister you want, isn't it? "*It is inadvisable to wander alone, despite the frequent police patrols on horseback or by car. . . .*" That is what Central Park is most famous for these days, and it is not hard to find. I have never been mugged in Central Park, never seen anyone else harmed either, but I have had my chill moments all the same. More than once, even as the joggers pad around their circuit, I have noticed perched distantly on the rocky outcrops which protrude among the dusty trees, groups of three or four youths, silently and thoughtfully watching. They wear dark glasses, as likely as not, and big floppy hats, and they recline upon their rock in attitudes of mocking but stealthy grace, motionless, as though they were fingering their flick-knives.

I waved to one such group of watchers once, as I walked nervously by: but they responded only by looking at each other in a bewildered way, and shifting their long legs a trifle uneasily upon the stone.

All around the city roars. Well, no, not roars—buzzes, perhaps. The energy of Manhattan is less leonine than waspish, and its concerns are, for so tremendous a metropolis, wonderfully individual and idiosyncratic. Despite appearances, Manhattan is an especially human city, where personal aspirations, for better or for worse, unexpectedly take priority.

Perhaps this is because, unlike either of the other global cities (for in my view there are only two, Paris and London)—unlike its peers, New York is not a capital. True, the headquarters of the United Nations is down by the East River, but architecturally it is the perfect reflection of its lackluster political self, and one hardly notices it. True too that the municipal affairs of this city, being on so momentous a scale, are equivalent I suppose to the entire political goings-on of many lesser republics. But it is not really a political city. Affairs of state and patriotism rarely intrude. Even the state capital is far away in Albany, and Manhattan conversations do not often turn to infighting within the Democratic party, or the prospects of Salt III.

There is not much industry on the island, either, in any sociological or aesthetic sense: few blue-collared workers making for home with their lunch boxes, few manufacturing plants to belch their smoke into the Manhattan sky. This is a city of more intricate concerns, a city of speculators and advisers, agents and middlemen and sorters-out and go-betweens. Many of the world's most potent corporations have their headquarters here, but their labor forces are mostly conveniently far away. Fortunes are made here, and reputations, not steel ingots or automobiles.

The pace of New York is legendary, but nowadays in my opinion illusory. Businessmen work no harder, no faster, than in most other great cities. But New Yorkers spend so much time contemplating their personal affairs, analyzing themselves, examining their own reactions, that the time left for business is necessarily rushed. Do not suppose, when the Vice-President of Automated Commercial leaves his office in such a hurry, that he is meeting the Overseas Sales Director of Toyuki Industries: good gracious no, he is leaving early because he simply must have it out face to face with Brian about his disgraceful behavior with that Edgar person in the disco last night.

More than any other place I know, to do business in New York you must understand your colleagues' circumstances. They often need worrying out. There are some telltale signs indeed, like tribal tattoos—short hair for Brian and Edgar, for example, droopy moustaches and canvas shoes for aspirant literary men, rasping voices and nasal intonations for girls who hope to get into television, hands in trouser pockets for Ivy League executives. But you should take no chances. The tangles of Manhattan marital and emotional life, which provide inexhaustible hours of instruction to the social observer, set the tone of this place far more than torts, share prices or bills of lading.

There is hardly a citizen of Manhattan, of any race, creed or social class, who does not have some fascinating emotional imbroglio to relate— and hardly a citizen, either, who fails to relate it. Nitter-natter, chit-chat, *you would hardly believe it, so I said never, so she said absolutely*—sibilantly across this city of gossip, from Wall Street clubs to bars of Harlem one seems to hear the tide of confession and confidence, unremitting as the flood of the traffic, rattly as the clang of the subway trains which now and then emerges from grilles beneath one's feet.

Is this inbreeding? Certainly there is something perceptibly incestuous about Manhattan, now that the diversifying flow of immigration has abated. This is no longer the lusty stud of the world. Ellis Island, through whose lugubrious halls so many millions of newcomers passed into the land of fertility, is only a museum now, and ethnically Manhattan has lost its virile momentum. You feel the migratory thrust far more vividly in Toronto, and most of New York's contemporary immigrants are hardly immigrants at all, in the old risk-all kind, but are Puerto Ricans joining their relatives, or Colombians cooperatively financed by the drug-rings of Jackson Heights.

They are seldom inspired, as their predecessors were, by any flaming spirit of release or dedication, and they very soon fall into the Manhattan mode. "Well it's like I say, see, I got this lady I used to know back in Bogotá. She says to me, 'Leon,' she says, 'I wantya to know, I'm fond of you, truly I am, but there's this problem of Juan's baby, see?' 'To hell with Juan's baby,' I says, 'what's Juan's baby to me?' And she says, 'Leon honey,' she says, 'listen to me. . . .' "

"Give me your tired, your poor, your huddled masses yearning to breathe free. . . ." An occasional Russian dissident appears in New York these days, to endure his statutory press conference before being whisked away to CIA debriefing or associate professorship somewhere. But the loss of the grand old purpose, so stoutly declaimed by the Lady of Liberty out there in the bay, means that Manhattan is recognizably past its prime.

Every city has its heyday, the moment when its purpose is fulfilled and its spirit bursts into full flower, and Manhattan's occurred I think in the years between the Great Depression, when the indigents squatted in Central Park, and the end of World War II, when the GIs returned in splendor as the saviors of liberty. In those magnificent years this small island, no more than a fantastic dream to most of the peoples of the world, stood everywhere for the fresh start and the soaring conception. Manhattan was Fred Astaire and the sun-topped Chrysler Building! Manhattan was the Jeep and Robert Benchley! Manhattan was rags-to-riches, free speech, Mayor La Guardia and the Rockettes!

No wonder nostalgia booms on Broadway. Those were the days of the American innocence, before responsibility set in, and every dry and racy old song of the period, every new Art Deco furniture boutique, is an expression of regret. European Powers pine for their lost glories with bearskin parades or jangling cavalry: New York looks back with *Ain't Misbehavin'*, or the refurbishing, just as it was, of that prodigy of Manhattan gusto, Radio City Music Hall (whose designer reportedly had ozone driven through its ventilator shafts, to keep its audiences festive, and toyed with the idea of laughing gas too. . .). Fortunately the old days come quickly in a city that is not yet 300 years old, and the authentic bitter-sweetness is relatively easy to achieve. I was touched myself by the furnishing of a restaurant equipped entirely with the fittings of one of the old Atlantic liners, those dowagers of the Manhattan piers, until I discovered that the ship concerned was the *Caronia*, whose launching I remember as clear as yesterday.

The memories of that time are legendary already, and moving fast into myth. Nothing in travel stirs me more than the dream of that old Manhattan, the Titan City of my childhood, when the flamboyant skyscrapers soared one after the other into empyrean, when John D. Rockefeller, Jr., pored over the plans for his Center like a modern Midas, when the great liners stalked through the bay with their complements of celebrities and shipboard reporters, and the irrepressible immigrants toiled and clawed their way up the line of Manhattan, from Ellis Island to the Lower East Side to the Midtown affluence of their aspirations. Its monuments are mostly there to see still, newly fashionable as the buildings of the day-before-yesterday are apt to become, and sometimes even now you may stumble across one of its success stories: the waiter proudly boasting that, since arriving penniless and friendless from Poland, he has never been out of work for a day—the famous publisher, in the penthouse suite of his own skyscraper, whose mother landed in Manhattan with a placard around her neck, announcing her name, trade and language.

Rockefeller Center is the theater of this mood. Raymond Hood, the creator of its central structure, the RCA Building, was reminded one day that he had come to Manhattan in the first place with the declared intention of becoming the greatest architect in New York. "So I did," he responded, looking out of the window at that stupendous thing, jagged and commanding high above, "and by God, so I am!" The magnificent brag, the revelatory vision, the ruthless opportunism, the limitless resource—these were the attributes of Rockefeller Center, as of Manhattan, in the heady years of its construction: and when at winter time they turn the sunken cafe into an ice rink, then in the easy delight of the skaters under the floodlights, some so hilariously inept, some so showily skillful, with the indulgent crowd leaning over the railings to watch, and the waltz music only half drowned by the city's rumble—then I sometimes seem to be, even now, back in those boundless years of certainty.

If the conviction is lost, the abilities remain. This is the most gifted of all the human settlements of the earth, and there are moments in Manhattan when the sheer talent of the place much moves me. I happened to be in the Pan Am Building recently when an orchestra of young people was giving a lunch-time concert in the central concourse. This is a common enough event in Manhattan, a place of inescapable music, but somehow it seized my imagination and twisted my emotions. No other city, I swear, could provide an interlude so consoling. The brilliant young players were so full of exuberance. The audience listened to their Brahms and Vivaldi with such sweet attention. The music sounded wonderfully tender in the heart of all that stone and steel, and seemed to float like a tempering agent down the escalators, through the bland air-conditioned offices, of that great tower of materialism. ("How beautifully they play," I remarked in my delight to a man listening beside me, but in the Manhattan manner he brought me harshly down to earth. "They gotta play beautifully," he replied. "Think of the competition.")

The cities of Europe have mostly lost their artists' quarters, swallowed up now in housing estates or ripped apart by ring roads. In Manhattan, Bohemia flourishes still, in many an eager alcove. This is a city of the streets and cafes, where human contact, carnal or platonic, is still easy to arrange, where no young artist need feel alone or benighted for long, and where no ambition is too extravagant. Manhattan probably has more than its fair share of artistic phonies, and SoHo, currently the most popular painters' quarter, certainly exhibits an adequate proportion of junkyard collages or knobs of inadequately sandpapered walnut labeled "Significant Others 3." But tucked away in the attics, cheap hotels, apartment blocks and converted brownstones of this island myriad genuine artists and craftsmen are at work, impervious to trend and disdainful of sham.

I like to spend Sunday mornings watching the *alfresco* circus down at Washington Square, the gateway to Greenwich Village, where wandering musicians and amateur jugglers compete for the attention of the sightseers with virtuoso frisbee throwers, classical in their skills and gestures, impromptu demagogues, chess players, itinerant idiots and Rastafari bravos. Often and again then, when I am sitting on my park bench watching this colorful world go by, I spot a fellow practitioner of my craft, alone on *his* bench with *his* notebook, and as our eyes meet I wonder if I ought to feel compassion for him, as the struggling artist from his austere garret somewhere, or envy, as the author of tomorrow's runaway best-seller.

Contrary to the world's conceptions, New York is rich in people of integrity. In a city of such attainments it has to be so. This is a city of dedicated poets, earnest actors and endlessly rehearsing musicians. Draft after draft its writers are rejecting, and there are more good pianists playing in New York every evening than in the whole of Europe— smouldering jazz pianists in the downtown clubs, crazy punk pianists on Bleecker Street, stuffed-shirt romantic pianists in the Midtown tourist spots ("Would you mind lowering your voice to a whisper, please, during Mr. Maloney's renditioning?"), smashing student pianists practicing for next year's Tchaikovsky competition, jolly young pianists accompanying off-Broadway musicals, drop-out pianists, drunk ruined pianists, mendicant pianists with instruments on trolley wheels, Steinway pianists flown by Concorde that afternoon for their concerti at Lincoln Center.

So I am never really deluded by the charlatan inanities of New York. I disregard the fatuous interviewers and repellent respondents of what we are gruesomely encouraged to think of as NBC's Today Family. I sneer not at the sellers of Instant Ginseng. I am not deceived by the coarse-grained editors, hag-ridden by their own accountants, or the ghastly company of celebrities. "Creativity" is so degraded a word in Manhattan that I hesitate to use it, loathing its translation into salesmen's acuity or publicity gimmick. But creative this place truly is: not in the old audacious style perhaps, but in the quieter, introspective, muddled but honest way that is more the Manhattan manner now.

It would seem inconceivable to Hood or John D., Jr., let alone Commodore Vanderbilt or Pierpont Morgan, but actually in 1979 Manhattan feels a little old-fashioned. The Titan City has come to terms, and recognizes that everything is *not* possible after all. They build more thrilling buildings in Chicago now. They do more astonishing things in Houston. There are more aggressive entrepreneurs in Tokyo or Frankfurt. It is no good coming to Manhattan for the shape of things to come: Singapore or São Paulo might be more reliable guides. In the days of the Great Vision the New Yorkers built an airship mast on the top of the Empire State Building almost as a matter of course, sure that the latest and greatest dirigibles would head straight for Manhattan: it was years, though, before New York was reluctantly persuaded, in our own time, to allow supersonic aircraft to land at JFK.

Manhattan is no longer the fastest, the most daring or even I dare say the richest. For a symbol of its civic energies now, I recommend an inspection of the abandoned West Side Highway, the victim of seven years' municipal indecision, which staggers crumbling on its struts above a wilderness of empty lots, truck parks and shattered warehouses, the only signs of enterprise being the cyclists who cheerfully trundle along the top of it, and the railway coaches of the Ringling Bros., Barnum and Bailey Circus which park themselves habitually underneath.

The falter came, I believe, in the fifties and sixties, when Manhattan began to see laissez faire, perhaps, as a less than absolute ideology. Doubts crept in. The pace slowed a bit. The sense of movement lagged. All the great ships no longer came in their grandeur to the Manhattan piers; the New York airports were far from the island; today even the helicopters, which were for a couple of decades the lively familiars of Manhattan, are banned from their wayward and fanciful antics around the skyscrapers. Bauhaus frowned down upon Radio City Music Hall, in those after-the-glory years, and most of Manhattan's midcentury architecture was, by Hood's standards, timid and banal. The truly original buildings were few, and worse still for my taste, the swagger-buildings were not built at all.

When, in the early 1970s, the World Trade Center was erected in a late spasm of the old hubris—the two tallest towers on earth then, beckoning once more the world across the bay—all Manhattan groaned at the change in its familiar skyline, and to this day it is hard to find a New Yorker willing to admit to admiration for that arrogant pair of pylons. The fashionable philosophy of smallness strongly appealed to New Yorkers, in their new mood of restraint, and nowadays when citizens want to show you some innovation they are proud of, they generally take you to a dainty little curbside park with waterfalls, or Roosevelt Island, an itsy-bitsy enclave of sociological good taste. Suavity, discretion and even modesty are the architectural qualities admired in Manhattan now, and the colossal is no longer welcomed.

And believe it or not, *quaintness* approaches. Mr. Philip Johnson's latest building is to be crowned with a decorative device like the back of a Chesterfield sofa: so does old age creep up, all but unsuspected, upon even the most dynamic organisms—Time's A-Train, hurrying near! Manhattan is no longer critical in the atomic sense: "No Nukes" is a proper slogan for this gently decelerating powerhouse.

It is not a sad spectacle. I find it endearing. If New York has lost the power to amaze, it is gaining the power to charm. They did not mean it seriously, when they called this city Little Old New York, but the phrase is losing its irony now. Old Manhattan inevitably becomes—small geographically it always was—little and old in the figurative sense, in the cozy familiar endearing sense. Manhattan telephone operators, who used to be mere human mechanisms, call one "dear" nowadays: and at the New York Hilton, that very shrine of impersonal efficiency, there is somebody down in the kitchens who actually recognizes my voice, every time I go there, and sends me up my breakfast with kind endearment and inquiries after my family.

It happened that when I was in Manhattan Bonwit Teller, for generations one of the smartest stores on Fifth Avenue, closed its doors to make way for a building development. I went along there on the last day, and what a sentimental journey that was! Tears came to saleswomen's eyes, as they pottered for the last time among the atrocious hats, unsellable ceramics, belts and bent coat hangers which were all that remained of their once-delectable stock: and an elderly customer I buttonholed by the elevators seemed almost distraught—something beautiful was going out of her life, she said, "a bit of New York, a little bit of me."

Bonwit's was quick to remind us, in the next day's *New York Times*, that they have plenty of stores elsewhere, but still the event really did touch some heart-chords in New York. Sentimentality, eccentricity, Earl Grey tea—all these are signs of a society growing old, but doing it, on the whole, gracefully. There is much that is jaded or curdled, of course, to the culture of Little Old New York. Violence really is a curse of the place, circumscribing the lives of hundreds of thousands of people, and blighting whole districts of the city—when the donor of the East River Fountain was asked why it had not been spouting recently, he said he assumed it was clogged with corpses. More people in Manhattan, as it happens, suffer from human bites than from rat bites—764 recorded in 1978, as against 201 from the rats.

Yet I am of the opinion all the same that Manhattan, whose very name is a byword for the mugging, the fast practice, the impossible pressure and the unacceptable vice, has become in its maturity the most truly civilized of the earth's cities. It is where mankind has, for good or for

bad, advanced furthest on its erratic course through history, and in unexpected places, in unforeseen situations, its mellowness shows.

I spent a few hours one night with a squad car of the Fifth Precinct,
operating out of Elizabeth Street on the Lower East Side, and found it,
to my astonishment, a curiously gentlemanly exercise. I am not overfond
of policemen as a breed, and have heard the worst about New York's
Finest, but I can only report that my experiences that night were altogether disarming.

My pair of cops were textbook, almost comic-book, figures: burly
fellows as you would expect, bulging slightly at the belt, with guns
sagging heavy at their hips and that peculiar akimbo sort of gait, as
though they are about to enter a Japanese wrestling bout, which is peculiar to American policemen. Our calls too were as you might foresee: a
potential suicide on the Brooklyn Bridge, some kids starting a fire, a
molester in a tenement house, an elderly householder shot through the
head by a thirteen-year-old robber. We progressed around town, within
limits as closely defined as a fox's hunting territory, with the proper
alternation of creep and crash, now nosing insidiously into back alleys,
where the junkies stared blankly at our passing, now switching our
yelper on and exploding through the traffic in our battered sedan as
though wild horses were carrying us.

But I was surprised, whenever we got there, by the moderation of these
Fifth Precinct heavies. I have ridden with big-city policemen in many
countries, Bolivia to Hong Kong, and these fellows seemed to me the
nearest of them all to the neighborhood cops of long ago. The Brooklyn
jumper turned out to be a merry fellow, brandishing a bunch of flowers
above his head, who said he was merely responding to the Challenge of
the Waters, and was given a lift to somewhere less stimulating. The kids
were putting out their fire by the time we reached them, and we did not
interfere. At the scene of the shooting the local population of Puerto
Ricans, Italians and Colombians, far from melting into the night when
we and eight other police cars appeared helter-skelter on the scene, howl-
ing and flashing, crowded seriously around to help, and were treated I
thought with rough but sensible courtesy.

A lucky night? Untypical cops? Perhaps, but nevertheless my night down at the Fifth Precinct, cruising from Chinatown to Mafialand, from Ratner's restaurant still aglow to the seafood joint where they show the bullet holes that killed a Godfather seven years ago—my night down there left me indefinably beguilded and conciliated by Manhattan. I stopped off at an all-night cafe on my way uptown, and had a pancake. There were a couple of grotesquely painted old ladies in there, looking as though the funeral parlor cosmetician had prematurely had a go at them, and a slob distastefully wiping the last of the egg off his plate with a piece of greasy bread, and two or three night-workers mildly chatting up the waitress, and an obvious Englishman, in a striped tie, grinning and bearing it through the jet lag, the time change and the behavior patterns of the Manhattan midnight.

They used to say of it that it would be a fine place when it was finished. I think in essentials they have completed it now. They are no longer tearing down its buildings, and throwing up new ones, with the fury of their youth. Whole districts are no longer changing character year by year under the impact of the immigrants. Manhattan has jelled, I think. A feeling not of complacency but perhaps of wry experience pervades Little Old New York now: when, in the Russian Tea Room that day, I caught the eye of Mr. Allen, truly the laureate of Manhattan in its silver age, it seemed to me that his expression was rather *wistful*.

Actually it is Woody Allen, not that bear, who should be encaged in Central Park, to stand as a focal symbol for peregrinating Welsh essayists. But let me end anyway with one more visit to the Park, that zipless blank at the heart of Manhattan, for a lyrical *envoi* to this piece. I chanced one day, off the joggers' circuit, to come across a young black man fast asleep upon a bench below the lake. His overcoat was thrown over him, his boots were placed neatly side by side upon the ground. His head upon his clasped hands, as in kindergarten plays, he was breathing regularly and gently, as though bewitched.

Even as I watched a gray squirrel, skipping across the green, leapt across his legs to the back of the bench, where it sat tremulously chewing, as squirrels do: and suddenly, almost at the same time, there arose one of those brisk gusts of wind, tangy with salt, which now and then blow a breath of the ocean invigoratingly through New York.

A scatter of leaves and fallen blossoms came with it, flicked and eddied about the bench. The squirrel paused, twitched again and vanished. The black man opened his eyes, as the breeze dusted his face, and seeing me standing there bemused, smiled me a slow sleepy smile. "Be not afeared," I said ridiculously, on the spur of the moment, "the isle is full of noises."

"Yeah," the man replied, stretching and scratching mightily in the morning. "Bugs, too."